The Small-Boat Skipper's Handbook

GEOFF LEWIS

Illustrations by Geoff Page

HOLLIS & CARTER

LONDON SYDNEY

TORONTO

© G. G. E. Lewis 1977
ISBN 0 370 10319 X
Printed in Great Britain for
Hollis & Carter
an associate company of
The Bodley Head Ltd
9 Bow Street, London WC2E 7AL
by Unwin Brothers Limited, Woking
Set in Monotype Baskerville
First published 1977

CONTENTS

List of Illustrations

List of Tables

FOREWORD

Sailing is a game about which you can't possibly know too much. The more you know, the more you realise how much remains to be learnt. There are therefore many books which attempt to record one or another of the many facets of owning, sailing and maintaining small craft. This present book places in one volume a wealth of knowledge arranged for quick and easy reference in the cabin or cockpit of powered and sailing craft.

The book is in three parts. The first deals with basic facts about the boat and her equipment in concise and where possible tabular form. The second part offers the information needed to handle and navigate a boat efficiently and safely, whether on a short evening sail or on a cruise to foreign waters. The third part is unique in books of this nature. It is designed for recording vital data on one's own craft. By completing these pages the owner has immediate access while ashore to information which would otherwise require a journey to the boat to find out, for instance, how much of what sort of rope to buy for a new jib halyard, or what type of sparking plug is needed for the motor.

No attempt is made to replace the nautical almanac, whose tidal and astronomical data are ephemeral. Rather, this is a book of permanent reference and increasing value to all who own a sail or power craft as well as to those who aspire to do so.

Readers may notice an apparent randomness in the use of metric and Imperial units; this is intentional, for in some cases the metric system has already been adopted in Britain for the measurement of articles and materials whereas in others the Imperial system still prevails. Where appropriate, both systems have been quoted. This work has been prepared in two editions, a British one of basic utility to any yachtsman in the English-speaking world, and an American one more specifically geared to the needs of the North American yachtsman.

ACKNOWLEDGMENTS

In compiling this *Small-boat Skipper's Handbook* every attempt has been made to provide data from the most reliable and authoritative sources. This would not have been possible without the generous cooperation of a number of Government Departments, publishing organisations, industrial companies and individuals in Britain, Canada, the United States and Australia.

To name them all is impossible; I am indebted in particular to the Editor of *Practical Boat Owner* for permission to reproduce material which has been published in that excellent magazine, to the American Boat and Yacht Council and the American Plywood Association, to the Bristol Wire Rope Company and C C L Swaging Systems Ltd., to Marlow Ropes Ltd. for data on ropes, knots and splices, and to the Timber Research and Development Association. Ken Dangerfield provided valuable data on working with resinglass from recent first-hand experience. Material provided by the Meteorological Office and the Marine Division of the Department of Trade is reproduced with the permission of the Controller of Her Majesty's Stationery Office.

To all these and to the many individuals who have made useful contributions to the text, I offer my sincerest thanks, especially to Pat Munday, whose painstaking work in checking, improving and typing the manuscript is beyond praise.

Geoff Lewis
JUNE 1976

I

Sea Sense

Sailing is essentially a light-hearted business. When the buoy-rope goes over the side the cares of the world should go with it. But that doesn't mean that one can then adopt a carefree attitude of irresponsibility. New and to some extent greater responsibilities immediately fall on the shoulders of the yacht skipper, for the safety of his crew and of his boat, for the safety of everyone else using the same patch of water. These can still be discharged light-heartedly, provided that the skipper has cultivated that intangible quality called 'sea sense'. It comes with knowledge and experience of a whole range of seamanlike abilities. More than just knowing how to sail a course and navigate, or repair a sail and tuck a neat eye-splice, it comes to skippers and crews who are constantly alert to everything going on around them. Such people immediately sense when all is not well and will have taken the necessary remedial steps long before the situation becomes desperate.

Human beings are more prone to failure than the components of a well-found boat. A yachtsman with sea sense keeps an eye on the way in which even the simplest tasks are carried out, not only by his crew but also by himself. He need not be carping in his criticism, but the avoidance of crises, big or small, makes for happiness afloat. Constant alertness produces a wealth of information, each bit of which may be individually small, but collectively adds up to something which helps materially in the good running of the ship and the well-being of the crew. Morale drops, often unnoticed, when the sun sets or the skies cloud over and the rain begins, and with it drops efficiency. This is a time for even greater alertness.

This book contains information on very many sailing matters, grouped for convenience into discrete chapters, but the skipper with sea sense will not package the data in separate compartments of his mind. The sight of a main halyard beginning to chafe at the masthead coupled with the arrival of wind-foretelling cirrus cloud on the western horizon and a known shortage of fuel in the tank may lead him to opt for a nearer port than his intended destination, where he can sort things out more easily than at sea. However good a landfall he may have made after an extended passage, the skipper may find insufficient land-marks on a featureless coast to identify exactly the entrance to a harbour. But this may sometimes be determined by the tracks of other shipping approaching the coast, or aircraft flying towards an airfield known to be near the port. Nevertheless, the prudent skipper knows that these are not infallible signs, and he uses the information with caution until it is obviously right. The tide may be flooding into an estuary, but when it comes to anchoring or picking up a mooring the direction in which nearby boats are lying will show whether there may be an eddy running contrary to the tide.

Advice or suggestions should never be spurned or ignored; they may not in the end be used but should certainly be taken into consideration when making decisions. Once a decision has been made, it should be acted upon. This does not prevent a change of plan to deal with changed circumstances, but rapid and frequent alterations are confusing and demoralising. Indecision is criminal at sea.

A smart ship is a happy ship, not merely because she looks good but also because one avoids the unhappy consequences of slovenliness. Ropes trailing over the side foul propellers, articles left on the cabin ladder steps get trodden on and broken. Halyards left swinging free have a habit of running up the mast out of reach; shackle pins placed on deck while the shackle is threaded through an eye roll over the side or into the bilge; nails or screws left lying around soon find their way into someone's bare foot.

An important part of sea sense is the instinctive ability to plan ahead, whether it be for a transatlantic voyage or for picking up a mooring. And the plan should visualise the possibility of things not working out exactly, in which case an alternative plan must be ready for instant use. 'One-shot-only' plans can be disastrous.

It may appear spectacular to roar through an anchorage creating a great wash, but this is unlikely to earn the lasting friendship of anyone whose dinghy is alongside and whose children are just getting into it.

A reputation for good seamanship is earned by caution, not bravado. There's nothing undignified in sounding your way into a strange harbour, though it may appear pointless if a large merchant vessel has just gone in ahead of you. On any passage lasting overnight or more than a few hours, a proper system of watchkeeping is essential, and those off watch must rest even if they do not sleep. The standard four-hour watches kept in navies and merchant ships may be found satisfactory by some yachts' crews, but three-hour watches have often been found to result in more alert crews. In any event, a trick at the helm should not exceed two hours except in emergencies, particularly in bad weather. A tired helmsman is unlikely to steer an accurate course; on a running course he may allow the mainsail to gybe 'all standing', with a serious risk of losing the mast. It is misplaced kindness to allow anyone off watch to sleep on when he should have relieved the watch on deck; similarly no responsible skipper minds being aroused from his fitful sleep if those on deck have any doubts about the boat or her position or if the weather should appear to be changing.

These are just a few examples of sea sense; summed up they may be seen to be an ATTITUDE OF MIND rather than a particular expertise which might be learnt by rote. Anyone who realises this while applying the techniques described in this book is entitled to call himself a good skipper. A crew of people with sea sense is a winning crew; it can't be beaten; it's a team in the best sense of the word. As sailing folk we're supremely lucky that our hobby provides such a splendid quality free, gratis and for nothing.

2

Boat Design and Construction

Boat design is as much an art as a science; it is the art of optimising a number of conflicting restraints and criteria to produce the best design for the purpose for which the boat is intended. The most obvious criteria are that she shall be seaworthy, stable and easily driven, but these are relative terms and one feature or another may have to be sacrificed in the interest of the overall design, which may be constrained by rating rules, accommodation required, range of operation and a host of other desirable features.

Boat construction is (or should be) an art too. The many forms of wooden, resinglass and metal construction all require different types of expertise, and few boatyards possess them all. Two similar boats built to the same drawings by different yards may turn out to have subtly different characteristics.

This chapter does not attempt to teach boat design or construction; both are highly skilled professions, but if a boat owner understands a few of the fundamentals he is better equipped to maintain or modify his craft.

See also Chapter 9 for Maintenance

SOME FUNDAMENTALS OF DESIGN

Displacement is the weight of water displaced from the hole in the sea in which the boat floats. It is equal to the total weight of the boat and all her equipment if weighed on land.

Buoyancy is the upward thrust of the water displaced; it is also equal to the weight of water displaced. An adequate reserve of buoyancy is necessary so that a boat will not sink if a moderate amount of water is shipped or heavy loads embarked.

The buoyancy must be distributed in the design of a boat so that the bow and stern will be lifted by an advancing wave before it breaks inboard. Similarly the buoyancy of the beam and bilges must restore the boat to an upright condition when she rolls or heels.

Centre of buoyancy is an imaginary point in the bowels of the boat through which the upward thrust of the buoyancy may be assumed to act. Its position moves as the boat rolls or pitches.

Centre of gravity is an imaginary point through which the whole weight of the boat may be assumed to act. Its position is fixed (unless ballast or heavy weights are moved) and must be on the centre line of the boat if it is to float upright.

When a boat is afloat and at rest, the C of B and the C of G are in the same vertical line. When a boat heels, the C of B moves to one side so that the upward thrust of the buoyancy and the downward thrust of the boat's weight form a 'couple' which provides **righting moment.**

Stability is a boat's resistance to heeling forces. It depends on the vertical distance between the C of B and the C of G and on the shape of the hull. It is greatest when the C of G is kept low down; hence heavy weights (ballast, batteries, water tanks, etc.) should be located as low as possible in the boat.

A safe boat will have sufficient stability to right her after she has been knocked down (heeled to over 90 degrees).

Metacentre is the point at which a vertical line through the C of B when the boat is heeled intersects the 'upright' centre line through the C of G (for small angles of heel). Its height is a measure of *stiffness*; a high metacentre gives a stiff boat suitable for sheltered waters but uncomfortable in a seaway, and a low metacentre provides an easier motion appropriate to sea-going vessels.

Ballast ratio is the weight of ballast to the weight of the complete hull, expressed as a percentage. In general, the larger the ballast ratio the greater will be a boat's stability, but this is only partially true, since the righting moment depends on the depth as well as the weight of the ballast keel. A deep keel with light ballast can produce the same righting moment as a shallow keel with a big ballast ratio.

Resistance to a boat's motion is caused by frictional drag of the underwater body, by induced drag caused by heeled or yawing hulls, by the energy lost in wave making as the boat thrusts the water aside, and to a much lesser degree by air drag and eddies in the flow of water past the hull.

Both frictional drag and wave making resistance increase with speed; a highly-polished bottom may minimize frictional resistance but cannot eliminate it. Wave making is a function of the length and shape of the hull; at high speeds it becomes the predominant retarding influence. Eddies can be minimized by streamlining such underwater excrescences as the propeller aperture and depth sounder or log fairings. Air resistance matters most in high-speed power craft.

The **maximum speed** of any boat is that at which the propelling force (wind or motor) can no longer overcome the increase in total resistance which increased speed would cause. The longer a boat is, the faster she will be, given sufficient net propulsive force to overcome hull resistance.

Speed-length ratio is normally quoted in terms of the

speed in knots divided by the square root of the waterline length in feet. The maximum value of 'vee-over-root-L' rarely exceeds 1·35 in sailing craft; a fast cruiser might achieve 1·25 when reaching in a good breeze on a flat sea. Beating to windward this might be reduced to about 1·0 or 0·75 in a seaway.

Planing dinghies and catamarans are not subject to the 'vee-over-root-L' rule when actually on the plane; they then offer much less hull resistance than displacement boats.

Motor craft can be forced beyond a speed-to-root-length ratio of 1·35 by increasing propulsive power at the expense of fuel consumption, which rises rapidly as speed is increased in a hull of given length. (See page 106).

Lateral resistance is the extent to which the keel area and underwater hull form of a sailing boat prevent her from being pushed sideways (to leeward) when beating or reaching and a power craft from skidding during fast turns. The **leeway angle** may be between 3 and 6 degrees in a well-designed modern boat and up to 10 degrees in older boats and motor sailers.

Centre of lateral resistance is an imaginary point at which the forces keeping the boat up to windward (or from skidding) may be assumed to be concentrated. Its position changes with angle of heel, and may be estimated by balancing a cardboard cut-out of the underwater profile on a pinpoint. The position of the pin is roughly the CLR of the profile.

Centre of effort of a sail plan is an imaginary point at which the net propulsive thrust of the wind on the sails may be assumed to act. For each individual sail the CE is approximately at the intersection of the median lines drawn from each corner to the mid-point of the opposite side. The overall CE is on a line joining the individual CEs; if this line is divided in the same proportions as the respective sail areas the overall CE is approximately at the point of division.

Balance and trim: a well balanced and trimmed sailing craft should carry slight weather helm, so that if the tiller is released the boat will slowly luff up into wind. This is achieved by the correct location of the CLR and the CE with respect to each other and to the load waterline (LWL).

To get a good balance, the CE needs to be ahead of the CLR by about 3 to 6 per cent of LWL in a fine-lined keelboat, 4 to 7 per cent in a dinghy and 8 to 16 per cent in a beamy sloop with a long keel. Not all authorities agree on these numbers, and individual boats may show big differences, but in general if a boat won't balance when these conditions are met the rake or position of the mast may be at fault or the sail plan unsuitable.

SOME FUNDAMENTALS OF CONSTRUCTION

Whether built in timber, resinglass or metal, a boat **structure** consists of a watertight hull and deck stiffened in appropriate places to provide strength and to keep the hull in shape.

A **skeleton** is built first for wooden and metal boats; this is then covered with a **skin** of **planking** or **plating.** The skeleton consists of transverse **ribs** and **frames** attached to the inner **keel,** to which are also attached the **stem** and **sternposts.** See Fig. 1.

All heavy loads and thrusts are carried by the skeleton; the skin of planking or plating is not intended to carry any but light loads. The keel is the backbone of the skeleton, and must eventually carry all loads imposed on the boat from within or without. This should be remembered when adding any load-bearing fitting or device to a boat.

The principle is the same in resinglass boats, except that

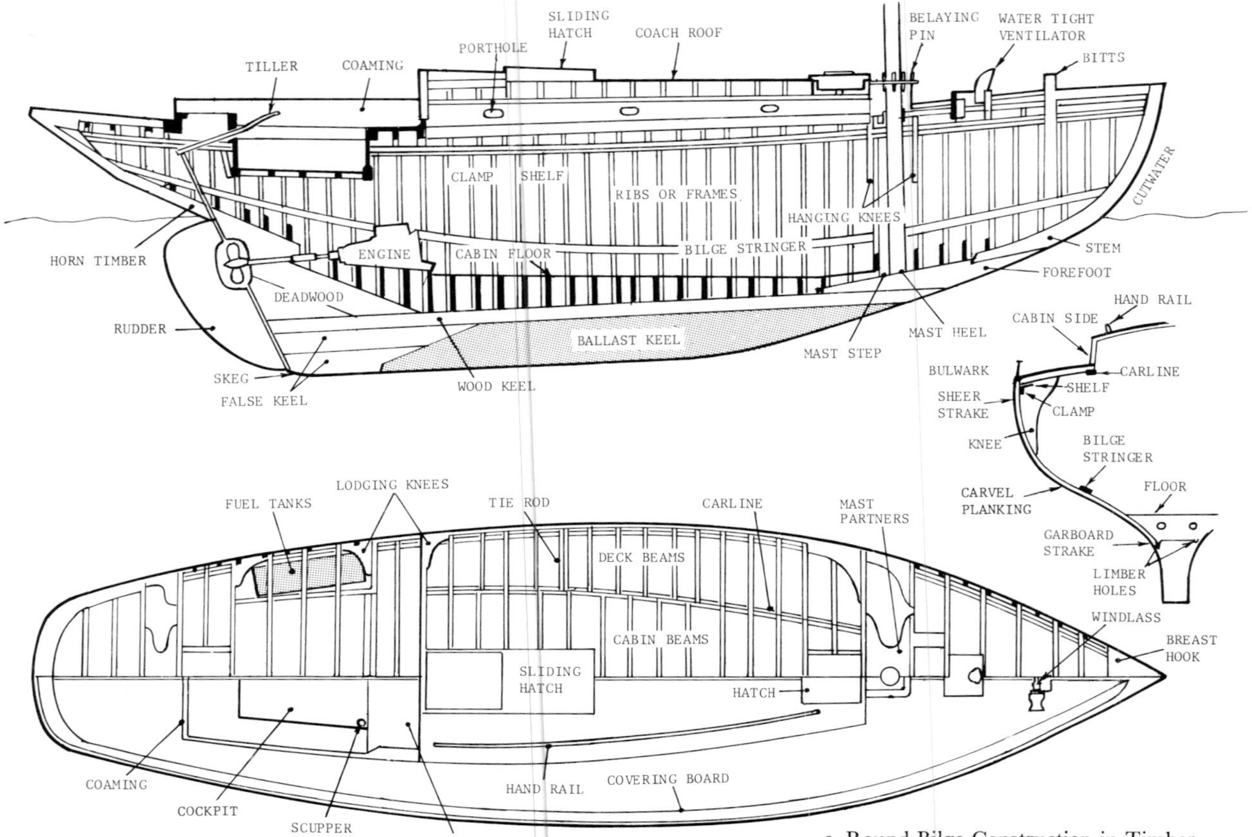

SLIDING HATCH
COACH ROOF
BELAYING PIN
WATER TIGHT VENTILATOR
BITTS
PORTHOLE
TILLER
COAMING
CUTWATER
CLAMP
SHELF
RIBS OR FRAMES
HANGING KNEES
HORN TIMBER
ENGINE
CABIN FLOOR
BILGE STRINGER
STEM
FOREFOOT
DEADWOOD
HAND RAIL
CABIN SIDE
RUDDER
BALLAST KEEL
MAST HEEL
MAST STEP
BULWARK
CARLINE
SHELF
SKEG
FALSE KEEL
WOOD KEEL
SHEER STRAKE
CLAMP
KNEE
BILGE STRINGER
LODGING KNEES
FUEL TANKS
TIE ROD
CARLINE
MAST PARTNERS
CARVEL PLANKING
FLOOR
GARBOARD STRAKE
DECK BEAMS
LIMBER HOLES
WINDLASS
CABIN BEAMS
BREAST HOOK
SLIDING HATCH
HATCH
COAMING
COCKPIT
SCUPPER
HAND RAIL
COVERING BOARD

1 Round Bilge Construction in Timber

the skeleton is moulded integrally with the skin, and the skin itself is made thicker in heavily-loaded regions.

Wooden Construction

Wooden construction uses an oak or other hardwood skeleton, planked with mahogany, pine or other straight-grained timber. In **carvel** construction, the planks are butted edge-to-edge and the seams rendered watertight with caulking cotton. **Clinker** (or **clincher** or **lapstrake**) construction has its planks overlapping like tiles on a roof. See Figs. 2 and 3.

Fastenings secure the planking to the skeleton; they may be copper nails or rivets clenched over copper washers known as roves, or silicon bronze screws. Brass screws are undesirable below the waterline as they lose their zinc content and soften ('dezincify'); stainless steel screws while excellent elsewhere are avoided underwater as they are subject to 'crevice corrosion'.

Butt straps are wooden blocks used to span the joints where planks are butted end-to-end. Such joints are kept clear of ribs and frames.

Floors are wooden or metal strips or sometimes welded metal structures spanning the inner keel and bolted to the lower parts of certain ribs to stiffen and strengthen the skeleton. They often carry the weight of the ballast keel via the keel bolts.

Deck beams are part of the structure just as much as the ribs; they carry not only the weight of the deck and anything placed upon it but also the loads imposed by sheet blocks and cleats and perhaps the mast, though in this case it is usual for a **bulkhead** to be located internally to help carry the weight of the mast and the tension of the standing rigging.

Moulded construction is an alternative method of planking: several thin skins are applied in succession to

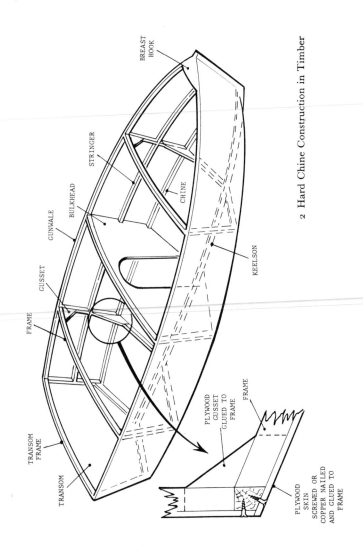

BREAST HOOK

STRINGER

BULKHEAD

GUNWALE

CHINE

GUSSET

KEELSON

FRAME

TRANSOM FRAME

TRANSOM

PLYWOOD GUSSET GLUED TO FRAME

FRAME

PLYWOOD SKIN SCREWED OR COPPER NAILED AND GLUED TO FRAME

2 Hard Chine Construction in Timber

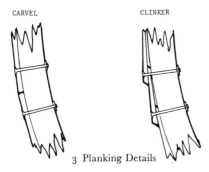

CARVEL   CLINKER

3 Planking Details

the skeleton with the grain of each skin running diagonally to the adjacent skin and glued with synthetic resin.

Decks are either laid like carvel planking or may consist of sheets of marine plywood.

Plywood construction: Resin-bonded marine plywood if properly chosen and used is a good material for building wooden boats. In Britain the only suitable plywood is to specification BS 1088 with weather and boil-proof bonding to BS 1203. (The corresponding material in the United States is defined in US Product Standard PS 1·74.)

Plywood boats are usually of **hard-chine** or **multiple-chine** construction on frames forming a simpler skeleton than for a conventionally-planked boat (Fig. 2). By nature, plywood can be made to bend in only one plane. When so curved it makes a very strong structure, but the subtle double curvatures found in planked and resinglass boats cannot be made from sheets of plywood.

The edges of plywood sheets are vulnerable to damage and ingress of water unless suitably protected. When two edges are butted together the joint should be backed up by a butt strap 6 to 8 inches wide in a dinghy and 12 to 15 inches wide in a heavier boat. Merely to butt two plywood sheets together along the edge of a frame is asking for trouble.

To minimise the risk of delamination (separation of the plies through glue failure) the edges of plywood sheets should be sealed against moisture by allowing several applications of thinned (10 per cent white spirit) varnish to soak in until no more can be absorbed. This is advisable even if the wood is subsequently to be painted.

Some cheaply-constructed plywood boats have large areas of thin skin unsupported by an adequate framing. Such areas have been known to burst inwards when struck by a heavy wave, with obvious consequences. Small fast runabouts are particularly prone to this fault. Similarly, certain stitched-and-bonded hulls built from do-it-yourself kits are easily holed when grounded on a rock.

Adequate support from closely-spaced frames not only adds to the strength of a boat but helps to prevent 'drumming' in resonance with certain engine speeds.

Some **timbers recommended for boat-building** by the Timber Research and Development Association are listed in Table 1. Some traditionally-used timbers have almost disappeared or become prohibitive in price, but other less well-known varieties have taken their places. The properties to look for are weight, durability, working qualities and whether it comes in the sizes required.

Metal Construction

Hulls of **steel** or aluminium are built on a skeleton basically similar to metal craft, with the plates rivetted or welded to the frame. Steel construction is extremely strong and durable and very suitable for work boats; it may however be too heavy for small yachts.

Sea air and salt water play havoc with unprotected steel, and frequent repainting is necessary to keep corrosion under control. Rust must first be chipped away and the bare metal primed with red oxide or yellow chromate before applying undercoat and enamel.

Ship & Boat-building Timbers

HARDWOODS

Timber	Description	Ave. Wt. Lb./Cu. Ft.	Durability Classification	Working Qualities	Uses Recommended
*AFROR-MOSIA (Afrormosia spp.)	Yellowish brown with brown markings. Shallowly interlocked grain, and fine even texture. Moderately hard, but strong. Seasons well.	43	Very Durable	Fairly easy to work, finishes smoothly. Glues & polishes well. Needs care in nailing as it has a tendency to split. Stains when in contact with ferrous metals under moist conditions. Very stable.	Planking, working decks, superstructures as Teak alternative.
AFZELIA/ DOUSSIE (Afzelia spp.) Trop. Africa	Light reddish brown, darkening to reddish brown. Grain irregular commonly interlocked, texture coarse but even. Hard and strong. Seasons slowly.	51	Very Durable	Moderately hard to work, takes a good finish. Difficult to nail and screw and recommended to be prebored. Glues and polishes satisfactorily. Very stable.	Keels, stems, hogs, superstructures.
AGBA/TOLA (Gossweilerodendron balsamiferum) Trop. Africa	Light brown or pinkish brown with a wide sapwood; sticky resin occurs in pockets or streaks; conversion wastage; straight grained, fine textured; seasons	32	Durable	Easy to work with little dulling effect; sharp cutting edges necessary for fine finish, takes stain and paint, can be glued.	Planking, decking, stringers, shelving, superstructures, and veneers for moulding.

27

Timber	Description	Ave. Wt. Lb./Cu. Ft.	Durability Classification	Working Qualities	Uses Recommended
	well; strength comparable to Honduras Mahogany.				
ASH (*Fraxinus excelsior*) Europe	Whiteish with occasional pinkish tinge. Straight grained & rather coarse texture. Moderately hard, excellent bending properties.	43	Perishable	Works fairly easily and finishes smoothly. Glues, nails, screws & polishes well. Stains satisfactorily. Liable to distort, if not properly seasoned.	Tiller handles, boathooks, cleats, canoes.
CEDAR, HONDURAS (*Cedrela* spp.) Trop. America	Pinkish to reddish brown. Usually straight grained with a moderately coarse and uneven texture. Soft.	36	Durable	Easy to work and finishes well. Nails, screws and glues excellently. Varnishes, stains and polishes satisfactorily. Stable.	Skins of light craft, planking, cabin work.
DANTA (*Nesogordonia papaverifera*)	Reddish brown. Fine even texture. Pin knots may be present.	40	Moderately Durable	Works fairly readily with some blunting effect. Tends to split in nailing, glues well, finishes well, can be bent.	Keels, stems, framing, planking & bent timbers.
ELM, ROCK (*Ulmus thomasi*)	Pale brown, straight grained with moderately fine texture. Hard, strong and elastic.	44	Non-Durable	Moderately hard to work but takes a smooth finish. Takes nails, screws and glues satisfactorily and paints, stains and varnishes well.	Rubbing strakes, fenders, timbers, gunwales, risings.

Timber	Description		Durability	Working properties	Uses
ELM, WYCH (*Ulmus glabra*) Europe	English dull brown. Fairly straight grained & medium textured. Moderately hard, strong & elastic.	42	Non-Durable	Fairly easy to work and takes a good finish. Nails, glues, stains and varnishes well.	Keels, deadwoods, planking of small craft.
*GREEN-HEART (*Ocotea rodiaei*) Guyana	Light to dark olive green. Fine even textured, straight grained.	64	Very Durable	Fairly hard to work; finishes well; requires pre-boring to eliminate splitting. Will glue.	Keels, engine bearers.
GUAREA (*Guarea* spp.) West Africa	Light pinkish or orange brown. Straight brown. Medium hardness.	36	Durable	Works easily and takes good finish. Nails and screws & glues well. Gum present which may exude. Moderately stable.	Planking, decking, framing.
*IROKO/ MVULE (*Chlorophora excelsa*)	Light yellow brown when fresh, ageing to medium brown or dark reddish brown. Grain interlocked, texture moderately coarse. Strong and hard.	40	Very Durable	Moderately easy to work, takes a good finish. Nails, screws and glues satisfactorily. Stable timber, though irregular grain may result in distortion.	Could be used as an alternative for teak, with careful selection.
MAHO-GANY, AFRICAN (*Khaya* spp.) Trop. Africa	Reddish brown. Grain broadly interlocked, texture coarse, fairly even. Medium hardness.	35/44	Moderately Durable	Easy to work, takes a good finish. Nails, screws and glues well. Stable.	Planking, decking, framing.

29

Timber	Description	Ave. Wt. Lb./Cu. Ft.	Durability Classification	Working Qualities	Uses Recommended
MAHOGANY, HONDURAS (*Swietenia macrophylla*)	Light reddish to yellowish brown, even textured. Slight interlocked grain, very stable.	34	Durable	Easy to work with little dulling effects. Finishes well, stains, paints and glues satisfactorily.	Planking, decking, superstructures.
*MAKORE (*Mimusops heckelii*) W. Africa	Pinkish to dark reddish brown. Grain generally straight, texture fine & even. Hard and fairly strong.	39	Very Durable	Works moderately well, but has blunting effect on cutting edges. Nails, glues and screws well. Takes an excellent finish. Stable.	Planking for underwater parts. Veneers for moulding.
MERANTI, DARK RED (*Shorea* spp.) Malaya	Dark red in colour, grain tends to be interlocked; coarse to even texture.	43	Durable	Works fairly well. Nails and screws easily. Glues well. Stains & finishes well after filling.	Planking, thwarts.
OAK (*Quercus* spp.) European	Light brown to medium brown. Grain commonly straight, texture coarse and uneven. Hard and strong with fairly good bending properties.	45	Durable	Variable in working qualities, but generally medium in working. Nails, screws and glues well. Staining when in contact with ferrous metals under moist conditions.	Stems, framing, stringers, etc.
OBECHE/ WAWA (*Triplochiton scleroxylon*) W. Africa	Creamy white to pale yellow. Grain often interlocked, texture medium soft, but has good strength properties for its weight	24	Non-Durable	Works easily, and takes a good finish. Nails and screws well, but its holding properties are not great. Has good staining and glueing. Fairly stable.	An alternative for softwood, interior cabin-work, but needs preservation

SAPELE (*Entendrophragma cylindricum*) Trop. Africa	Pinkish to reddish brown, grain narrowly interlocked, texture fairly fine. Hard and strong.	35/43	Moderately Durable	Works fairly well. Nails, screws and glues well, finishes and polishes excellently. Not particularly stable.	Planking, decking, etc. Veneers for moulding.
SERAYA, WHITE (*Parashorea* spp.) N. Borneo	Pale straw coloured. Grain sometimes shallowly interlocked, texture medium to coarse. Medium hardness.	35	Moderately Durable	Easy to work. Nails, screws & glues well. Takes a good finish and polish. Stable.	Decking, planking, etc.
*TEAK (*Tectona grandis*) Burma, Thailand India and Java	Golden brown to medium brown. Grain generally straight, texture medium, sometimes coarse. Moderately hard, but strong.	41	Very Durable	Moderately easy to work. Nails satisfactorily, tends to split near edges. Screws and glues well. Very stable.	Too well known to need comment.
UTILE (*Entandrophragma utile*)	Reddish to purplish brown in colour similar to Sapele; somewhat open in texture, irregular striped grain.	34/47	Durable	Works fairly readily with tools with slight dulling effect. Nails, stains & glues satisfactorily.	Planking, decking, thwarts, etc. Considered to be better than Sapele. Veneers for moulding.

31

SOFTWOODS

Timber	Description	Ave. Wt. Lb./Cu. Ft.	Durability Classifica-tion	Working Qualities	Uses Recom-mended
CEDAR, WESTERN RED (*Thuya plicata*) Canada	Reddish brown, non-resinous wood. Straight grained medium to coarse textured. Soft.	24	Durable	Easy to work, takes good finish. Nails and screws well; tends to stain by ferrous metal under moist conditions. Glues and stains satisfactorily. Stable.	Canvas covered decks.
FIR, DOUGLAS (*Pseudotsuga taxifolia*) Canada & U.S.A.	Reddish yellow to light orange red-brown. Generally straight grained some-times wavy or spiral texture medium. Medium hardness.	33	Moderately Durable	Fairly easy to work. Nails, screws and glues satisfactorily, requires various finishing treat-ments as raised grain & resin may be trouble-some. Medium stability.	Decking, planking, thwarts, piling, floors, masts and spars, stringers and shelving.
LARCH, EUROPEAN (*Larix decidua*) Europe	Light orange red-brown. Normally straight grained, medium textured. Medium hardness.	35	Durable	Fairly easy to work, except when resinous. Nails, screws and glues well. Takes satisfactory finish. Medium stability.	Planking, decking, stringers, shelving knees, beams.
PINE, PARANA (*Araucaria angustifolia*) Brazil	Pale straw coloured with brownish and reddish streaks; straight grained, fine even textured. Variable in density, generally	34	Non-Durable	Easy to work, tends to split when nailed and screwed near edges. Takes smooth finish, stains polishes well. Not particularly stable.	Little used in this field as yet.

32

Species	Description		Durability	Working properties	Uses
(Pinus spp.) U.S.A. & British Honduras	...brown spring-wood, with reddish summer-wood. Straight grained medium texture. Very resinous. Hard and strong.	44	Durable	Moderately hard to work due to its resinous nature. Moderately hard to nail and screw. Needs careful preparation before finishing.	Decking, keels, keelsons, planking, masts, stringers, shelving.
REDWOOD, EUROPEAN (Pinus sylvestris)	Pale yellowish brown to light reddish brown. Straight grained medium textured, fairly resinous. Moderately hard and strong.	31	Moderately Durable	Fairly easy to work, takes a good finish. Nails, screws & glues well. Takes paint and varnish satisfactorily. Stable.	Planking, decking, for canvas covering, thwarts, floors, etc.
SPRUCE, SITKA (Picea sitchensis)	Light pinkish brown, with high lustre. Straight grained, uniform textured. Commonly free from resin. Moderately soft but strong for its weight.	28	Non-Durable	Easy to work and takes fine finish. Nails, screws and glues well. Takes paint, varnish and other treatments readily. Stable.	Spars, oars, paddles, decking, canoes, canvas covered. High strength wt. ratio.

DURABILITY: The classifications are based upon the Forest Products Research Laboratory definitions arrived at from graveyard tests of 2″ × 2″ stakes driven into the ground, viz.—

Very Durable	—	More than 25 years.
Durable	—	15—25 years.
Moderately Durable	—	10—15 years.
Non-Durable	—	5—10 years.
Perishable	—	Less than 5 years.

All the lower categories will be considerably enhanced by the application of wood preservatives.

*These timbers have good resistance to Teredo.

Corrosion occurs most rapidly in places where pools of water can form, such as in the bilge and in the bottoms of tanks. Such areas are often built more heavily than elsewhere to allow for loss of metal by corrosion.

Dents and buckled plates resulting from collision with a pier or another craft should be examined to assess whether rivets have loosened, welding cracked or other structural damage caused. A seriously buckled frame may affect the structural integrity and safety of a steel hull.

Aluminium and its alloys are employed in building hulls of lighter weight than comparable steel craft. Construction methods are similar, but welding needs greater care and skill. Rivets are comparatively soft and may tend to work loose; where plating has suffered a blow it may be advisable to replace all its rivets.

Electrolytic corrosion is possible anywhere in an aluminium craft where a different metal is in contact with the aluminium. Even if fittings are electrically insulated from the deck or hull the bolts or screws attaching them tend to bridge the insulation; these points should frequently be examined for corrosion.

Resinglass Construction

Resinglass, otherwise known as glass-reinforced plastic (GRP) and glassfibre, is best suited to the quantity-production of strong and durable boat hulls. These are built on a male or female mould which places some restrictions on hull shape; re-entrant curves may make it impossible to remove the hull from the mould or vice versa.

A skin of polyester resin reinforced with chopped glass-fibre mat is applied to the mould, its thickness varying with the structural loads to be borne by different parts of the moulding. Ribs are moulded integrally with the skin to stiffen and strengthen the hull and to provide attachment points for keels, bulkheads, engine bearers and other heavily-stressed components.

Decks and cabin tops are moulded separately and resin-bonded to the completed hulls. This joint is a potential source of weakness and should be periodically inspected for cracking and leaks.

Contrary to popular belief, a resinglass boat is not a no-maintenance boat; size for size such a boat needs the same amount of attention as any other boat to mast, spars, sails, rigging, motor, equipment, everything except the bare hull.

Even the hull needs proper attention; the shiny exterior gel coat is vulnerable to scratches and cracks which may expose the internal glass mat to sea or rainwater. This will seep through and ultimately weaken the structure, especially if the water absorbed becomes frozen during the winter. Scratches and cracks should thus be sealed as soon as possible with a local application of gel coat.

The causes of scratches will be obvious, but more serious cracks may occur through unfair stresses being placed in localised areas: an ill-distributed mast loading, a deck fitting whose load is inadequately spread, an internal bulkhead jammed too tightly into the hull, all these can cause damage which can only be repaired by replacing the affected area.

Fastenings whereby deck fittings or internal furniture are attached to a resinglass hull call for comment. Unless they carry a very light load, screws (including the self-tapping variety) are unreliable. Heavily-loaded fittings such as guardrail stanchions, sheet blocks and cleats should be through-bolted, the load being spread by means of a wooden block resin-bonded to the underside of the deck or moulding.

The underwater surfaces of a resinglass boat need anti-fouling to prevent barnacles adhering to the gel coat, as their removal is liable to roughen the coat, and penetration may ensue. A special etch primer is needed before the antifouling composition will adhere to the smooth surface.

Chapter 9 gives further information on working in resinglass.

No boat lasts for ever. The effects of age and perhaps lack of adequate maintenance show up sooner or later. The life of a wooden boat may range from ten years for a lightly-built and perhaps overpowered runabout to over a century in the case of sturdy fishing craft converted into yachts.

Much the same applies to steel-built craft. In the end timber rots, steel rusts away, fastenings no longer hold the hull together. Planking, timbers and fastenings may be replaced in limited areas, but where the members of a wooden boat are generally soft no amount of refastening will keep her watertight. Her day is done.

Prevention is the best form of cure. If timber is kept well painted and varnished all the year round it will last much longer than wood with bare patches.

Ill-ventilated areas are more prone to rotting than others. Watch out for **dry rot** (Merulius Lachrymans) up in the forepeak, inside the transom and in similar usually in-accessible places. Once this disease is established it spreads like wild fire, reducing the affected timber to the con-sistency and strength of a breakfast cereal. Early treatment with copper naphthalate ('Cuprinol') will stop it spreading but will not restore lost strength. Only complete replace-ment can do that.

Wet rot is more common than dry rot; watch for it in places where rainwater leaks through the deck or cabin top, under stanchions or deck fittings which have not been properly bedded in with white lead or similar stopping, or almost anywhere a pool of water can lie. Be alert for areas where the paint is lifting; this may be a sign of wet rot beneath it.

Damage caused by ship-worm (commonly gribble and teredo) occurs mainly in tropical waters, but it is not unknown in higher latitudes, especially in estuaries whose water is warmed by industrial effluent or by power stations. Modern antifouling compositions are effective against these borers if renewed frequently in accordance with local practice.

Antifouling applied hastily between tides or just before launching may have gaps which allow ship worm to penetrate. Areas which have been abraded against a stone quay or on the sea bed are similarly vulnerable. So is the underside of a rudder. The only cure for rotten or worm-riddled timber is to replace it.

Collision Damage

Damage caused by collision or by squeezing between a quay and a larger boat may be superficially frightening but structurally unimportant, or it may be the very reverse. If the damage seems considerable, it would be wise to engage a professional surveyor to report on the repairs needed. His fees would be covered several times over if he locates unsuspected weaknesses in what may be thought unlikely areas.

Damage to planking and easily visible ribs and frames will be obvious, but by the very nature of their construction wooden boats tend to transmit unfair stresses around the structure until the weakest member breaks, perhaps in an obscure corner.

If the damage is confined to one or two planks, it is not sufficient to replace the damaged area with short lengths of timber; the new planking should span several ribs on each side of the damaged area and take into account existing joints so that there are no short sections.

Single cracked ribs may be repaired with doubling pieces, preferably of stronger section than the broken one, and it would be prudent to reinforce adjacent ribs and those opposite with similar doublers if the original crack occurred naturally and without evidence of unfair treatment.

Traditionally, timbers are either steamed to the required shape or selected from wood naturally grown to that form; if these become broken one may take advantage of modern techniques by replacing them with laminated members constructed by gluing thin strips together in a suitable jig. These are very strong and have no inbuilt stresses.

FASTENINGS IN TIMBER

Always use non-ferrous fastenings; mild steel screws and nails corrode rapidly, lose their grip and disfigure surrounding woodwork. Below the waterline, copper nails properly clenched or rivetted over roves are best, unless silicon bronze fastenings are available. Brass tends to lose its zinc content, and stainless steel suffers from crevice corrosion underwater.

Above water and for internal work stainless steel and brass screws are reliable.

Sometimes mild steel tie rods, bolts and nuts are unavoidable; they should be hot-dip galvanised; failing this ideal mild steel components can be painted with Kurust and lead paint to prolong their lives.

Synthetic resin glues (Aerolite 306 or other ureaformaldehyde adhesives) make wood-to-wood joints stronger than the timber if properly used. See Adhesives, pp. 131-2.

SOME USEFUL DIMENSIONS

Bunks and **berths** less than 77 inches long are too short for a moderately tall occupant. Their width should be at least 20 inches; 22 inches wide is better and 24 inches luxurious. If space is scarce a bunk can be tapered to 13 inches at the foot without discomfort.

Foam mattresses are uncomfortable if less than 3 inches thick; 4 to 5 inches is better but for real luxury 6 inches.

Chart tables to take a once-folded chart must be at least 28 by 22 inches; 30 by 27 inches is better. There is no standard size of marine chart but they will all fit into a chart locker or drawer 29 by 21 inches. A chart folio for keeping charts under a bunk mattress measures 28 by 22 inches.

Book racks and **shelves** need to be at least $8\frac{1}{2}$ inches wide to hold Pilot Books and Almanacs; some reference books are as much as $8\frac{1}{2}$ inches wide and 12 inches high.

Hanging lockers for shore-going clothes on coat hangers need a minimum width of 20 inches and a depth of 40 inches below the hanging rail.

Water closet seats are most comfortable and efficient if their height off the cabin sole is between 11 and 13 inches. A minimum of 38 inches head room over the seat is essential.

Galley sinks and **worktops** should in general be higher than is normal ashore; a good height is 36 inches.

Guard rails should be at least 24 inches high; anything less is more likely to trip you over the side than to keep you inboard.

Water tanks should contain enough fresh water for one gallon per man per day. With economy one can get by with much less. If two or more separate tanks are installed the first one running dry will serve as a reminder of how much is left. A cubic foot of fresh water in any country weighs $62\frac{1}{2}$ pounds; an Imperial gallon weighs 10 pounds, a US gallon 8·3 pounds. There are about 4·5 litres to an Imperial gallon and 3·8 to a US gallon.

Outboard motors are usually designed for a standard transom height of 15 inches; long-shaft versions for 20 inches.

TONNAGES

No tonnage rule completely describes the size of a boat or her proportions. Different rules have evolved for different purposes.

Displacement tonnage is the weight of water pushed aside from the hole in the sea in which a boat floats. It happens to be exactly the same as the total weight of the boat and all her gear if weighed on dry land (Archimedes' Principle).

Thames tonnage is an archaic rule formulated for yachts when they were all of much the same proportions. It is determined by the formula:

$$\frac{(L - B) \times B \times \frac{1}{2}B}{94}$$

where L is the overall length in feet on deck from the forward side of the stem post to the after side of the stern post, B is the maximum beam in feet at any level but excluding rubbing strakes, and 94 is an arbitrary number decided by the Royal Thames Yacht Club many years ago. Hence the name.

As the Thames measurement formula takes no account of draught, a light shallow-draught boat will have the same tonnage as a heavy deep-draught boat of the same length and beam.

Registered tonnages are assigned in the UK by the Department of Trade by the same rules as apply to merchant ships. The **Gross Registered Tonnage** is the number of hundreds of cubic feet contained in the hull below the main deck, with additions for deck houses or any space above the main deck which may contain crew or passengers, cargo or stores under cover. This is an estimate of the 'earning capacity' of a merchant ship.

The **Net Registered Tonnage** is obtained by deducting the volumes which do not contribute directly to earning capacity (chart room, engine room, tank spaces, etc.) from the Gross Registered Tonnage.

Both GRT and NRT are recorded in a vessel's Certificate of Registry, and the GRT is carved indelibly in the main deck beam. In resinglass yachts this usually means that an engraved brass plate is bonded into a corresponding part of the cabin.

Registration of private pleasure craft is not compulsory in Britain, but it carries certain privileges and advantages.

3

Ship Safety and Insurance

In the ultimate, safety at sea comes from the competent handling of a well-found craft within the limits of both vessel and crew. Constant alertness for possible dangers is preferable to a lot of safety equipment which nobody on board knows how to use. (For seamanship in emergencies see Chapter 17.) Even so, prudence suggests (and for boats over 13·7 metres [45 feet] the British law demands) that certain safety equipment shall be carried.

The Marine Division of the British Department of Trade recommends the following scales of equipment for sea-going pleasure craft:

CRAFT OF LESS THAN 5·5 METRES (18 FEET) OVERALL LENGTH

Personal Safety Equipment

Lifejackets of Department of Trade accepted type or BSI or other national specification except those wholly dependent upon oral inflation. One for each person on board. Alternatively, in sheltered waters, one **buoyancy aid,** of the Ship and Boat Builders National Federation approved type, for each person on board. Always wear a lifejacket or buoyancy aid when there is a risk of being pitched overboard.

Rescue Equipment for Man Overboard

Lifebuoy, one, and a 30-metre (100 feet) **buoyant line** (minimum breaking strain of 115 kilos [250 lb]), where practicable. Alternatively, one Department of Trade accepted **rescue quoit.** A second lifebuoy should be carried on motor cruisers and, where practicable, on other craft.

General Equipment

Anchor of sufficient size and with a long enough mooring line or cable, according to the type and size of craft and the possible areas of operation. (See Chapter 7, *Anchors, Cables and Moorings*). A spare anchor and tow-line of 18 metres (10 fathoms) is advisable, especially for sea-angling trips.

Efficient **bilge pump,** and a **bailer** or **bucket with lanyard** (even if the yacht is fitted with a sea-bailer). For powered craft, the bilge pump should be fixed. On other craft a portable bilge pump which can draw water from the sea may be useful for fire fighting.

Paddle or **oar with rowlock,** one at least; two if practicable.

Distress signals, two at least. Even in sheltered waters adequate distress signals should be carried. (See pp.232–3).

Compass for motor cruisers, anglers' craft, dinghy cruising and racing.

First-aid kit (see p. 272).

Water-resistant torch.

Radar reflector of adequate performance, at least 12 inches, preferably 18 inches, for craft engaged in sea-angling and cruising in the open sea.

Radio receiver for craft engaged in sea-angling and cruising in the open sea.

Engine tool kit (see pp. 134–5).

Fire-fighting Equipment

One **fire extinguisher** of not less than 1·4 kilos (3 lb) capacity, dry powder (where fuel is carried), or two if galley is also fitted. Carbon dioxide (CO_2) or foam extinguishers of equal extinguishing capacity are alternatives to dry powder appliances. BCF (bromo-chloro-difluoro-methane) chemical extinguishers may be carried, but people on the boat should be warned that the fumes given off are toxic and dangerous in a confined space and a similar notice should be posted at each extinguisher point. A blanket or rug soaked in the sea may also be effective in fighting fires.

Bucket with lanyard, one. (May be the one used as a bailer).

Your craft should have been designed and built with the object of keeping fire risks to a minimum, but a check may be made on such 'built-in' precautions by referring to the Home Office pamphlet 'Fire Precautions in Pleasure Craft'.

Overloading

Never overload. The number of people or the amoun of equipment a boat can carry is generally shown on a plate fitted by the builder.

Sea-angling vessels should be more restricted and the following scale is recommended:

Craft of

4·9 metres (16 feet) but less than 5·5 metres (18 feet): 4 persons

4·3 metres (14 feet) but less than 4·9 metres (16 feet): 3 persons

3·7 metres (12 feet) but less than 4·3 metres (14 feet): 2 persons

Sea-angling from craft of less than 3·7 metres (12 feet) in length is hazardous.

CRAFT OF BETWEEN 5·5 METRES (18 FEET)
AND 13·7 METRES (45 FEET)

Personal Safety Equipment

Safety harness made to BSI specification. One for each person on sailing yachts. One or more on motor cruisers as may be needed when on deck. An adequate temporary harness may be made out of a length of 12 mm ($\frac{1}{2}$-in) nylon with an eye splice at each end and long enough to go round a waist plus 12 inches. Fit the free end with a snap shackle or carbine hook. Wear a safety harness on deck in bad weather or at night. Make sure it is properly adjusted. Experience has shown, however, that a harness can be dangerous if you go overboard at speeds of 8 knots or more.
Lifejackets of Department of Trade accepted type or BSI or other National specification except those wholly dependent upon oral inflation. One for each person on board. Keep them in a safe place where you can get at them easily. Always wear one when there is a risk of being pitched overboard.

Rescue Equipment for Man Overboard

Lifebuoys, two at least. One lifebuoy should be kept within easy reach of the helmsman. For sailing at night, it should be fitted with a self-igniting light.
Buoyant line, 30 metres (100 feet) (minimum breaking strain of 115 kilos [250 lb]). This too should be within easy reach of the helmsman.

Additional Flotation Equipment for Vessels Going More than Three Miles Out, Summer and Winter

Inflatable liferaft of Department of Trade accepted type, or equivalent—to carry everyone on board. It should be carried on deck or in a locker opening directly to the deck and should be serviced annually; OR

Rigid dinghy with permanent, not inflatable, buoyancy, and with oars and rowlocks secured. It should be carried on deck. It may be a collapsible type; OR

Inflatable dinghy built with two compartments, one at least always kept fully inflated, or built with one compartment, always kept fully inflated, and having oars and rowlocks secured. It should be carried on deck. If the vessel has enough permanent buoyancy to float when swamped with 115 kilos (250 lb) added weight, a dinghy with two compartments may be stowed. In sheltered waters a dinghy may be towed. Check that the tow is secure.

Additional Flotation Equipment for Vessels Going Not More than Three Miles Out

In Winter (1 November to 31 March):

Inflatable liferaft or alternatives, as above. In sheltered waters the summer-scale equipment, listed below, may usually be adequate. Liferafts may not be necessary on angling boats operating in organised groups when the boats are continually in contact with each other.

In Summer (1 April to 31 October):

Lifebuoys (30-inch); OR

Buoyant seats of Department of Trade accepted type, one for every two people on board. Lifebuoys carried for 'man overboard' situations may be included. Those smaller than 30-inch diameter should be regarded as support for one person only.

General Equipment

Anchors, two, each with warp or chain of appropriate size and length. Where warp is used at least 5·5 metres (3 fathoms) of chain should be used between anchor and warp. (See Chapter 7, *Anchors, Cables and Moorings*).

Bilge pump.

Efficient compass and spare.

Charts covering intended area of operation.

Distress flares, six with two of the rocket parachute type. (See pp. 232–3).

Daylight distress (smoke) signals. (See pp. 232–3).

Tow-rope of adequate length.

First-aid kit with anti-seasickness tablets. (See p. 272).

Radio receiver for weather forecasts.

Water-resistant torch.

Radar reflector of adequate performance, at least 12 inches, preferably 18 inches, but as large as can be conveniently carried. Preferably mounted at least 3 metres (10 feet) above the sea.

Lifeline, also useful in bad weather for inboard lifeline.

Engine tool kit (see pp. 134–5).

Name, number or sail number (generally recognised), should be painted prominently on the vessel or on dodgers in letters or figures at least 22 centimetres (9 inches) high.

Fire-fighting Equipment

For vessels over 9 metres (30 feet) in length and those with powerful engines, carrying quantities of fuel:

two **fire extinguishers** should be carried, each of not less than 1·4 kilos (3 lb) capacity, dry powder, or equivalent, and one or more additional extinguisher of not less than 2·3 kilos (5 lb) capacity, dry powder, or equivalent. A fixed installation may be necessary.

For vessels of up to 9 metres (30 feet) in length with cooking facilities and engines:

two fire extinguishers should be carried, each of not less than 1·4 kilos (3 lb) capacity, dry powder, or equivalent.

For vessels of up to 9 metres (30 feet) in length, with cooking facilities only or with engine only:

one fire extinguisher should be carried, of not less than

1·4 kilos (3 lb) capacity, dry powder, or equivalent. Carbon dioxide (CO_2) or foam extinguishers of equal extinguishing capacity are alternatives to dry powder appliances. BCF (bromo-chloro-difluoro-methane) chemical extinguishers may be carried, but people on the boat should be warned that the fumes given off are toxic and dangerous in a confined space, and a similar notice should be posted at each extinguisher point.

Additionally for all craft:

Buckets, two, with lanyards.

Bag of sand, useful in containing and extinguishing burning spillage of fuel or lubricant.

Your craft should have been designed and built with the object of keeping fire risks to a minimum, but a check may be made on such 'built-in' precautions by referring to the Home Office pamphlet 'Fire Precautions in Pleasure Craft' (HMSO).

CRAFT OF OVERALL LENGTH 13·7 METRES (45 FEET) AND OVER

In the UK these craft must conform with the safety equipment regulations laid down in the Merchant Shipping (Life Saving Appliances) Rules 1965. Obtain from H.M.S.O.

ADDITIONAL SAFEGUARDS

Yachtsmen making a coastal passage are strongly advised to contact the local Coastguard Station, and in the UK to complete a **Coastguard '66' Passage Report Form** (see p. 265). This ensures that the Coastguard Service has full particulars regarding the craft, her occupants, her equipment and intended voyage, for use should search and rescue action be needed. At his destination, the yachtsman reports his arrival to the nearest Coastguard Station. THERE IS NO CHARGE FOR THIS SERVICE.

A brass or plastic **whistle** attached by a lanyard to the collar of each lifejacket may make it easier to locate a man overboard in a rough sea.

All craft are required, by law, to be equipped with adequate **navigation lights** when at sea between sunset and sunrise, and means of giving **sound signals** to conform to the International Regulations for Preventing Collisions at Sea. (See Chapter 12.)

DISTRESS SIGNALS

See Chapter 16 on Sea Signalling.

SMALL-BOAT INSURANCE

Boat insurance is not at present compulsory in Britain, but like house insurance it is usually advisable. Finance companies covering a marine mortgage or hire purchase deal will of course insist on appropriate insurance until the boat is paid for.

A marine insurance policy usually covers loss of or damage to the boat herself and claims from third persons for damage to or loss of other craft or property, including injuries or loss of life. It will not cover the owner himself or his crew and passengers unless this has been specifically requested. Nor will it cover their personal effects unless they have been detailed and included in the total value of the boat.

Most companies classify boats into three major groups— over 16 feet long, under 16 feet with a maximum speed not exceeding 17 knots (i.e. dinghies and small motor craft), and fast power craft under 16 feet but whose speed can exceed 17 knots.

Cruising boats are usually over 16 feet in length, and the

cost of insuring them depends on their size, age, cruising limits, how long in commission during the year, where moored, whether laid up ashore or afloat, the amount for which the boat is to be insured and the limit of third-party cover.

Lower premiums are sometimes asked for boats with diesel engines, but petrol-driven craft may not be penalised if an approved fire-extinguishing system is installed.

In Britain, cruising limits are graded as tideless inland water, coastal waters of the UK within the 3-mile limit, coastal waters of the Continent from the River Elbe to Brest, and world-wide.

The term 'in commission' does not imply that the boat is actually in use; it means 'available for use'. Similarly, 'laid up' means that the boat is clearly not available for immediate use, as her mast or motor or some such important feature has been removed, or possibly she is laid up ashore and cannot be launched without the aid of a crane.

The third-party element of the insurance is sometimes limited to the insured value of the boat, but the cost of extra cover is modest and worth paying as claims may exceed that value considerably, particularly if personal injury or loss of life is involved.

Dinghies used as tenders to larger craft and their out-board motors should be specified separately, as they are not automatically included as part of the bigger boat's gear.

Sailing dinghies and small runabouts are often not laid up and may be used on a crisp day during the off-season. The extra cost of insuring them for 12 months in commission is quite small.

In the event of a mishap afloat, when the possibility arises of an insurance claim, skippers are expected by their insurance companies to take all possible steps to minimise the amount of the claim. In cases of theft, it helps to have a record of such data as the serial numbers of the outboard motor, the DF radio, the binoculars, etc. See Chapter 20, *Own Ship's Data*. When a theft is discovered, inform the authorities as soon as possible (Harbourmaster, police, Customs officer) as well as the insurance company.

If damage has been caused by immersion, it can be minimised by hosing down with fresh water and other early treatment. See p. 99 if the outboard motor gets a ducking.

Collision damage involves a third party, unless the object collided with was a rock. Other craft, piers, jetties all have owners and they too may have sustained some damage and wish to claim the cost of repairs. Liability should never be admitted, as it may prejudice future negotiations. Include if possible, in any claim, the name of the third party's own insurers.

The loss of a dinghy at sea will elicit little sympathy from the insurers if the name and port of registration (or yacht club) of the parent vessel is not clearly marked on the dinghy.

If you should find a lost or abandoned dinghy (or any other craft) at sea and can bring it safely into harbour, the appropriate British authority to inform is the Receiver of Wrecks, usually to be found in the local Custom House, unless of course you can restore the boat directly to its owner.

4

Ropes, Lines and their Uses

Natural organic fibre ropes are now an anachronism in small craft; this section is about modern synthetic ropes.

The **strength** of a rope depends on its cross-section area and material.

Ropes are **measured** by their overall diameter, in millimetres in the UK and in inches in the USA. The British practice of measurement by circumference is now obsolete, but the tables show all three equivalents.

Nylon rope is the strongest, size for size, with Terylene (Dacron) close behind.

Polypropylene ropes are lighter and cheaper than Nylon and Terylene but are not so strong. As they are buoyant they make good mooring and heaving lines.

Polyethylene ropes are buoyant and cheaper still, but they have the lowest strength.

Terylene (**Dacron**) ropes are excellent for halyards and sheets. In their pre-stretched form they do not slacken under load. Their strength is such that often it is necessary to use a larger rope than the load demands to avoid cutting the hands. The smallest size one may comfortably handle is about 8 mm ($\frac{5}{16}''$) in a dinghy and 10 mm ($\frac{7}{16}''$) in larger craft.

Nylon is excellent for anchor warps and mooring lines since it stretches under load and absorbs shocks.

Normal 3-strand rope is suitable for all applications and

is easy to splice. Nylon and Terylene ropes are also available in plaited (braided) form; this is easy to handle but more difficult to splice.

No rope should be used at the limit of its strength; the slightest accidental overload will break it. Nylon and Terylene ropes can be used to 90 per cent of their breaking strength but this should not be repeated frequently, especially when spliced.

The comparative working strengths and other characteristics given in Tables 2 and 3 compiled by Marlow Ropes Ltd. have been reliably proved in practice. (*For converting metric to Imperial measurements see Table 17, page 144.*)

Handling Synthetic Fibre Ropes

Synthetic ropes are more slippery than natural fibre ropes; take at least three turns round winches, capstans, mooring posts, bitts and cleats.

Avoid kinks, especially when coming under load.

Avoid damage caused by passing through an acute angle through eyebolts, shackles, fairleads, chocks.

Coil ropes down in a clockwise direction for right-hand lays.

Plaited (braided) ropes won't coil down like laid ropes; flake them down in a plastic bucket.

Synthetic ropes won't rot if put away wet, but salt crystals are abrasive and should be washed out periodically with fresh water.

Ordinary detergents will help to clean ropes, but paint removers will damage them.

Fusing the ends of ropes in a small flame is a satisfactory and easy alternative to whipping to avoid fraying. But heating the middle of a rope will certainly weaken it.

Avoid chafe and lengthen the life of rope by protecting it from abrasion. A length of plastic hosepipe for a permanent mooring rope, a strip of old rag or plastic tape for

Table 2
Typical Strengths of Synthetic Fibre Ropes
Guaranteed Working Strength (kg) (1 kg = 2·2 lb)

Diam. mm	Diam. in	Circ. in	TERYLENE/DACRON POLYESTER					NYLON		POLY-PROPYLENE	8-Plait	POLY-ETHYLENE	Diam. mm
			3-Strand Standard	3-Strand Pre-Stretched	8-Plait Pre-Stretched	8-Plait Matt Finish	16-Plait Matt Finish	3-Strand	Braided		8-Plait		
1·5	$\frac{1}{16}$	$\frac{3}{16}$	—	—	65	—	—	—	—	—	—	—	1·5
2	$\frac{3}{32}$	$\frac{1}{4}$	140	—	75	—	—	—	—	—	—	—	2
3	$\frac{1}{8}$	$\frac{3}{8}$	230	230	165	—	—	—	—	—	—	—	3
4	$\frac{3}{16}$	$\frac{1}{2}$	295	295	295	204	—	320	—	—	—	180	4
5	$\frac{7}{32}$	$\frac{5}{8}$	400	400	400	305	—	550	—	—	320	—	5
6	$\frac{1}{4}$	$\frac{3}{4}$	565	565	565	470	—	750	—	550	500	360	6
7	$\frac{9}{32}$	$\frac{7}{8}$	770	770	770	—	—	1050	—	—	—	—	7
8	$\frac{5}{16}$	1	1015	1015	1015	560	1120	1350	—	960	910	630	8
9	$\frac{3}{8}$	1 $\frac{1}{8}$	—	1270	—	940	—	1500	—	—	—	—	9
10	$\frac{7}{16}$	1 $\frac{1}{4}$	1590	1590	1590	1015	2000	2080	—	1425	1360	980	10
12	$\frac{1}{2}$	1 $\frac{1}{2}$	2270	2270	2270	1590	3000	3000	—	2030	—	1386	12
14	$\frac{9}{16}$	1 $\frac{3}{4}$	3180	3180	—	—	3300	4100	—	2790	—	1880	14
16	$\frac{5}{8}$	2	4060	—	—	—	3500	5300	5300	3500	—	2510	16
18	$\frac{3}{4}$	2 $\frac{1}{4}$	4570	—	—	—	3850	6700	6700	4450	—	—	18
20	$\frac{7}{8}$	2 $\frac{1}{2}$	5580	—	—	—	5580	8300	8300	5370	—	—	20

Table 3

Recommended Rope Sizes (Minimum)
Halyards
(Pre-stretched Terylene/Dacron)

OVERALL BOAT LENGTH metres	MAIN Diam. mm	JIB Diam. mm	SPINNAKER Diam. mm	BURGEE Plaited Diam. mm
4–7	6	7	6	1·5
8–10	9	9	7	3
11–13	10	10	7	3
14–16	12	12	8	3

Sheets
(Pre-stretched or Braided Terylene/Dacron)

OVERALL BOAT LENGTH metres	MAIN or JIB Diam. mm	GENOA Diam. mm	SPINNAKER Diam. mm	SPINNAKER LIGHT WEATHER Diam. mm
4–7	10	10	6	6
8–10	10	10	10	6
11–13	10	12	12	6
14–16	12	16	16	10

Mooring Ropes and Dock Lines

OVERALL BOAT LENGTH metres	MINIMUM SIZE Terylene/Dacron Diam. mm	Polyprop/ Polyethylene Diam. mm	Nylon Diam. mm
4–7	6	8	6
8–10	12	16	10
11–13	14	20	12
14–16	16	24	14

Lengths: Head and stern lines ⎱ equal to length of boat.
Fore and aft springs ⎰
Breast lines: at least half length of boat.

Anchor Warps: see Table 6, page 85.

temporary use. Ropes with particles of grime and grit embedded in the lay will have a short life, so keep them clean.

Sheets and halyards abrade mainly where they pass through blocks and sheaves. Turning them end-for-end each season changes the abraded section. If new ropes are cut a few feet longer than is necessary, they can be subsequently shortened to change the point of abrasion.

A REEL FOR STOWING KEDGE WARPS

Short mooring and other lines are easily coiled down by hand and stowed in a locker. Longer warps for kedge anchors are more difficult and should be kept on a reel. A 12-inch diameter reel with a 4-inch diameter core 4-inches long is a convenient size; it will hold approximately the following amounts of different size ropes:

Rope size (Diam. in inch/mm)

$\frac{1}{4}''$/6 mm	$\frac{5}{16}''$/8 mm	$\frac{7}{16}''$/10 mm	$\frac{1}{2}''$/12 mm	$\frac{9}{16}''$/14 mm
540'/160m	420'/130m	240'/73m	140'/42m	100'/30m

Capacity in feet/metres

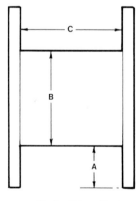

4 Kedge Warp Reel

Referring to Fig. 4, the approximate capacity of any other size drum may be calculated from the formula:

$$\text{Capacity in feet} = K \times C \times A(A + B)$$

where the constant K for different size ropes is:

$\frac{1}{4}''$/6 mm	$\frac{5}{16}''$/8 mm	$\frac{7}{16}''$/10 mm	$\frac{1}{2}''$/12 mm	$\frac{9}{16}''$/14 mm	$\frac{5}{8}''$/16 mm
4·2	3·2	1·9	1·1	0·8	0·7

KNOTS, BENDS AND HITCHES

Knots are strictly ornamental rather than functional, **bends** secure one rope to another and **hitches** secure a rope around a spar or through a ring. But the terminology is inconsistent. A small repertoire of bends and hitches will meet almost all requirements in a small boat.

A **round turn and two half hitches** (Fig. 5) will suit a number of needs, like attaching a rope to a ring, fenders to a guard rail, the dinghy painter to the parent craft. The free end should always be long enough not to slip back through the second half-hitch; if this end is lashed ('frapped')

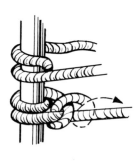

5 Round Turn and Two Half Hitches

57

to the standing part with thin cordage the hitch can never come undone involuntarily. The complete round turn is essential to security; a single half-turn will slip under load.

A **fisherman's bend** (Fig. 6) is preferred by some for dinghy painters, anchor rings and similar occasions where the load may jerk and cause a synthetic rope to slip. An extra half-hitch will make it more secure still.

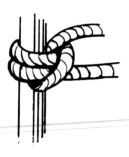

6 Fisherman's Bend

The **bowline** (Fig. 7) is essentially a temporary method of making an eye at the end of a rope; it serves to attach a heaving line to a mooring rope to send it ashore, as a lifeline for someone going up the mast on a bosun's chair or to send the tool bag up to him. It does not jam, and can be opened easily after carrying a heavy load. If you can tie a bowline single-handed in the dark with the rope under tension it may save your life if you fall overboard from a moving vessel.

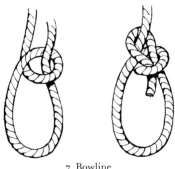

7 Bowline

A **clove hitch** (Fig. 8) secures a rope to a rail or spar at a point remote from both ends of the rope. It may tend to jam and is difficult to untie after being under load, and will slip if the load is applied obliquely.

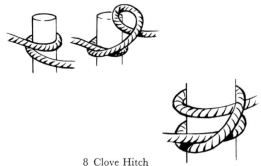

8 Clove Hitch

A **rolling hitch** (Fig. 9) is a clove hitch with an extra hitch to prevent it from sliding. Often used to attach burgee sticks to halyards, it has many similar applications. The two adjacent turns should be on the end from which the tension comes.

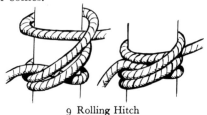

9 Rolling Hitch

59

10 Reef or Square Knot

A **reef knot** or **square knot** (Fig. 10) is strictly for joining reef points on sails without roller reefing, **but** can be used for attaching two ropes of equal size together. If subjected to strain, or if the ropes are of unequal size or stiffness, it is liable to 'capsize' and let go.

A **sheet bend** (Fig. 11) is better for joining two unequal ropes; a double sheet bend better still.

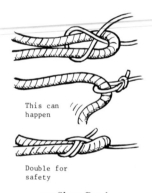

This can
happen

Double for
safety

11 Sheet Bend

A **marling hitch** (Fig. 12) is often used for lashing sails to spars; it is an obvious choice for tying long bundles of anything together.

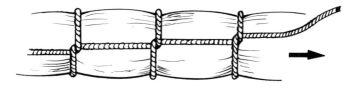

12 Marling Hitch

A **figure of eight knot** (Fig. 13) prevents a sheet or other rope from pulling through a block or fairlead. It is less likely to jam than an overhand knot, which is not a complete knot in itself but only a step in making other knots.

13 Figure-of-Eight (Stopper) Knot

SHORT SPLICES AND EYE SPLICES

A **short splice** (Fig. 14) is used to join two ropes together semi-permanently; while quite adequate for repairing or lengthening mooring ropes it does reduce the overall strength by about an eighth and it cannot be used for running rigging (halyards or sheets) as its diameter will no longer pass through a block or sheave of the correct size for the rope. Make five full tucks in any synthetic rope splice.

An **eye splice** (Fig. 15) provides a permanent eye at the end of a rope such as a halyard or spinnaker sheet. For some applications a simple 'soft' eye is adequate, but if the eye is to be used with a shackle or other metalwork of small

61

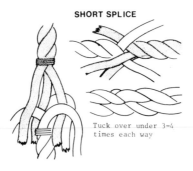

14 Short Splice

diameter a thimble should be included to avoid damage to the rope. In this case it becomes a 'hard' eye or 'thimble' eye. Every size of rope has an appropriate size of thimble; too small a thimble will cut into the rope and too large may chafe adjacent ropes. A large eye splice for a permanent mooring rope can be protected from chafe by making it through an appropriate length of plastic hose-pipe or sewing on a heavy Terylene sailcloth sheath.

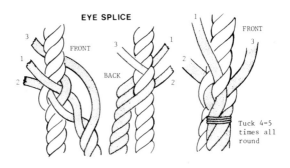

15 Eye Splice

Long Splices, it is true, will pass through blocks and sheaves intended for the particular size of rope, but they are a relic of the times when sailing ships might be at sea for a year or more. In these days of good cheap and durable synthetic ropes they are a false economy.

Splicing braided ropes (Figs. 16 and 17). The easiest way of making an eye in braided rope is the 'sew and serve' method. Unless the stoppings, sewing and serving are really tight the result will be a weak untidy splice. Waxed Terylene whipping twine should be used for sewing and or serving.

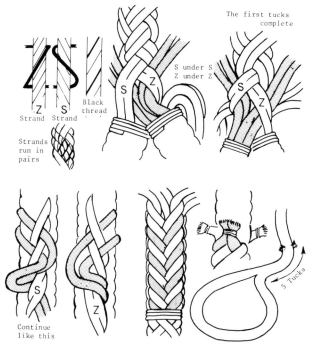

16 Splicing Braided Ropes

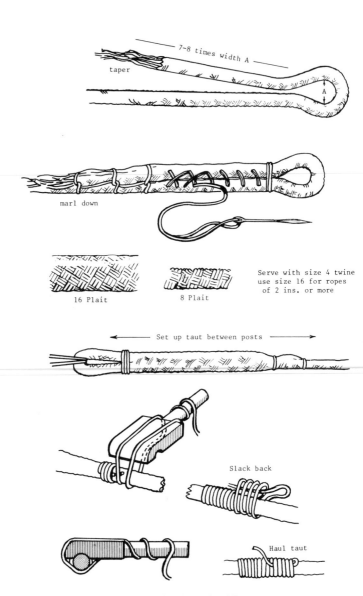

7–8 times width A

taper

A

marl down

16 Plait

8 Plait

Serve with size 4 twine
use size 16 for ropes
of 2 ins. or more

Set up taut between posts

Slack back

Haul taut

17 Eye Splice in Braided Ropes

64

WIRE ROPES

Standing rigging usually consists of stiff rope of 7 strands, each of 7 or 19 wires; the exact size of each wire depends on the strength required of the rope as a whole.

In running rigging the rope is made flexible by surrounding a central fibre or plastic core with 6 strands, each of 7 or 19 wires.

Wire ropes may be terminated in hand-made eye-splices, hydraulically-swaged terminals or Talurit splices. A good hand-made splice reduces the strength of the rope by about 15 per cent, a bad one by considerably more. The makers of machine-made terminations claim that the strength of their splices exceeds that of the rope. Typical strengths and other properties are given in Table 4.

Temporary eyes in wire rope may be made in emergency by Bulldog grips.

Flexible wire rope halyards may be spliced into a soft rope tail to facilitate handling; the method is the same as

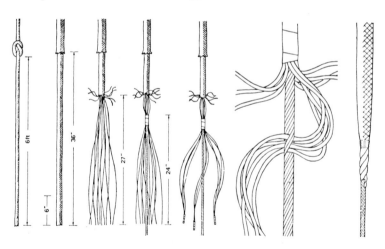

18 Splicing Braided Ropes to Wire

for splicing fibre ropes except that the 6 wires are grouped into 3 pairs and treated as 3 strands.

The method recommended by Marlow Ropes Ltd. for splicing a plaited rope to a wire is shown in Fig. 18.

Table 4

Properties of Small Wire Ropes

CONSTRUCTION	DIAM. (NOMINAL)		WEIGHT (approx)		MIN. BREAKING LOAD	
	mm	in	kg/100 m	lb/100 ft	kg	lb
7 × 19	3	$\frac{1}{8}$	3·34	2·24	588	1294
Steel Core	4	$\frac{3}{16}$	5·94	3·99	1040	2288
	5	$\frac{7}{32}$	9·29	6·24	1630	3586
	6	$\frac{1}{4}$	13·4	8·98	2350	5170
	7	$\frac{9}{32}$	18·2	12·2	3200	7040
7 × 7	2	$\frac{3}{32}$	1·51	1·01	276	607
Steel Core	3	$\frac{1}{8}$	3·39	2·28	629	1384
	4	$\frac{3}{16}$	6·05	4·07	1120	2464
	5	$\frac{7}{32}$	9·46	6·36	1750	3850
	6	$\frac{1}{4}$	13·6	9·14	2520	5544
	7	$\frac{9}{32}$	18·5	12·4	3430	7546
6 × 19	3	$\frac{1}{8}$	3·02	2·03	498	1096
Fibre Core	4	$\frac{3}{16}$	5·37	3·61	885	1947
Flexible	5	$\frac{7}{32}$	8·41	5·64	1380	3036
	6	$\frac{1}{4}$	12·1	8·13	1990	4378
	7	$\frac{9}{32}$	16·5	11·1	2710	5962
6 × 7	2	$\frac{3}{32}$	1·39	0·93	239	526
Fibre Core	3	$\frac{1}{8}$	3·12	2·09	538	1184
Flexible	4	$\frac{3}{16}$	5·55	3·73	957	2105
	5	$\frac{7}{32}$	8·68	5·83	1500	3300
	6	$\frac{1}{4}$	12·5	8·38	2150	4730
	7	$\frac{9}{32}$	17·0	11·4	2930	6446

PURCHASES AND TACKLES

. Purchases give more power to your elbow for handling heavy loads; levers, winches, capstans, blocks and tackles, all these are forms of purchase, and all are found in one place or another in most small craft.

While levers, winches and capstans are usually installed permanently for a specific purpose, blocks and tackles are portable devices which can be applied to many different tasks, like hoisting out the engine, hauling a boat up a slipway, even lifting a boat to get at the underside of the keel.

The main sheet is a common example of a block and tackle system in a sailing craft, and so is the kicking strap or vang.

A tackle must have at least one moving block to gain any mechanical advantage; a single fixed block can only alter the direction of a rope's pull.

Mechanical advantage is the gain in lifting power obtained from a tackle; it is simply the ratio between the weight lifted and the force applied to the free end (the fall) of the rope. Apart from frictional losses, the mechanical advantage of a tackle is the same as the number of parts of the rope at the moving block. In practice, friction reduces this somewhat.

Blocks with multiple sheaves give a greater mechanical advantage than single blocks; use the block with the greater number of sheaves as the moving block to maximise this effect.

There is a right and a wrong way round to use the same tackle to gain greater mechanical advantage. See Fig. 19.

When rigging any block and tackle system, be sure that the fixed block is adequately supported; it may have to carry not only the weight of the object being lifted but

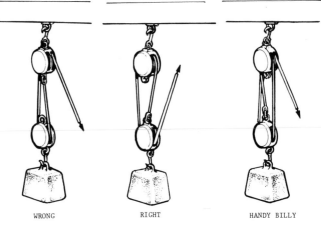

WRONG   RIGHT   HANDY BILLY

19 Blocks and Tackles

also the pull applied to the fall of the rope.

When it is necessary to support a weight on a tackle for a period of time and the fall of the rope cannot be cleated, it is wise to wind and tie several turns of thinner rope round the tackle between the blocks. This is known as 'racking' and it will prevent the tackle from moving accidentally.

A temporary method of supporting the weight is to jam the fall of the rope between the weight-bearing parts of the tackle and one of the blocks. Called 'choking the luff', this should only be used for short periods and for light loads, as heavy loads are liable to damage the rope.

A useful tackle to have in a boat is a **'handy-billy'** (Fig. 19). It consists of a double block at the fixed end and a single block with becket at the moving end to which is attached a length of 12 mm ($\frac{1}{2}$-inch diameter) rope. This will lift half a ton with a more-than-adequate margin of safety.

Slinging a Load

More accidents happen through faulty slinging than through failure of the tackle itself.

The most useful form of sling for general purposes is a strop; this is a rope spliced to form an endless loop. When placed around the load and passed back through itself it grips the load and reduces the risk of slipping. Two such slings will lift a spar or packing case if they are properly spaced so that they make an angle of about 45 degrees where they are attached to the tackle or crane hook.

A greater angle places an unfair load on the slings; in an extreme case (150 degrees between the slings) the load on each sling is twice the total weight of the object to be lifted.

Although a sling may be strong enough to lift a given load, it may be cut or damaged by sharp edges or an acute bend in the rope, like a shackle of small diameter. To avoid this, pad the edges of packing cases underneath the slings, and if the crane or lifting tackle has no hook, use a big shackle to attach the slings or fit a metal thimble in each sling.

Awkward loads like boat motors need special treatment; if no lifting eyes are fitted it is usually necessary to put one sling under the gearbox, a second sling round the flywheel or other strong point at the opposite end and a third sling to the top of the middle of the engine to prevent it from overturning when lifted.

Before taking the weight completely on the slings, they should be adjusted for length, taking care that they cannot slip off projecting parts, nor damage piping or other components.

Never leave a load in mid-air for a moment longer than is needed; slings can break, crane ratchets can slip, the wind may set a load swaying uncontrollably, and even if nobody gets hurt a long drop may prove expensive. Keep the load no more than an inch or two above the deck or ground when manoeuvring it.

Always lift a load vertically; it will otherwise swing when the strain is taken and may cause injury or damage. A heavy load may be manoeuvred sideways by hauling on it with a second tackle.

5

Sails and Sailcloth

There's no better way of knowing how your sails set than to get someone else to handle the boat on all points of sailing while you watch critically from another boat. Alternatively, get someone else to take photographs or make a movie from the other boat while you sail your own boat.

Don't expect too much; a heavy cruiser rarely points closer to the true wind than 50 degrees, an average cruiser or ocean racer about 45 degrees, and racing machines and some dinghies about 35 degrees.

A lot can be learnt from tell-tales sewn to each side of the main and foresails; these should be short lengths of nylon yarn or ribbon, located in the position of maximum curvature of the sail, usually about one third of the luff length up from the foot and one third of the foot length back from the luff. Similar tell-tales tied to the shrouds and backstay show the direction of the apparent wind at any instant.

Foresail Sheeting Arrangements

The sheeting angle, that is the angle between the foot of the foresail and the centreline of the boat, is very important if maximum performance is desired. In one-design boats you have no choice, but in many quantity-produced cruising boats the angle is often not optimized.

Sheeting angles of 10 to 20 degrees are quoted by various sources, but for any particular boat the exact figure is best found by experiment. It will, moreover, be different for every foresail used, every wind strength and every course sailed on or off the wind. You can deal with these variables by fitting tracks on the deck for sliding sheet blocks or by having several pairs of sheet blocks in different positions, or at least eyes for them.

Either of these measures may not be justified in a small boat; in this case it is usual to settle for a sheet block location optimised for beating to windward in Force 3 or 4 with the foresail normally used in those conditions.

To find this location experimentally, sail the boat hard on the wind with the sheets correctly trimmed, then luff up very slowly. If the luffs of the foresail and the mainsail begin to lift at the same moment, the sheeting angle is about right. If the mainsail luff lifts before the foresail, the sheet blocks may be moved outwards, and *vice versa*. The exact amount may be estimated by pulling the sheet itself inwards or outwards as necessary and noting where the line of the sheet from the clew of the sail would meet the deck.

The position of the sheet blocks in a fore-and-aft direction is equally important. This again will vary with the sizes of the foresails, etc., and several sheet block locations may be needed for best performance. The criterion is that the sheet angle in the vertical plane should be such as to give the same tension on the foot of the sail as on the leech so that each takes up a natural curve. Generally, if the leech flutters move the block forward, if the foot flutters, move it aft.

Various rules of thumb quote angles between the extension of the sheet line and the mitre seam of the sail, but since this seam may or may not bisect the angle at the clew of the sail it is better to experiment with each foresail carried and optimise the sheet leads for your own boat.

A Barber hauler is useful to control the actual direction in which a jib sheet pulls. A temporary one will show whether any change is needed in the positions of sheet blocks; fitted permanently it can control the size of the slot between the mainsail and foresail.

See p. 55 for appropriate sizes of rope for sheets and p. 82 on sheet winches.

STOWING SAILS

Modern synthetic sails don't need drying out as cotton sails did to prevent mildew when bagged and stowed away. Even so, a little care in stowing them will pay off in efficiency and ease of handling.

Sail bags should be amply big enough to hold their contents without ramming the sail in tightly; creases are formed this way and spoil the airflow over the surface. For the same reason no heavy weight should be placed on a bagged sail.

When bagging a sail, it should be lightly flaked down in the bag in the reverse order to that in which it is raised, so that the head comes out first for a mainsail and the tack for a jib, staysail or genoa. A spinnaker should be bagged with all three corners visible at the top of the bag so that the halyard and both sheets may be attached before unbagging the sail.

Mainsails of cruising boats are often stowed along the boom and not bagged. If such a sail is flaked down across the boom any creases which form will be in the direction of the airflow and less likely to disturb it than if the sail is merely bundled up under a tight sail cover.

Lower sail battens which are substantially parallel with the boom may be left in position, but any upper battens which are at an angle with the boom should be removed before stowing a mainsail. They may otherwise force the

73

sail into an unnatural shape while stowed.

Mainsails which are stowed on a boom should be protected from sunlight and dirt by a cover; PVC cloth with nylon reinforcement is an excellent material for this purpose.

SAILCLOTH WEIGHTS

The right weight of cloth for any sail is the lightest which will stand the wind it is to be used in.

A rough approximation of the weight in ounces per square yard of Terylene (Dacron) for working sails may be obtained by dividing the waterline length of the boat in feet by 3.

Table 5 gives more precise figures, but the sailmaker's advice should be sought regarding ghosters, heavy-weather spinnakers and other special requirements.

Table 5

Sailcloth Weights

BOAT	MAINSAIL, WORKING FORESAILS	GENOA	LIGHT GENOA	SPIN-NAKER (*Nylon*)
	Ounces per sq. yd. of Terylene/Dacron			
Light Dinghy	4	4	–	$1\frac{1}{2}$
Heavy Dinghy	5	5	–	$1\frac{1}{2}$
Light Keelboat	$6\frac{1}{2}$	$6\frac{1}{2}$	4–5	$1\frac{1}{2}$
Cruisers:				
Waterline Length				
15–17 feet	5–7	5–7	4–5	$1\frac{1}{2}$
18–20	6–8	6–8	4–5	$1\frac{1}{2}$
21–25	8–$9\frac{1}{2}$	6–$9\frac{1}{2}$	5–6	$1\frac{1}{2}$
26–30	$9\frac{1}{2}$–$10\frac{1}{2}$	6–$10\frac{1}{2}$	5–6	2

Cloth width is normally 36 inches in UK and USA.

The weight of European metric cloth in grams per square metre is 33 times the figures in Table 5.

Darning Small Tears

The diagram shows the method of darning a straight or right-angled rent. (Fig. 20). Start from the under side at point X at end of tear.

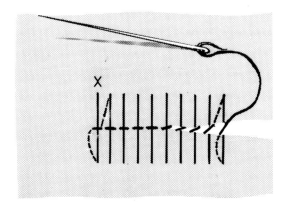

20 Darning a Sail

Draw every stitch taut and finish off with a back-stitch through the holes made by the last stitch.

A sailmaker's leather palm makes sewing heavy cloth easier.

Use Terylene thread for Terylene sails and for nylon spinnakers.

75

Thread size is measured by its breaking strength in pounds. For small repairs use a poundage equal to half the cloth weight, (4 oz. cloth—2 lb. thread, etc.)

Wax the thread with a block of beeswax or a candle; this makes it easier to work and helps the darn to lie flat.

Needles come in Standard Wire Gauges; the most useful sizes in small craft are numbers 17, 18 and 19.

A small rent can be held together temporarily until a

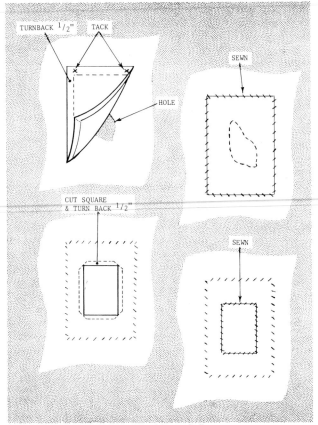

21 Patching a Sail

more permanent repair is possible by covering it with sticking plaster from the first aid kit.

Patching Holes

The diagrams show the sequence. (Fig. 21). The patch should be of the same weight cloth as the sail to be repaired, and should extend about 2 inches beyond the hole after its ragged edges have been cut square.

Thread and needle sizes as above for small darns.

If the hole is larger than half the width of the cloth the whole cloth should be replaced over a suitable length.

Cleaning Soiled Sails

Scrub sails in hot water and detergent to remove dirt and grime. Areas of heavy soiling can be soaked in liquid detergent before scrubbing, preferably overnight.

Rust stains can be removed by soaking the area affected in a weak oxalic acid solution (one half-pound of oxalic acid crystals to each gallon of hot water, or pro rata). Wash carefully in fresh water afterwards; oxalic acid is toxic. Don't use this solution on coloured sails; the dye may be bleached and the final result worse than the original stain.

Grease and **oil stains** can be dissolved in any commercial degreasing agent such as trichlorethylene. A mixture of 'trike' and detergent applied by brushing will loosen obstinate grease marks. But in practice you are more likely to have Swarfega or a similar jelly hand-cleaner aboard, and this will dissolve grease or oil which can then be washed out in cold water.

Paint and **varnish stains** should be removed by acetone; in no circumstances use paint stripper on sails.

Blood stains can usually be removed by a weak ammonia solution (half a pint in a gallon of cold water), followed by a fresh water wash with detergent.

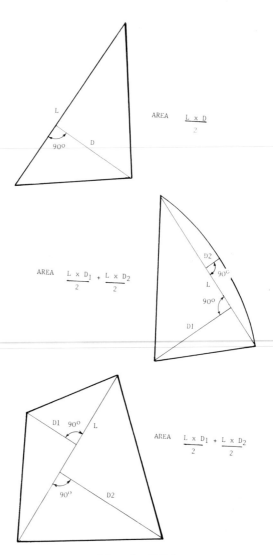

22 Measuring Sail Area

CALCULATING SAIL AREAS

The area of a triangular sail with substantially straight luff, leech and foot is simply half the length of the leech (L) multiplied by the perpendicular distance (D) from the clew to the leech. (Fig. 22).

If the leech or foot have significant curvature (roach) the additional areas to be added to the basic triangle may be estimated by the same method: half the straight-line distance from clew to head (or tack) multiplied by the maximum projection of the leech (or foot) beyond that line.

The area of a gaff mainsail or other quadrilateral sail is measured by dividing the sail diagonally into two triangles, calculating the area of each triangle as above and adding the two results.

Spinnakers are difficult to measure, as their shape and fullness varies so greatly. An approximation is obtained by multiplying the lengths of the leech and the foot and subtracting 10 per cent for the area lost at the head.

'Percentage' sail measurements indicate the actual area of a foresail/jib/genoa relative to the area of the fore triangle, which is one half I times J, where I is the height from the deck to the foresail halyard block and J is the distance along the deck from the mast to the foot of the forestay. A 100 per cent sail has the same area (though not necessarily the same shape) as the fore triangle.

6

Standing and Running Rigging

Modern synthetic fibre and stainless steel wire ropes have taken much of the agony and expense out of rigging, but a certain amount of attention is still required; failures can be inconvenient, perhaps expensive, in the limit fatal.

Incipient failure of fibre ropes is obvious from examination; abraded and chafed lengths can on occasion be cut out and the ends respliced, but if the rope has to run through a block, sheave or small fairlead it may be necessary to replace it completely. See section on running rigging, p. 81.

Galvanised wire standing rigging eventually loses its protective coat of zinc and rusts, particularly at the lower ends which are exposed to salt spray. Such a wire may be good for another season but it should be treated with suspicion.

Any wire from which short strands project to cut or prick the hands is obviously weakened and should be replaced in the interest of safety, both of the boat and of her crew.

Standing rigging wires have been known to fatigue through wind-induced vibration, often where bending stresses are concentrated at the ferrule of a splice.

Short needles of stainless steel found on deck are a sign of fatigue in a wire somewhere in the rigging. Wire running rigging may break into such needles at a sheave, or round a winch drum.

SETTING UP STANDING RIGGING

The object is to get the mast absolutely straight and upright, though a little rake aft may be desirable.

First slacken off all forestays, backstays (and runners if fitted).

Slacken off lower shrouds and adjust masthead shrouds until the mast is upright in the thwartships plane.

Adjust masthead forestay and backstay rigging screws until the mast is upright (or correctly raked) in the fore-and-aft plane.

Tighten up lower shrouds and inner forestay (if fitted) while taking care that the centre of the mast is not bent.

Sight up the mast track to check that it is dead straight.

When all is well lock the rigging screws; seizing wire is more reliable than locknuts.

No wire should be slack, nor should it be so taut that it twangs like a violin string. Experience will decide the right tension; the lee shrouds may be expected to slacken when sailing in a fair breeze.

Occasionally check that the mast is still straight when sailing hard on the wind and when running before it.

Runners should be adjusted for tension when actually sailing; they must remove any curve from the mast when under load on both tacks.

The pins of all shackles aloft should have been wire-locked before the mast was stepped. Where fork-ends are used their split pins should be of stainless steel.

Wire with strands sticking out like barbed wire is dangerous and should be replaced.

LOOKING AFTER RUNNING RIGGING

Running rigging suffers most from chafing. Sheets and halyards become chafed locally where they pass through blocks or rub against shrouds and guard rails.

The life of running rigging may be extended by turning it end-for-end occasionally, maybe each season, certainly before serious abrasion is obvious.

A length of polythene tubing over the regions of contact with shrouds and guard rails will minimise chafe. Thread the tubing over new wire rope before splicing the terminations; split the tubing longitudinally and tape it round existing wires.

New running rigging should be a few feet longer than the minimum necessary; it can subsequently be shortened to remake a splice or to move the point of chafe along the rope.

Experiment with the lead of foresheets; the best run is usually a little lower than the extension of the line formed by the mitre seam of the sail. The foresheet block will be in a different position for each size of foresail. See p. 71.

Recommended sizes of ropes for halyards and sheets for various sizes of craft are given on p. 55.

It is conventional for main halyards to be cleated on the starboard side of a mast and jib and foresail halyards on the port side. Not all mass-producers of small sailing craft appear to have heard of this.

SHEET WINCHES

Sailing dinghies and boats with a foresail area of less than about 50 square feet rarely need winches, but some mechanical help is needed to sheet in the genoa of quite a small cruiser in a strong wind.

Sheet winches should be chosen to deal with the maximum sheet tension expected, but this will not necessarily come from the biggest sail in the wardrobe. For instance, a huge 'ghoster' used only in light weather conditions will exert a smaller pull than a working genoa used in winds up to Force 5.

Some winch makers work on a rule of 5 pounds tension for every square foot of sail. A 100 square feet foresail would thus exert a maximum pull of 500 lb; if one assumes that a normal crew-member can exert a force not exceeding 100 lb on the winch handle, a 'mechanical advantage' of not less than five is required.

Mechanical advantage is assessed by dividing the length of the winch handle (measured from the centre of the winch drum) by the radius of the drum. A 12-inch handle on a 4-inch diameter drum would thus have a mechanical advantage of 6.

In the larger sizes, sheet winches have internal gearing to obtain the required mechanical advantage for a big sail; otherwise the length of winch handle needed would be unwieldy.

7

Anchors, Cables and Moorings

All but the smallest boats need two anchors: a main or 'bower' anchor and a kedge.

The **bower** anchor should be heavy enough to hold in any conditions of wind, sea and holding ground you are likely to encounter.

The **kedge** may be lighter; it is invaluable for 'mooring ship' to two anchors in a crowded or restricted harbour or anchorage, also for laying out with the dinghy to haul off when you have run aground, and to anchor temporarily when waiting for wind or tide.

Plough and Danforth type anchors are most popular for small craft; weight for weight they hold much better than fisherman anchors, and are easier to stow on deck or below.

Chain cable is the best for cruising boats' bower anchors; it should be at least 3 times as long as the greatest depth of water you are likely to anchor in. You can extend it with a rope if this is ever necessary.

A 'shackle' of chain (15 fathoms, 30 metres) is often enough for a 4- or 5-tonner, two shackles for larger boats.

Nylon warps are satisfactory for kedge anchors and, with reservations, for bower anchors. They should have at least three fathoms (5·5 metres) of chain between the anchor and the nylon. This keeps the pull on the anchor horizontal and minimizes abrasion on a rocky bottom.

Nylon anchor warps should be at least 5 times the depth of the deepest likely anchorage. A minimum of 50 metres (150 feet) will suit the smaller boat, twice that for larger boats.

Two or more lengths of chain should be joined with proper joining shackles; they are stronger than ordinary shackles and will pass over the gipsy of the anchor winch without difficulty. They are however not as strong as the chain, so get a full unbroken length if possible.

The inboard end of the chain should be secured in the chain locker to prevent the end being lost overboard accidentally. A Terylene lashing is preferable to a shackle; it may be necessary to slip the chain in a hurry to avoid being run down or to add a length of rope when dragging. In these circumstances it may be impossible to undo a shackle under load, but the lashing can be cut.

If you have to slip the end of the chain overboard for any reason, put a buoy (e.g. a plastic fender) and line on it so that it may be retrieved later.

Table 6 gives recommended anchor weights and chain and warp sizes for various craft:

Table 6

Recommended Anchor Weights, Chain and Warp Sizes

LENGTH OVERALL		BOWER ANCHOR WEIGHT		KEDGE ANCHOR WEIGHT		CHAIN SIZE	NYLON WARP SIZE Diam.	
feet	metres							
		lb	kg	lb	kg	in	in	mm
13–23	4–7	15	7	—	—	$\frac{3}{16}$	$\frac{5}{16}$	8
26–32	8–10	35	16	20	9	$\frac{5}{16}$	$\frac{9}{16}$	14
36–43	11–13	45	20	25	11	$\frac{3}{8}$	$\frac{5}{8}$	16
46–52	14–16	45	20	25	11	$\frac{7}{16}$	$\frac{7}{8}$	20

It is helpful to know how much chain you have down at any time; any private colour code painted on the links at intervals will achieve this.

Retrieving a foul anchor: see section on boatwork, p. 243.

PERMANENT MOORINGS

A mooring should be more than just adequate for the size of boat and the shelter offered by the location. In the owner's absence the boat may be subjected to strong tides and gale force winds, and break adrift if the mooring is too light.

Some harbour authorities lay permanent moorings for local and visiting craft; the harbourmaster will know which moorings are appropriate to the tonnage and draught of particular yachts. These moorings are usually on 'trots', or long heavy chains anchored to the sea bed with less heavy chains rising at intervals, one for each boat to be accommodated. See Fig. 23.

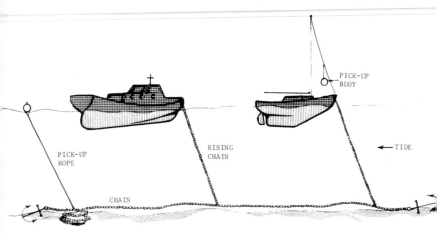

23 Trot of Permanent Moorings

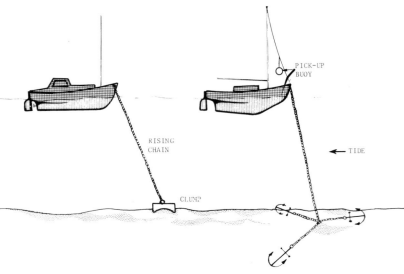

24 Single Permanent Moorings

A pick-up buoy and rope is attached to each rising chain; when mooring, the buoy-rope should be brought completely inboard and the boat made fast to the chain. Failing this, the rope may chafe through or allow the boat to foul the next boat on the trot.

It is sometimes possible to find a location where owners may lay their own private moorings. Such a mooring would consist of a heavy cast iron or reinforced concrete clump of suitable weight and with a concave underside whose suction will add to holding power, Fig. 24. The weight required depends on the nature of the seabed and the drag and the windage of the boat; the weight of the boat is immaterial except insofar as bigger boats have greater windage and drag.

A sandy or muddy bottom will have the best holding power; soft silt has little to be said for it though a clump may sink through it to a harder foundation. Rocky bottoms have no holding power whatsoever and should normally be avoided; similarly thick weed, though anchors may be used instead of a clump (see later).

A clump will withstand a horizontal pull on a sandy bottom a little less than its own weight, and about $1\frac{1}{2}$ times its weight on a soft muddy seabed. As with an anchor, the pull must be horizontal or the clump will merely lift off the bottom.

The rising chain should thus be about $2\frac{1}{2}$ times as long as the depth of water at High Water Spring Tides. It should be attached to the ring of the clump by a heavy shackle whose pin has been rivetted over (or at least wire-locked).

It may be desirable to put a swivel between the clump and the rising chain, especially if the boat is not often used.

The buoy rope should be a foot or so shorter than the depth at Low Water Spring Tides; this will prevent it chafing on the bottom at any state of the tide. Accordingly the buoy itself should be able to support the weight of chain lifted off the seabed at High Water Springs. You'll have to calculate this for your own local range of tides, using Table 7:

Table 7

Mooring Buoys Reserve Buoyancy

WEIGHT OF CHAIN (lb/ft)		RESERVE BUOYANCY OF HALF-IMMERSED SPHERICAL POLYTHENE BUOYS (lb)	
in	lb/ft	Diam. in	lb
$\frac{1}{4}$	0·75	12	13
$\frac{5}{16}$	1·0	15	25
$\frac{3}{8}$	1·5	18	45
$\frac{7}{16}$	2·0	21	70
$\frac{1}{2}$	2·5	24	110

Table 8 suggests some suitable clump weights and chain and rope sizes for various boats:

Table 8

Mooring Clump Weights, Chain and Rope Sizes

LENGTH OVERALL		CLUMP WEIGHT		CHAIN SIZE	POLYPROPYLENE BUOY ROPE DIAM.	
(feet)	(metres)	(lb)	(kg)	(in)	(mm)	(in)
13–23	4–7	900	400	$\frac{3}{8}$	16	$\frac{5}{8}$
26–32	8–10	1500	700	$\frac{7}{16}$	20	$\frac{7}{8}$
36–43	11–13	2200	1000	$\frac{1}{2}$	20	$\frac{7}{8}$
46–52	14–16	3300	1500	$\frac{1}{2}$	20	$\frac{7}{8}$

In estuaries where a strong tide runs and in harbours with a thick carpet of weed on the bottom, it is advisable to use anchors and a ground chain instead of a clump. The idea is to have a span of chain between two anchors and the rising chain attached to the middle of the span.

The length of HALF the span plus the rising chain should be at least $2\frac{1}{2}$ times the depth at High Water Springs. The rising chain itself must be at least the depth at HWS plus enough to bring inboard and secure; from this the whole span length can be calculated.

The anchors should be at least as heavy as are used for the boat's main bower anchor; old heavy fisherman anchors long since abandoned for sea-going work are ideal and cheap, but bend down one fluke to touch the anchor stock so that it doesn't stick up and become foul of someone else's anchor chain.

Old worn and rusty chain can similarly be used for the span, provided that enough metal remains at the worn part of the links; a really heavy worn chain provides added security by its surplus weight.

Laying this type of mooring can be tricky; the anchors must be dropped with the span fully extended in an up- and down-stream direction; if laid across tide the strain may be too great for the anchors to hold.

As with a clump mooring, the buoy rope should be of such a length that it doesn't quite touch the bottom. If the name of the boat and her tonnage are painted on the buoy it is less likely to be picked up by a craft large enough to drag the mooring.

8

Engines and Electrics

The following pages contain check lists which simplify the diagnosis of faults in different types of boat motor in a logical and methodical manner. Originally published in *Practical Boat Owner* as Skippers' Check Cards, these (and many other equally useful check cards) are still available in the form of loose cards from the publishers of that magazine.

Perhaps the most common cause of faults in boat engines is inadequate laying-up and recommissioning; if carried out in the manner recommended later in this chapter, these tasks will minimize faults and prolong the life of marine engines. The information is also taken from *Practical Boat Owner* Skippers' Check Cards.

FOUR-STROKE PETROL/GASOLINE
ENGINE FAULT FINDING

ENGINE WILL NOT START

Starter not turning engine:

>Battery flat or disconnected.
>Broken lead or dirty connections.
>Starter switch defective.
>Starter motor defective.

Starter cranks engine slowly:

>Battery nearly flat.

Terminals dirty or loose.
Starter motor faulty.
Sump oil too thick.

Starter turns engine:

FUEL CHECK: Fuel in carb?　NO
Then check:　Fuel tank empty.
Fuel line air leak.
Fuel line blocked.
Fuel pump defective.
Tank vent blocked.
Filters blocked.

FUEL CHECK: Fuel in carb?　YES
Then check:　Jets blocked.
Choke defective.
Water in fuel.
Carb dirty.
Hole in carb float.
Air leak in inlet manifold.

Ignition checks:

Spark at plug gaps?　NO
PLUG CHECK: Plugs oiled up.
Insulators cracked or dirty.

Spark at plug leads?　NO
DISTRIBUTOR
CHECK:　Rotor arm damaged.
Cap faulty.
L.T. lead loose.
Points defective.
Carbon brush defective.
Condenser defective.

Spark at H.T. lead?　NO
COIL CHECK: Coil burnt out.

H.T. lead defective.
Ignition switch defective.
Points maladjusted (not opening
  or closing L.T. circuit).

BATTERY
CHECK: Flat.
Leads dirty or loose.

ENGINE MISFIRES

Ignition:

Plug leads shorting/mixed up.
Spark plug gaps incorrect.
Insulators dirty or cracked.
Battery connections loose.
Distributor cap defective (check
  for tracking).

Fuel:

Fuel line partly blocked.
Water in carb.
Fuel pump defective.
Filters partly blocked.
Needle valve defective.

Mechanical:

Valves sticking.
Valves burnt.
Valve spring broken.
Valve clearance wrong.

ENGINE STARTS AND THEN STOPS

Ignition:

L.T. connection loose.
Ignition switch defective.
Contact points dirty.

Fuel:

Tank vent blocked.
Fuel line blocked.
Dirty fuel.
Fuel pump defective.
Needle valve sticking.
Air leak in fuel line.
Fuel nearly exhausted.

ENGINE RUNS AT FULL THROTTLE ONLY
Fuel:

Slow running jet blocked.
Slow running setting screw maladjusted.

Mechanical:

Valve sticking.
Valve burnt.
Valve spring broken.

ENGINE NOT GIVING FULL POWER
Fuel:

Fuel supply defective.
Inlet manifold air leaks.
Jets partly blocked.

Ignition:

Ignition retarded.
H.T. lead shorting
Distributor cap defective.

Mechanical:

Valves burnt.
Valves not seating correctly.
Valve clearance incorrect.

ENGINE RUNS BUT NOT PERFECTLY
Fuel:

Weak mixture.
Fuel feed faulty.
Carb flooding.

Ignition:

Ignition timing incorrect.

Mechanical:

Inlet valves not closing.

ENGINE KNOCKS

Ignition:

Timing too far advanced.
Plug leads crossed.

Mechanical:

Bearings or piston loose.
Engine needs a de-coke.

TWO-STROKE ENGINE FAULT FINDING

*ENGINE WILL NOT START, OR
STOPS WHILE RUNNING*

Fuel:

Fuel tap turned off.
Over choked.
Dirty fuel.
Carb main jet blocked.
Carb fuel filter blocked.
Tank vent blocked.

Ignition:

Spark plug fouled.
Spark gap too large.
Contact breaker points dirty
    or maladjusted.
Magneto wet.
H.T. lead to plug broken.

Mechanical:

Engine needs a de-coke.
Oil or water in crankcase.

ENGINE WILL NOT GIVE FULL OUTPUT

Fuel:

Carb out of adjustment.   95

Ignition:

Spark plug fouled.
Contact breaker gap too big/too small.
Ignition retarded.

Mechanical:

Engine needs a de-coke.
Exhaust pipe blocked.
Exhaust pipe unsuitable.
Cooling system blockage.
Propeller fouled by weed or rope.

ENGINE RUNS ROUGHLY

Fuel:

Fuel contaminated.
Carb main jet blocked.
Carb fuel filter blocked.
Tank vent blocked.

Ignition:

Spark plug fouled.
Insulation leaks.

ENGINE KNOCKS

Mechanical:

Overheating due to cooling
water blockage.
Engine needs a de-coke.

Ignition:

Ignition too far advanced.

DIESEL ENGINE FAULT FINDING

ENGINE WILL NOT START

Fuel system   Is there fuel at injection pump?   NO
checks: Air in system.
                     Choked filter.

Defective lift pump.
Fuel tank empty.
Tank vent blocked.

Is there fuel at injection pump? YES
Control rod sticking.
Excess fuel control.
Defective injectors.

**Mechanical
checks:**

Air cleaner blocked.
Defective compression.
Wrong injection timing.
Defective air throttle.
'Stop' control stuck out.

ENGINE STARTS AND THEN STOPS

**Fuel system
checks:**

Air in system.
Choked fuel filter.
Defective lift pump.
Faulty injectors.
Tank vent blocked.

**Mechanical
checks:**

Injector timing too early.
Bearings worn.
Pistons worn.
Broken valve spring.

FAULTY INJECTORS

(The adjustment of injectors calls for expert knowledge and spares should be carried. The following information is for use *in extremis* only).

Excessive leak-off:

Loose nozzle nut.
Nozzle/body faces distorted.
Needle or nozzle worn.

Nozzle opening pressure incorrect:

> Check spring adjusting screw.
> Check spring.
> Check spray holes.
> Seized needle.

Nozzle drips:

> Check nozzle and body
>   face for distortion.
> Check needle.
> Seating faulty.

Spray form distorted:

> Check nozzle spray holes.
> Nozzle tip damaged.

ENGINE SMOKES EXCESSIVELY
(Warning signs of further trouble to come)

White smoke—then check for:

> Air leaks.
> Poor compression.
> Fuel injection phase angle incorrect.
> Defective fuel pump timing.

Black smoke—then check for:

> Excess fuel device stuck out.
> Max. stop screw wrongly set.
> Fuel injection pump delivery
>   valve defective.
> Fuel injection pump calibration
>   incorrect.
> Faulty injector.

ENGINE WILL NOT START

Check spark plug.
Check fuel.
Check fuel filter.
Blocked fuel line.
Broken fuel pipe.
Cold engine not choked.
Hot engine flooded.

ENGINE WILL NOT IDLE

Carb needs adjustment.
Defective sparking plugs.
Wrong fuel mixture.

ENGINE VIBRATES BADLY

Broken or bent prop.
Fouled prop (check for weed or rope).
Carb needs adjustment.

ENGINE RUNS BUT BOAT SLUGGISH

Fouled prop (check for weed or rope).
Drive pin sheared.
Clutch slipping.

ENGINE LOSES POWER

Carb needs adjustment.
Defective sparking plugs.
Fuel system partly blocked.
Dirty fuel.
Engine overheating.

IF ENGINE FAILS TO START

Remove plugs and squirt in oil.
Remove carb drain plug.

Pull engine over on starter cord.
Squirt in more oil and pull over.
Fit clean dry spark plugs.
Reassemble carb.
Try to start engine.
If engine runs and then stops:
    Change oiled-up plug.
    Restart—Run for 20 minutes.

ENGINE STILL REFUSES TO START

Probably the electrics have suffered. The engine should be returned to an agent for overhaul. Before returning, oil up the inside and wash down exterior with fresh water.

WARNING: The Longer that the Engine is Immersed in Water—the Greater Damage it will Sustain.

LAYING-UP PROCEDURE:
FOUR-STROKE AND TWO-STROKE PETROL/GASOLINE ENGINES

Run engine until hot.
Drain sump, gearbox, reduction gear of oil.
Change oil filter element.
Refill with new oil.
Grease water pump system.
Drain water from cylinder block.
Drain water from exhaust system while hot.
Remove water pump impeller (if fitted). Store.
Oil cylinders (using inhibiting oil).

Oil valve gear.
Fit old spark plugs.
Plug exhaust pipe end.
Plug carb air intake.
Oil starting chain, sprocket, etc.
Remove electrical gear. Store.
Remove battery. Store, charge monthly.
Grease engine controls.
Repaint engine surfaces or grease with
rust inhibitor.

Fuel systems

Drain system.
Clean or replace filters.
Dismantle carb.
Clean float chamber.
Clean jets and refit.
Blank off air intake.

Two-stroke only

Drain crank case.
Remove magneto. Store.

*Check Appropriate Operating Manual
for Special Instructions.*

RECOMMISSIONING PROCEDURE:
FOUR-STROKE AND TWO-STROKE
PETROL/GASOLINE ENGINES

Remove plugs from carb air intake
and exhaust pipe end.
Check and grease stern tube.
Remove old spark plugs.
Oil cylinders with engine oil.
Rotate engine by hand.
Check gears, etc.

Drain oil from crankcase
(two-stroke only).
Fit new spark plugs.
Fit battery.
Fit electrical gear and adjust.
Check cooling system.
Refit water pump impeller.
Check carb and fuel filters.
Refill fuel tank.
Check oil levels in sump and gearbox.
Start engine.
Engage drive and warm up engine.
Check prop shaft alignment.
Stop engine. If sump or gearbox filled
with storage oils or contaminated,
replace with new oil.
Check and grease remote controls.
Check all nuts, bolts, unions, clips, etc.
Clean engine exterior.

*Check Appropriate Operating Manual
for Special Instructions.*

LAYING-UP PROCEDURE: DIESEL ENGINES

Run engine until hot.
Drain sump, gearbox, reduction
gear of oil.
Refill with new or inhibiting oil.
Grease water pump system.
Drain fuel tanks.
Clean and replace filters.
Refill tank with storage fuel.
Bleed fuel system.
Run engine for a few minutes.

Shut off sea cocks.

Drain cylinder block and exhaust
  system while hot.

Leave taps open.

Remove water pump impeller. Store.

Lubricate valve gear, etc.

Remove injectors and inhibit cylinders.

Replace injectors.

Plug air intake and exhaust.

Remove battery. Store, charge monthly.

Remove electrical gear. Store or return
  to maker for servicing.

Grease engine controls.

Clean and touch up engine paintwork.

*Check Appropriate Operating Manual
for Special Instructions.*

RECOMMISSIONING PROCEDURE: DIESEL ENGINES

Remove plugs from air intake and
  exhaust.

Check and grease stern tube.

Remove injectors and oil cylinders.

Turn engine by hand.

Check gears and moving parts.

Refit injectors.

Refit electrical gear.

Fit battery.

Check cooling system.

Refit water pump impeller.

Check and clean fuel filters.

Check fuel flow.

Drain storage oil (if recommended).

Drain oil if contaminated.

Bleed fuel system.

Check all oil levels.
Start engine and warm up.
Check cooling water circuit
  for leaks, blockages, etc.
Stop engine. Drain storage oil
  from sump and gearbox.
Refill sump and gearbox with new oil.
Lubricate all remote controls.
Check all nuts, bolts, unions, clips, etc.
Clean engine exterior.
Check prop shaft alignment.

*Check Appropriate Operating Manual
for Special Instructions.*

LAYING-UP PROCEDURE FOR OUTBOARD ENGINES

Run outboard engine in fresh water.
Stop engine by turning off fuel tap.
Drain engine water system while hot.
Remove carb.
Drain fuel tank.
Remove spark plugs.
Inhibit each cylinder.
Replace spark plugs.
Strip and clean carb. Reassemble.
Drain gearbox and flush.
Refill gearbox.
Drain water pump and grease.
Clean and touch up paintwork.
Blank off carb air intake and exhaust.
Grease all controls.

*Check Appropriate Operating Manual
for Special Instructions.*

RECOMMISSIONING PROCEDURE FOR
OUTBOARD ENGINES

Clean engine exterior.

Remove plugs at carb air intake and exhaust.

Remove spark plugs.

Oil cylinder with two-stroke oil.

Turn engine by hand.

Check moving parts.

Fit new spark plugs.

Check and adjust electrical system.

Check gearbox oil.

Lubricate and check remote controls.

Check all nuts, bolts, unions, clips etc.

Clean carb and fuel filters.

Fill fuel tank.

Fit engine to boat or for tank test.

Start engine and check cooling system.

Clean and refit spark plugs.

FUEL CONSUMPTION

A very rough rule of thumb for estimating fuel consumption of an **inboard petrol/gasoline engine** is to divide the horsepower developed by 10; this gives the number of gallons used per hour.

Diesel engines use about half that quantity. **Outboard motors** vary considerably from make to make, but they are always more thirsty than inboard engines of the same power. (And outboard 'powers' quoted are rarely true powers, so they are not strictly comparable with inboard powers.)

See Figs 25 and 26 for graphs of engine power requirements.

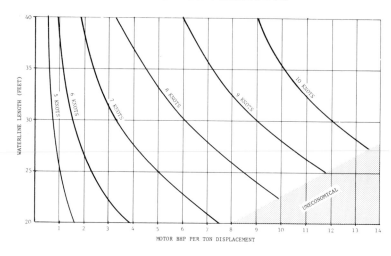

25 Engine Power Requirements: Power Craft

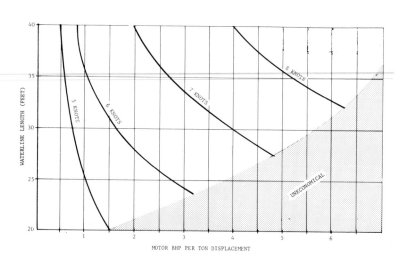

26 Engine Power Requirements: Auxiliary Sailing Craft

PROPELLERS

A big, slow-turning propeller is always more efficient than a small one running at high speed. In small craft 'slow' usually means under 1,000 rpm and 'fast' means substantially above it.

At high speeds propeller cavitation occurs; water cannot conform with the rapidly-moving surface of the blades and voids or cavities are left, effectively reducing the useful working area of the blades and increasing 'slip'. Slip is the difference between the speed at which the propeller would advance were it turning in a solid medium (as would a screw in a nut) and its true speed of advance through the water.

The **diameter** of a propeller is of course the diameter of the disc swept out by the blade tips; the **pitch** is the distance the propeller would advance if rotated one revolution in the hypothetical solid medium.

The diameter and pitch are often stamped in inches on the boss of a propeller; failing this they can easily be found by measuring the propeller on a sheet of paper. See Fig. 27.

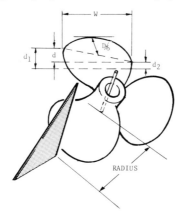

27 Measuring Propellers

If W is the width of the blade one sixth of the diameter D in from the tip, pitch is:

$$\frac{2 \cdot 1 \times D \times (d_1 - d_2)}{W}$$

A propeller is said to be 'right-handed' if it revolves clockwise as seen from astern when driving the boat ahead, 'left-handed' if anticlockwise.

Three- or four-bladed propellers are more efficient than those with two blades; the latter are sometimes fitted however to auxiliary sailing craft, since when sailing, their drag may be minimized by aligning the blades vertically behind the deadwood just ahead of the propeller.

SOME NOTES ON ELECTRICS

Boat electrics are usually a low-voltage low-powered system somewhat akin to automobile electrics, but simpler.

Lighting and engine starting systems depend on a battery which is kept charged by a generator driven by the main engine or by a separate charging set.

Most small craft systems use a 12-volt car-type battery and generator (or alternator), but some power craft have a 24-volt system. All spares or accessories bought should be of the correct voltage.

It is important not to overload the generator or battery. The generator is capable of producing a certain maximum number of ampères of current; this has to serve for charging the battery and running the electrical equipment and must not be exceeded.

The maximum power available from a generator is the product of its voltage and its amperage; a 12-volt generator providing 30 ampères is running at 360 watts.

The capacity of a fully-charged battery is measured in ampère-hours; a 50 amp-hour battery will provide one ampère for 50 hours, 5 ampères for 10 hours and so on before needing to be recharged. If the battery is connected to the generator permanently it will of course be recharged fully or partially whenever the engine is run.

A sailing craft with 10-watt port, starboard and stern navigation lights will consume 30 watts, or $2\frac{1}{2}$ ampères on a 12-volt system (30 divided by 12 equals $2\frac{1}{2}$). A fully-charged 50 amp-hour battery will provide current for these lights for 20 hours (50 divided by $2\frac{1}{2}$ equals 20). The same type of calculation can be made for other loads.

The usual car-type battery consists of lead plates immersed in a dilute solution of sulphuric acid. If not kept topped-up with distilled water and regularly charged it will deteriorate and soon become useless.

The state of charge of a lead-acid battery can be found with a hydrometer; this measures the specific gravity of the acid. In a fully-charged battery the S.G. of the acid is about $1\cdot250$; when this falls to $1\cdot180$ the battery is fully discharged and should be recharged immediately.

The terminals of boat batteries tend to corrode more rapidly than car batteries; they should be regularly cleaned and greased, and moisture should be wiped away.

Alkaline batteries are used in some craft; they consist of nickel and iron plates immersed in a solution of potassium hydroxide (caustic potash). This type is lighter and less easily damaged than the lead-acid type. While it can remain unharmed in a discharged state, this is imprudent as it makes it more difficult to start the engine to recharge the battery.

The S.G. of the electrolyte in an alkaline battery is about $1\cdot22$ but this does not change with the state of charge, so a hydrometer is of no use. A 12-volt alkaline battery should be recharged when its voltage has fallen to 10 volts.

Alkaline batteries need topping-up with distilled water in the same manner as lead-acid batteries.

Many marine engines are fitted with alternators instead of the older type of direct current generators; this name is somewhat misleading as they are equipped internally with rectifiers and the output at the terminals is still D.C. Do not run an alternator if it is not wired to a battery. If you need to run the engine without a battery connected, first remove the belt-drive to the alternator.

Electric Wiring

Electric wiring is often of a poor standard in small craft, with the attendant risks of fire and electrochemical decay in timber as well as failure of the electric circuits.

Ideally a 2-wire fully insulated system should be used; this is not always possible, for the negative pole of an engine-driven generator may be earthed internally, precluding the total isolation of the system from earth.

Even so, if double-pole isolating switches are fitted between the battery and the distribution system and between the distribution system and each individual distribution box, the amount of time the system is at risk is limited to the periods when the electrics are actually in use.

The cables themselves should be insulated with butyl rubber or ethylene-propylene rubber enclosed in a polychloroprene or chlorsulphonated polythene sheath, manufactured to British Standard Specification 6993 or American B Y C Standard E-9.

Alternatively, PVC-insulated and sheathed cables are satisfactory, though prone to cracking at low temperatures.

Multi-stranded conductors are preferable to single strands as they are stronger and more flexible.

Cables are now supplied in the UK in metric sizes. Table 9 shows the current carrying capacity and the voltage drop for some common sizes of wiring, assuming 2-core PVC insulated cable.

Table 9

Current-carrying Capacity and Voltage Drop

CABLE SIZE (sq mm)	MAX. CURRENT (amps)	VOLTAGE DROP* (millivolts)
1·0	11	40
1·5	13	25
2·5	18	15
4·0	24	10
6·0	30	7
10·0	40	4

* For every ampère of current and metre of length

Example of calculating correct cable size:

What size cable is needed for a pair of navigation lamps of 18 watts each, fitted to the pulpit and supplied from a 12v battery in the cockpit? Length of cable run is 20 metres.

$$\text{Current carried} = \frac{2 \times 18 \text{ watts}}{12 \text{ volts}} = 3 \text{ amps.}$$

Smallest cable which will safely carry current is 1 sq mm. Will voltage drop be acceptable?

$$\text{Voltage drop} = 3 \text{ amps} \times 20 \text{ metres} \times 40 \text{ millivolts}$$

$$= \frac{3 \times 20 \times 40}{1000} \text{ volts}$$

$$= 2 \cdot 4 \text{ volts.}$$

Voltage remaining at navigation lamp connections

$$= 12 - 2 \cdot 4$$

$$= 9 \cdot 6 \text{ volts.}$$

Therefore, although the 1 sq mm. cable will carry the current safely, the lamps will not reach full brightness, and a heavier cable is needed. Recalculate for larger sizes.

Domestic fittings are of little use in small craft; they usually contain steel components which corrode rapidly in a marine environment. Non-ferrous switches and fittings repay their extra cost by their much longer life.

Watertight deck sockets ought to be fitted with a tube for cables passing through the deck; this not only protects the cables but helps to keep the deck watertight.

The dry batteries used in radios and depth sounders as well as in torches and hand-lamps corrode rapidly when discharged. Even if not replaced immediately they should be removed to avoid damage to the equipment.

Avoid if possible batteries with a cardboard case; they tend to disintegrate quickly in the moist atmosphere afloat.

Metal-cased batteries can be lightly smeared with petroleum jelly to retard corrosion.

The International Regulations for Prevention of Collision at Sea require certain minimum luminous intensities of ships' navigation lights. Table 10 converts these into lamp wattages; it has been factored to give a margin of safety above minimum requirements and to allow for loss of light through the coloured glasses of side lights.

There is virtue in having more powerful lights still, provided that they do not cause undue glare.

Table 10

Minimum Luminous Intensities of Ships' Navigation Lights

	Required Range of Visibility		
	1 mile	2 miles	3 miles
All White Nav. Lights	5 watts	10 watts	18 watts
Red or Green Side Light	10 watts	18 watts	—

9

Maintenance and Ship Doctoring

Painting Wooden Boats

The better it's done, the longer it will last. Good preparation is the secret of success.

New Bare Wood: Give it a coat of preservative (Cuprinol or similar).

When dry, sand the surface smooth with glass paper or wet-and-dry used dry. Remove all dust on the surface and in the vicinity with a vacuum cleaner if possible.

Apply one coat of metallic pink primer thinned with 10 per cent of its volume with white spirit to assist penetration of the grain.

Apply one coat of metallic pink primer unthinned.

End grain of plywood should receive several coats of primer to penetrate as deeply as possible.

Fill any major blemishes with stopping applied in layers not thicker than $\frac{1}{8}$-inch. Allow each layer to harden before applying another.

Fill minor blemishes with trowel cement.

Stopped or cemented areas should be sanded flat before applying the next coat of primer or paint.

Apply at least 2 coats of undercoat, with a light rub down between each. Wet-and-dry wetted with soapy water or white spirit will speed up this work, but the surface must be quite dry before the next coat of paint is applied.

A final light rub with dry paper will improve adhesion. Finish off with a single coat of yacht enamel.

An extra-durable finish may be obtained by lightly removing the gloss from the enamel with wetted wet-and-dry and applying a second coat of enamel.

Bare wood previously painted but which has been burnt off should be rubbed down with coarse glasspaper to remove traces of old paint from the grain, then rubbed down with medium glass paper or wet-and-dry (used dry) to eliminate scratches.

If paint stripper has been used, neutralise all traces with white spirit, especially in stopped or cemented areas.

Then treat as for new bare wood.

Painted wood in reasonably good condition need not be burnt off or stripped back to bare wood.

Rub down with wet-and-dry used wet followed by a dry rub down.

Fill in abraded areas with trowel cement and single coat of undercoat before applying the final coat of enamel.

Deeply scratched or abraded areas may need stripping to the bare wood, allowed to dry out and a complete new skin built up starting with primer as for bare wood.

If the old paint has lifted because it had been applied to pamp wood, strip to the bare timber, allow to dry out and build up a new skin beginning with primer.

Epoxy resin and **polyurethane** paints are very durable indeed, but various proprietary makes require different treatments. Get the maker's instruction leaflet and follow it.

Painting Resinglass Boats

Sand down to a smooth matt surface of even texture.

If the surface is still greasy to the touch, brush on a proprietary oil-removing fluid and leave for half an hour. Wash off with fresh water and leave to dry.

Rub down lightly, remove all dust from the surface and the vicinity, preferably with a vacuum cleaner.

Apply a single coat of resinglass primer.

Apply polyurethane paint or lead-based undercoat the same day.

Blemishes should be filled or stopped with epoxy stopping on top of the first undercoat; it will not adhere to the primer.

Apply 2 or 3 coats of polyurethane or lead-based undercoat.

Finish with polyurethane paint or yacht enamel.

NOTE: At all costs avoid using ordinary paint stripper on resinglass; this and many other solvents will soften the gel coat and may cause permanent damage.

Painting Steel Boats

New unrusted steel should be degreased if necessary before applying a steel plate primer directly to the surface.

Rusted and scaly steel must be chipped bright before applying the primer.

Underwater surfaces need a different primer from upper works.

Apply 2 coats of primer for upper works, 3 for underwater areas.

Apply stopping or cement to blemishes. Rub down smooth and flat.

Apply 2 coats of undercoat, rubbing down lightly between each with wet-and-dry used wet. Be sure surface is dry before applying next coat.

Finish with enamel or polyurethane paint.

How Much Paint?

Calculate approximate areas to be painted:

Topsides: (length + beam) × 2 (average freeboard).

Bottom:	(beam + draught) $\times \frac{3}{4}$ (length) for medium draught cruisers.
	(beam + draught) $\times \frac{1}{2}$ (length) for bilge or fin keel boats.
Decks:	$\frac{3}{4}$ (length $\times$ beam) minus cabin top and cockpit areas.
Masts & Spars:	length $\times$ circumference (in same units).
	length $\times$ average circumference if tapered.

Then consult Table 11:

Table 11

Paint Coverage (approximate)

	Sq metres per litre	Sq feet per litre	Sq feet per U.S. pint	Sq feet per Imp. pint
Primer	11	118	56	67
Undercoat	12	129	61	73
Enamel (Lead based)	13	140	66	79
Enamel (Polyurethane)*	13	140	66	79
Antifouling Undercoat	10	107	50	61
Antifouling*	6–8	65–86	31–41	37–49
Yacht Varnish	13	140	66	79
Varnish: (Polyurethane One-can)	13	140	66	79
Varnish: (Polyurethane Two-can)	13	140	66	79

* Antifoulings and polyurethane paints vary considerably in covering capacity; check with makers' recommendations.

VARNISHING WOODWORK

New wood should be sanded smooth with glasspaper or wet-and-dry used dry. Rub only along the grain, NEVER across it.

Apply one coat of wood preservative; allow to dry 24 hours.

Apply one coat of thinned varnish (add 10 per cent white spirit and mix well).

Do NOT sand down fibres, or grain which rises; they assist adhesion.

When first coat is dry (6–24 hours, depending on temperature and humidity) apply second coat of unthinned varnish. .

Apply 3 more coats to exterior woodwork, 2 more coats to interiors, allowing full drying time between coats.

If several days elapse between consecutive coats, lightly rub down the surface with glasspaper or wet-and-dry before applying next coat.

Old varnish in good condition should be rubbed down and dusted with a rag moistened with white spirit.

Any flaky varnish should be removed by sanding to below the level of the flaking.

Build up a skin of varnish to the original level in these areas.

Finish off with one complete coat of varnish.

Plywood needs special treatment. The end grain should receive several applications of varnish until it no longer sinks in.

New plywood surfaces should receive 2 coats of thinned varnish before varnishing as above.

Discoloured woodwork can be restored prior to revarnishing by treating it with a strong solution of oxalic acid and leaving it to soak. Wash away all traces with several changes of fresh water and leave to dry thoroughly before applying varnish.

ANTIFOULING

Antifouling compounds are needed to prevent the underwater surfaces of boats kept afloat from collecting weed and barnacles, and from being attacked by marine borers and worm.

Apart from structural damage, a collection of weed and barnacles will slow down a sailing boat and cause a power craft to use extra fuel to achieve the same speed.

Dinghies and trailed boats which are always hauled out of the water after use need no antifouling provided that they are hosed down with fresh water.

Antifouling compounds of various strengths are marketed to deal with fouling conditions of differing severity. Local knowledge is invaluable; a strong antifouling is wasted in light fouling conditions but too weak a compound will need a new application several times a season.

'Soft' antifoulings should be immersed within 24 hours of application and should not subsequently be allowed to dry out.

'Hard' antifoulings are usually not so strong as 'soft' compounds but they can withstand exposure to the air and scrubbing; they are thus suitable for racing craft.

The recommended undercoat or prior surface treatment is essential if the correct 'leaching' rate is to be achieved. Leaching is the slow dissolving of the poison in the compound; it leaves a thin film of poisoned water adjacent to the hull to repel marine growths.

Quantities needed and drying rates vary greatly from compound to compound; the maker's advice should be heeded.

NOTES ON RESINGLASS
(See also pp. 34–6.)

Resinglass is a thermosetting polyester resin bonded together with very fine fibres of glass, which have ten times the tensile breaking strength of steel, weight for weight.

Sometimes called glass reinforced plastic (GRP) or Fiberglass, which is a trade name.

General-purpose 'lay-up' resin (Resin A) is used for most boat-building and repairs, with a colour-pigmented gel coat for the outside surface.

Resin will not harden until a separate catalyst is added; this hardener comes in paste or liquid form and must be thoroughly mixed with the resin. The resin sets more quickly in a warm dry atmosphere than in the cold and damp.

The catalyst is a peroxide material, dangerous to the skin and especially to the eyes. It should be handled with care.

Resin putty contains powdered fillers and has little tensile strength; it should only be used for filling gaps.

Glass reinforcement comes as chopped mat, strands wound together to form a rope (rovings) and as woven cloth or tape. The nature of the job will suggest the choice of reinforcement.

Small areas are best laid up with a brush, larger ones with a lambswool or mohair roller. A steel roller like a miniature harrow is used for consolidating the lay-up and working out air bubbles.

A syringe for accurately measuring the catalyst is essential; for large amounts use an automatic dispenser.

Chopped mat, rovings and glass cloth are easily cut with a sharp knife, and so is the laminate before it has fully hardened.

Fully-cured resinglass may be cut with a high-speed hacksaw blade and shaped with a Surform tool. It may also be ground with a Cintride disc, but a face mask should be worn while grinding, as resin dust and glass are not good to breathe. When clogged, Cintride discs may be cleaned in acetone.

Laying up should be undertaken in a temperature of at least 10°C, preferably 15–20°C, and the air should be dry.

Once the catalyst is added, the resin will harden whether it is used or not; therefore as much preparation as possible should be done before adding the catalyst to the resin.

Cut the glass material to shape, prepare the surface of the mould, apply a wax release agent and have a bowl of acetone handy for cleaning hands and tools, but remember that acetone is as inflammable as petrol and evaporates quickly.

For mixing resin and hardener, ordinary plastic bowls are satisfactory, as resin will not adhere to polythene.

If a coloured gel coat is to be used, the colour pigment should be thoroughly mixed with the resin before adding the catalyst. Gel coat is best applied with a soft brush with single sweeping strokes, the aim being to form a layer 0·010 to 0·020 inches thick.

The first few layers of main laminate under a coloured gel coat should be pigmented the same colour; this will make accidental chipping of the gel coat less noticeable.

It is sometimes necessary to put screws into resinglass to attach fittings. Self-tapping screws are suitable for solid laminates; make the pilot hole a little oversize and coat the shanks of the screws with an epoxy adhesive (Araldite or similar) to ensure a firm and watertight attachment. Captive nylon inserts are available for some applications.

Foam sandwich construction will not hold self-tapping screws; through-bolting is needed and the bolt should be bushed to avoid crushing the sandwich.

FRESH WATER TANKS

Water, water everywhere, nor any drop to drink . . .

Opinions vary vastly as to the amount a small boat should carry. One has to compromise between having to fill up every day or two and having a ton of water ballast to drag around at sea. Many boats manage comfortably on tankage for a week's supply at a gallon a day per person when cruising.

Even 28 gallons can be difficult to find room for in a small 4-berth cruiser; there are advantages in having several small tanks disposed around low down in the bilges; they are easier to fit than one large tank, the stability of the boat is not reduced when the centre of gravity is kept low down, the rate of consumption can be assessed if only one tank is switched on at a time, and if a single tank should leak or become contaminated the contents of the others will still be available.

Conventionally, fresh water tanks may be of 14-gauge mild steel, galvanised inside and out (domestic pattern), but many resinglass boats have moulded-in tanks, and nylon-reinforced PVC bag tanks will often fit well into an awkwardly-shaped space. Stainless steel is ideal but expensive compared with the alternatives.

Water tanks when full are heavy objects, whatever their material, and they should be supported adequately and chocked off to prevent them from breaking loose in a seaway. Bag tanks should in addition be protected from chafe which may occur in different places due to the changing shape of the bag.

Filler pipes of not less than 1-inch bore will permit quick filling by the usual half-inch quayside hose or a large funnel. The filler cap should of course be watertight, especially if it is flush with the deck. Air vent pipes in each tank need to be of about half the bore of the filler pipe to prevent airlocks and blow-backs. Bag tanks collapse as they empty and need no air vent pipe.

Connections from the tanks (each via its own stop cock) are best made with 'food-grade' PVC tubing; other grades may give the water an unpleasant taste. Food-grade tubing is not always labelled as such, and it is worth testing a sample by stopping up one end, filling the tube with water and tasting it after 24 hours. Alternatively, copper piping may be used; this is more trouble to install but is more durable than plastic pipe and leaves no taste.

Mustiness in tanks can be removed by washing them out with a solution of bicarbonate of soda, subsequently flushing well with several changes of fresh water. If bicarbonate doesn't remove the mustiness, a solution of formalin will. Incidentally, you can remove mustiness from lockers by wiping them out with a cloth wetted in formalin.

Galvanised tanks sometimes rust after a few years use. External rusting can be prevented by painting normally. Internal rusting can be dealt with (provided that the tank has an inspection hole) by an application of black water-tank paint, made by several paint companies.

Water is usually stored in a very small boat in plastic erry-cans; these are manageable in sizes up to three gallons and should for preference be made of a dark plastic to exclude sunlight; this sometimes tends to encourage the growth of algae in fresh water from some sources.

FUEL TANKS

The fuel tank capacity of many production-line boats is often determined by convenience and cost rather than the owner's particular requirements. A power craft is limited in range by the capacity of her tanks, and voyages have to be planned to allow for refuelling at convenient ports before the tanks are empty. This can be quite a constraint if one wishes to make a fast passage to a distant cruising ground.

Sailing craft with a small auxiliary motor are not so constrained, but windless periods are not unknown and it may be a comfort to know that the tank holds enough fuel for a cross-channel passage of up to 24 hours. Everyone's needs will be different, but it is rare for the standard tank to hold more fuel than will be needed.

Extra tankage can of course be arranged, either by replacing the existing tank by a bigger one, or if this is not feasible, by fitting an additional tank or tanks low in the boat to keep the stability. If the motor has a fuel pump, fuel can be drawn from extra tanks in any convenient part of the boat, but engines with a gravity-fed fuel system will need special arrangements.

Tanks should be deep and narrow to minimize the free surface area, and should be fitted with the long dimension along the fore-and-aft line of the boat to help stability when rolling. Stainless steel is a suitable material for tanks for all fuels, and mild steel for diesel fuel, but internal galvanising should be avoided as it causes sediment to form. Copper and brass are suitable for all fuels, though some say that petrol/gasoline tends to deposit gum in such tanks. If this should happen, it can be removed with acetone periodically.

No matter how careful one is to exclude it, water will collect at the bottom of the tank due to condensation. Sediment will also form. The bottom of the tank should thus be regarded as a sump to collect these foreign matters, and the fuel supply to the motor should be taken from an inch or two higher up. Certain fuel cocks fitted to the bottom of a tank have a short stand-pipe which projects above the level of water and sludge.

A bowl-type fuel filter and water separator fitted in the fuel supply line will exclude the last traces from the motor.

Pipe runs should be of copper tubing or Petroflex; plastic

piping is a fire hazard and should be avoided at all costs. If the motor is bolted solidly to the engine bearers, a coil formed in the fuel pipe will absorb vibration and minimize the risk of breaking, but motors on anti-vibration mountings need a Petroflex connection for the last foot or two.

Filler pipes of $1\frac{1}{2}$ or 2 inches diameter will take a refuelling hose nozzle and avoid blow-backs, provided that the tank is adequately vented. Air vents should be of half the diameter of the filling pipe and should if possible be brought out on deck so that accidental overfilling does not flood the bilges with fuel.

All metal parts in the fuel system should be electrically bonded together and to the motor; static electricity can otherwise build up and a spark at the refuelling hose nozzle could start a serious fire.

ELECTROLYSIS AND CORROSION

When two dissimilar metals are immersed in seawater and are connected together electrically or are in direct contact, an electric current flows between them. If this current flows for a long enough time one metal or the other will corrode away.

This corrosion may be avoided if there are no dissimilar metals in contact with the water, but this is rarely practicable.

The corrosion may be minimized by selecting certain metals which in conjunction cause least and slowest electrolytic action.

Table 12 shows which combinations to use and to avoid. If certain undesirable conjunctions are inevitable, the metals should be electrically insulated from each other by synthetic rubber bedding compounds or neoprene washers.

Mild steel is excluded from the list because it corrodes very rapidly in any marine environment, and should be avoided, unless galvanized.

Table 12

Seawater Corrosion of Metals

Metal to be protected	Safe combination	Avoid
Copper, Brasses and Bronzes	Copper Brasses Bronzes Monel Metal Stainless Steel	Aluminium Galvanized Iron Galvanized Steel Zinc
Stainless Steels	Copper Brasses Bronzes Aluminium Alloys Monel Metal	Galvanized Iron Galvanized Steel
Aluminium Alloys	Stainless Steel Galvanized Iron Galvanized Steel Cadmium Plated Steel	Copper Brasses Bronzes Lead

Corrosion of metallic underwater fittings may be minimized by fitting sacrificial zinc anodes to the underwater surfaces on both sides. They will need periodical replacement but it's much cheaper than renewing corroded fittings.

The zinc anodes should be located reasonably near to the metal to be protected and bonded electrically to it by an insulated cable of about 4 sq millimetres section, run internally through the boat. If it proves impossible to fit an anode within ten feet of all the metal it is to protect, separate anodes should be installed.

All metallic underwater fittings in wooden and resinglass boats should be bonded together electrically; this is not necessary with metal hulls. If a flexible rubber coupling is fitted in the propeller shaft, it is advisable to interconnect the metal on each side of the coupling with a short flexible lead.

LIQUID PETROLEUM GAS

Butane and propane gases in liquid form are available under various trade names. Both are highly inflammable and when mixed with air in the 'right' proportion are explosive.

Both are heavier than air, so any leaking gas will run into the bilges and may form an explosive mixture. The gas should always be turned off at the cylinder when not in use.

Bottles should be kept upright in a properly-designed stowage, with if possible a drain to the outside of the boat.

Take no risks; when lighting an appliance strike the match before turning the gas on.

After changing the bottle test for leaks with soapy water around the union nut. A leaking connection will form bubbles.

The same test should occasionally be applied to all other joints in the system.

The amount of gas remaining in a partly-used bottle may be estimated by subtracting the tare (empty) weight from the total weight. The most commonly-used British Calorgas bottle weighs about $12\frac{1}{2}$ lb. ($5 \cdot 7$ kg) empty and contains 10 lb. ($4 \cdot 5$ kg) of gas when full.

If gas should have leaked into the bilges, immediately

stop the motor, turn off all naked flames and prohibit smoking. A diaphragm-type bilge pump MIGHT get it out, a rotary pump will probably not, but a pair of dinghy-inflating bellows most certainly will if the outlet is connected to a length of hosepipe leading to the upper deck and overboard. The bellows should of course be operated as low down as possible in the bilge, but be careful to keep your head well above the gas while pumping. Don't be tempted to use an electric vacuum cleaner; sparking at the brushes could cause the explosion you are trying to avoid.

On a really breezy day a wind scoop rigged with a sail around the forehatch might help to blow the gas out through the cabin hatch.

SCREW THREADS

Boats and their engines and equipment contain a variety of different standards of screw thread, not often interchangeable with each other.

Metric threads are gradually replacing all other types in Britain but enough of the other standards are still to be found to justify publishing Tables 13 and 14 and to merit a short description of their uses.

Coarse threads (Whitworth/BSW and Unified/UNC) are often found on deck fittings, rigging screws and components not subject to vibration or rapid rotation.

Fine threads (British Standard Fine/BSF and Unified/UNF) are mainly found in British and American motors and gearboxes.

Small sizes of screws in instruments and electronic gear are often to the British Association (BA) standard.

Metric threads are universally used in machinery and equipment of Continental origin, and in some recently-designed British engines and gearboxes.

Table 13

Isometric Screw Threads

OD (mm)	Pitch (mm)	Tap (mm)	Tap (in)	Clear (mm)	Clear (in)
5	0·80	4·20	$\frac{5}{32}$	5·10	$\frac{13}{64}$
6	1·00	5·00	$\frac{13}{64}$	6·10	$\frac{1}{4}$
8	1·25	6·80	$\frac{17}{64}$	8·20	$\frac{21}{64}$
10	1·50	8·50	$\frac{21}{64}$	10·20	$\frac{13}{32}$
12	1·75	10·20	$\frac{13}{32}$	12·20	$\frac{31}{64}$
14	2·00	12·00	$\frac{31}{64}$	14·25	$\frac{9}{16}$
16	2·00	14·00	$\frac{35}{64}$	16·25	$\frac{41}{64}$
20	2·50	17·50	$\frac{11}{16}$	20·25	$\frac{51}{64}$

Inch sizes are approximate; metric drills
should be used for precision work.

Screw Threads

UNIFIED FINE (UNF) Screw Threads				UNIFIED COARSE (UNC) Screw Threads		
OD	TPI	TAP	CLEAR	TPI	TAP	CLEAR
1/4	28	No. 2	Ltr. F	20	7/32	Ltr. F
5/16	24	Ltr. I	Ltr. O	18	Ltr. F	Ltr. O
3/8	24	Ltr. R	Ltr. W	16	Ltr. O	Ltr. W
7/16	20	Ltr. W	15/32	14	Ltr. U	15/32
1/2	20	7/16	17/32	13	7/16	17/32
9/16	18	1/2	19/32	12	1/2	19/32
5/8	18	9/16	21/32	11	17/32	21/32
3/4	16	11/16	25/32	10	21/32	25/32
7/8	14	13/16	29/32	9	25/32	29/32
1	12	29/32	1 1/16	8	7/8	1 1/16

BRITISH STANDARD Whitworth Screw Threads				BRITISH STANDARD Fine Screw Threads		
OD	TPI	TAP	CLEAR	TPI	TAP	CLEAR
1/4	20	No. 11	Ltr. F	26	No. 5	Ltr. F
5/16	18	Ltr. D	Ltr. O	22	Ltr. G	Ltr. O
3/8	16	Ltr. N	Ltr. W	20	Ltr. O	Ltr. W
7/16	14	Ltr. S	15/32	18	3/8	15/32
1/2	12	Ltr. X	17/32	16	7/16	17/32
9/16	—	—	—	—	—	—
5/8	11	17/32	21/32	14	9/16	21/32
3/4	10	5/8	25/32	12	21/32	25/32
7/8	9	3/4	29/32	11	25/32	29/32
1	8	27/32	1 1/16	10	29/32	1 1/16

BRITISH ASSOCIATION
(BA) Screw Threads

	OD	TPI	TAP	CLEAR
0	0·236	25·4	No. 12	Ltr. B
1	0·209	28·2	No. 19	No. 3
2	0·185	31·4	No. 26	3/16 in
3	0·161	34·8	No. 30	No. 19
4	0·142	38·5	No. 34	No. 27
5	0·126	43	No. 39	No. 30
6	0·110	47·9	No. 44	No. 34
7	0·098	52·9	No. 48	No. 39
8	0·087	59·1	No. 51	No. 43
9	0·075	65·1	No. 53	No. 48
10	0·067	72·6	No. 55	No. 50

OD = Outside Diameter in inches
TPI = The number of Threads per inch
TAP = Tapping Drill Size
CLEAR = Clearance Drill Size

Table 14

Twist Drills

LETTER	Size in inches	LETTER	Size in inches	NUMBER	Size in inches
Z	0·413	M	0·295	1	0·228
Y	0·404	L	0·290	2	0·221
X	0·397	K	0·281	3	0·213
W	0·386	J	0·277	4	0·209
V	0·377	I	0·272	5	0·205
U	0·368	H	0·266	6	0·204
T	0·358	G	0·261	7	0·201
S	0·348	F	0·257	8	0·199
R	0·339	E	0·250	9	0·196
Q	0·332	D	0·246	10	0·194
P	0·323	C	0·242	11	0·191
O	0·316	B	0·238	12	0·189
N	0·302	A	0·234	13	0·185

NUMBER	Size in inches	NUMBER	Size in inches	NUMBER	Size in inches
14	0·182	27	0·144	40	0·098
15	0·180	28	0·141	41	0·096
16	0·177	29	0·136	42	0·094
17	0·173	30	0·129	43	0·089
18	0·170	31	0·120	44	0·086
19	0·166	32	0·116	45	0·082
20	0·161	33	0·113	46	0·081
21	0·159	34	0·111	47	0·079
22	0·157	35	0·110	48	0·076
23	0·154	36	0·107	49	0·073
24	0·152	37	0·104	50	0·070
25	0·150	38	0·102	51	0·067
26	0·147	39	0·100	52	0·064

EQUIVALENTS

Inch fraction to decimals and mm

Size in inches		mm	Size in inches		mm
1/64	0·02	0·4	1/4	0·25	6·4
1/32	0·03	0·8	17/64	0·27	6·7
3/64	0·05	1·2	9/32	0·28	7·1
1/16	0·06	1·6	19/64	0·30	7·5
5/64	0·08	2·0	5/16	0·31	7·9
3/32	0·09	2·4	21/64	0·33	8·3
7/64	0·11	2·8	11/32	0·34	8·7
1/8	0·13	3·2	23/64	0·36	9·1
9/64	0·14	3·6	3/8	0·38	9·5
5/32	0·16	4·0	25/64	0·39	9·9
11/64	0·17	4·4	13/32	0·41	10·3
3/16	0·19	4·8	27/64	0·42	10·7
13/64	0·20	5·2	7/16	0·44	11·1
7/32	0·22	5·6	29/64	0·45	11·5
15/64	0·23	6·0	15/32	0·47	11·9

Size in inches	mm		Size in inches	mm	
31/64	0·48	12·3	3/4	0·75	19·1
1/2	0·50	12·7	49/64	0·77	19·4
33/64	0·52	13·1	25/32	0·78	19·8
17/32	0·53	13·5	51/64	0·80	20·2
35/64	0·55	13·9	13/16	0·81	20·6
9/16	0·56	14·3	53/64	0·83	21·0
37/64	0·58	14·7	27/32	0·84	21·4
19/32	0·59	15·1	55/64	0·86	21·8
39/64	0·61	15·5	7/8	0·88	22·2
5/8	0·63	15·9	57/64	0·89	22·6
41/64	0·64	16·3	29/32	0·91	23·0
21/32	0·66	16·7	59/64	0·92	23·4
43/64	0·67	17·1	15/16	0·94	23·8
11/16	0·69	17·5	61/64	0·95	24·2
45/64	0·70	17·9	31/32	0·97	24·6
23/32	0·72	18·3	63/64	0·98	25·0
47/64	0·73	18·7	1	1·00	25·4

Table 15
Adhesives

METALS — 5,6,7,9

	1,2,3				
FABRICS AND TEXTILES — 1,2,3		1,2,5,7,9			
	1,2		1,2,3,5		
RUBBERS — 1,2,5,7,9		1,2,3		1,2,3	
	1,2,9		1,2,3,8		5,7,9
WOOD — 3,4,6,8		1		2,3,7		1,5,7,9
	1,3,8		1,2,9		1,2		1,2,7
PAPER AND CARDBOARD — 1,2,3,8		1,5,8,9		1,2,7		1,2
	1,2,3		1,4,5,6,9		1,2
CERAMICS — 5,7,9		1		1
	1,5,7,9		1
THERMOSETTING PLASTICS — 2,5,7,9		2,7
	1,2,7,9
THERMOPLASTIC MATERIALS — 1,2,7

131

ADHESIVE TYPES	*Example:*
1 Natural Rubber	Rubber solution
2 Synthetic Rubber	Evostik, Bostik
3 Resin Emulsion	Not applicable to amateur work
4 Amino Resin	Aerolite 306
5 Epoxy Resin	Araldite
6 Phenolic Resin	Cascophen PC-1
7 Polyester Resin	Lay-up Resin 'A'
8 Thermoplastic hot-melt	Not applicable to amateur work
9 Resin Blends	Cascophen RS-7

There are in general three sorts of adhesive: Natural and synthetic rubbers, synthetic thermosetting resins and synthetic thermoplastic resins. The first two classes are most suitable for amateur use.

Table 15 shows the appropriate adhesives for various combinations of materials; it is based on material first published by PERA and later by *Practical Boat Owner*.

Example 1. Metal to Wood.

Enter the chart at metal and wood. Where the two paths meet, suitable types of adhesives are given. i.e. 1, 2, 3, 5.

Example 2. Wood to Ceramic.

Enter the chart at wood and ceramic. Where the paths meet, suitable adhesives are given, i.e. 1, 5, 8, 9.

Example 3. Wood to Wood.

Enter the chart at wood and suitable adhesives indicated are 3, 4, 6, 8.

Examples of thermosetting plastics: resinglass (GRP) and similar polyester resins, Formica and Paxolin (phenolic resin), white electric switch mouldings (urea formaldehyde), and melamine.

Examples of thermoplastics: polyvinyl chloride (PVC),

Perspex/Plexiglass (acrylic), nylon (polyamide), polythene (polyethylene), and polypropylene.

Thermoplastics soften and melt when heated; thermo-setting plastics do not.

CHECK LISTS

Boatswain's Locker

Marline spikes and prickers, various sizes.

Wire-cutting pliers.

Cold chisel; steel block for anvil.

Adjustable wrench.

Small tin of thick grease. Some prefer lanoline.

Coil of stainless or galvanised locking wire.

Spare shackles and thimbles, stainless or galvanised, for every size used in the boat. Bulldog grips.

Spare bottle screw, stainless or galvanised, of every size used in the boat.

Spare winch handle, spare reefing handle, spare log rotator.

Bosun's chair, Terylene/Dacron with pockets for tools.

Sailmaker's Bag

Assorted needles, wrapped in grease-impregnated cloth.

Sewing palm, left or right-handed as appropriate.

Reels of Terylene/Dacron thread and twine, for sewing and whipping.

Beeswax for needles.

Pieces of sailcloth of same weight as sails.

Adhesive tape for temporary repairs.

A needle threaded ready for an emergency repair.

Set of spare sail battens.

Spare piston hanks and mainsail track slides.

Brass eyelets, punch and die.

Carpenter's Bag

Multi-blade saw.

Chisels, $\frac{1}{2}$-inch and 1-inch.

Surform tool, with spare blades.

Hammer.

Screwdrivers, large and small.

Brace and various bits, $\frac{1}{2}$-inch to 1-inch.

6-foot steel measuring tape.

Grease-impregnated cloths to wrap all these tools.

Copper and galvanised nails, $\frac{3}{4}$-inch to 3-inches.

Brass or stainless steel screws, assorted.

Brass or stainless screw eyes, cabin hooks, cup hooks.

Engineer's Store and Engine Spares

Full set of chrome-vanadium open spanners and ring spanners to fit all engine, gearbox and propeller shaft nuts and bolts.

Mole wrench.

Small, medium and large screwdrivers; Phillips' screwdriver.

Set of Allen keys if appropriate.

Rawhide hammer.

Electrician's pliers.

Tinman's snips.

Hacksaw and spare blades.

Files, flat, round and triangular.

Grease-impregnated cloths to wrap all these tools.

Grease gun for engine and gearbox nipples.

Pressure oil can.

Soldering equipment.

Set of new sparking plugs for main engine and outboard.

Spare vee-belts for dynamo, fan, etc.

Distributor brushes for main engine and outboard.

Contact breaker assembly.

Dynamo and starter motor brushes.

Spare bulbs and fuses for the electrics.

Selection of nuts, bolts, washers, split pins, hose clips, pipe unions, nipples.

Instruction books and spare parts lists for main engine and outboard.

Purser's Store

Contains the 'common-user' items not specific to any particular trade. Some items are duplicated in other kits, but there's merit in keeping a reserve stock for general use.

Araldite adhesive.

Sealant compound.

Evostik.

PVC tape; several colours are useful for identifying pipes and cables.

Calor gas pipe jointing cement.

Petroleum jelly.

Rubber bungs.

Plastic teaspoons for mixing and as applicators.

Paraffin (kerosene); methylated spirit (industrial alcohol).

A few candles in case of the worst, and matches in a sealed tin.

Spare batteries for torches (flashlights), radio, depth sounder.

Lamp wicks, mantles, Primus prickers, spare glasses for cabin and other lamps.

Personal Gear

About the most difficult thing to stow in a small boat is a rigid suitcase. A waterproof kit-bag is far better.

Clothing: take a complete change, not only for reasons of hygiene but in case you get a ducking.

At least one heavy sweater; it can be chilly at sea even in fine weather. Cold is demoralising and saps efficiency.

Oilskins to taste; orange or yellow are most easily seen if the wearer falls overboard.

Several strips of towelling to wear like a scarf and keep rain and spray from running down the neck.

Non-slip deck shoes or boots; boots are warmer when the spray flies.

Buoyancy aid of approved pattern, with whistle attached.

Safety harness (this might be kept on board).

Stainless steel seaman's knife on lanyard.

Toilet gear and towels.

Sunglasses (Polaroid clip-ons for spectacle wearers).

Electric torch (flashlight), waterproof and shockproof.

Provisions

This basic list may suit the needs of many people; it can obviously be modified to meet personal preferences:

Bacon	Biscuits
Booze	Bread
Butter	Cake
Cheese	Chocolate
Cocoa	Coffee
Cooking Fat	Detergent
Eggs	Flour
Fruit (Fresh)	Fruit (Tinned)
Fruit Juices	Ham
Jams	Lard
Marmalade	Matches
Meat (Fresh)	Meat (Tinned)
Milk (Fresh)	Milk (Powdered)
Peanuts	Pepper, salt, mustard
Porridge	Raisins
Salads (Fresh)	Salads (Tinned)
Sausages	Soups (packet)
Sugar	Sweets
Tea	Tobacco and cigarettes
	Vegetables (fresh)
Toilet paper	WATER
Vegetables (tinned)	

Check List: Going on Board

A lot of good sailing time may be gained and anguish avoided if the boat and her equipment are checked methodically before leaving the shore or mooring.

Individual boats will differ widely in the appropriate routine, but the following checks may prompt more suitable ones for your own boat.

Before leaving home, check the provisions and personal gear (separate check lists on pp. 136 ff.).

Work out a best routine for the dinghy; often it's best for two people to go first with the gear, then one can bring the dinghy back for the rest of the crew while the other stows the gear before their arrival on board.

Walk around the deck, casting a critical eye on everything. Check the standing rigging for tautness and the running rigging for chafe. Check that the anchors and other equipment on deck are in position; light-fingered characters are everywhere.

Hoist the burgee and then the ensign; bring the lifebuoys on deck if they have been stowed below.

Open the hatches and get some air through the boat, even if you have to close them again when you go to sea.

Check over the motor. Usually this will entail opening the sea-cocks, giving the water pump and stern gland greasers one turn, checking the oil level in the sump and the fuel contents of the tank. Turning the engine over by hand before starting it will add considerably to the life of the battery.

Start the motor, and check immediately that the cooling water is circulating. Test under load by going ahead and astern for a few seconds while still on the mooring. This check is worth doing even if you intend to stop the motor and sail away; you may need the motor later.

Check the navigation lights if you expect to stay out late or overnight.

Check that everything has been properly stowed below; a few moments spent doing this may save expensive breakages or clearing up a mess later.

When you are satisfied that all is well, bring up the sail-bags and make ready to hoist sail.

Last of all, fleet the dinghy astern preferably on a double painter, or bring it on deck and stow it securely.

You may then truthfully claim to be 'in all respects ready for sea'.

Check List: Leaving the Boat

Some folk manage to get ashore within five minutes of picking up the mooring. Either they are exceptionally well organised or they may pay for their neglect later.

After picking up the mooring and getting the sail off her, the first priority should go to mooring up safely. This means getting the mooring chain inboard as soon as possible and securing it with the correct 'scope'; not so taut that the bows are pulled down by the weight of chain nor so slack that you may foul adjacent boats when swinging with the tide.

The weight of the chain should be taken by the samson post or bitts, not by the brake on the winch, and a lashing put around the chain so that it cannot possibly slip.

When the sails have been lowered, bagged and stowed below, walk round the deck and check as you checked before leaving that the standing and running rigging are still sound, the anchors properly stowed and everything in position.

If the motor has been running and perhaps idling since arriving on the mooring, run it up for a few seconds to clear it before stopping it. Turn off the sea-cock, and the fuel cock of a petrol engine. (The fuel cock of a diesel engine is best left open). Give the stern gland and water pump greasers one turn and, for diesel engines, open the throttle wide. Put the engine into gear so that the tide cannot turn the propeller and cause needless wear on the shaft bearings.

Tighten the halyards and rig bungee shock cords so that the halyards cannot slap against the mast, causing both wear and annoyance to neighbours.

Put the boom crutch into position and tighten the main sheet; put the sail cover on if the mainsail isn't normally stowed below.

Carry out 'lower deck rounds'; see that everything which isn't to be taken ashore is properly stowed. Turn off the sea-cocks on the galley sink drain, the WC, and anything else which may have a sea-cock, such as a Pitometer log. Check that the liquid gas bottle is turned off, though the last user should have already done this.

Pump the bilges dry, and have a final critical look around.

Switch off the electrical supply (or battery isolator).

When you are satisfied that all is well, lower first the ensign and then the burgee, lock up all ports, windows and hatches, and row ashore feeling pleased with your work.

I can't do this in anything like five minutes, but a well-drilled crew can speed things up by sharing the load.

If all this sounds tedious, your reward will come if the weather turns foul before you next use the boat; you won't lie awake wondering what horrors are going on as she rolls and pitches unattended in a gale, and you could be saved a lot of trouble clearing up the mess when it's all over.

Check List: Laying up Ashore

See that the boat is securely chocked up, or the legs firmly bolted on.

Have a suitable cover ready, which reaches to the waterline on each side.

Scrub down the bottom before any weed and barnacles have hardened.

Scrub down the topsides, decks and cabin top.

Remove all loose gear; stow it ashore in a dry place.

Remove the battery and have it put on charge.

Examine the mast and its fittings thoroughly; welds in the fittings of metal masts are prone to crack during the sailing season.

Label all standing and running rigging; put it aside for closer examination during the winter evenings.

Take the sails home to wash them and check for needed repairs.

Haul the anchor chain out of its locker; flake it down on boards under the bow of the boat.

Remove internal ballast, numbering it if necessary to ensure correct replacement.

Scrub out the interior, the bilges and all lockers.

Remove the bilge drain plugs, if fitted.

Flush the bilges through and clean out the limber holes.

Flush the toilet with several gallons of hot water and detergent.

Deal with the motor as suggested on p. 100 ff.

Erect a ridge-pole the whole length of the boat; put the boat cover over it and lash it securely against winter gales.

Ensure ample ventilation by leaving open all portlights, lockers, ventilators, drawers, doors and the ends of the boat cover.

Make a list of all jobs needing attention; plan to complete them well before the next season begins.

Check List: Fitting out and Recommissioning

This process really begins the day you finished laying-up, if the boat is to be kept in tip-top condition.

Deal first with any lengthy processes, such as removing the motor for major overhaul, repairing sails or ordering new ones.

Give early attention to anything which could deteriorate further during the winter; touch up bare spots on a wooden or metal hull with primer; grease exposed metalwork.

Check over all the loose gear, sails, standing and running rigging, bunk cushions, galley equipment, navigation gear, during the wet winter evenings. Aim to have all this work complete before spring, when you'll need the time for outdoor work.

Come spring and fair weather, repaint, revarnish and antifoul the hull as suggested on pp. 113 ff.

Replace bilge drain plugs; check that any echo-sounder transponder, any skin fitting which may have been removed and any other orifice in the underwater surface is watertight before launching. Close sea-cocks.

Reinstall the loose gear; lubricate sheet halyard and anchor winches; erect the mast and provisionally tension the standing rigging.

Launch away! But before sailing away check and finally adjust the rigging tensions; see that all running rigging runs correctly and the sails go up and down smoothly; run the motor and test it under load ahead and astern while still on the mooring.

If you can bring yourself to undertake routine maintenance during the summer when the rest of the family is sunbathing and swimming, the winter refitting load will be considerably lightened. In any case, it's much nicer to work in warm weather.

10

Useful Tables

Table 16

Weights and Measures

Imperial Measures and Equivalents

LENGTH

1 inch		=25·4 mm
1 foot	=12 in	=0·304 m
1 yard	=3 ft	=0·914 m
1 statute mile	=1760 yds	=1·609 km
1 nautical mile	=6080 ft	=1·853 km
1 fathom	=6 ft	=1·83 m

SURFACE AREA

1 sq inch		=6·452 cm²
1 sq foot	=144 sq in	=0·093 m²
1 sq yard	=9 sq ft	=0·836 m²
1 acre	=4840 sq yds	=4046 m²
1 sq mile	=640 acres	=259·0 hectares

CAPACITY

1 cu inch		=16·38 cm³
1 cu foot	=1728 cu in	=0·028 m³
1 cu yard	=27 cu ft	=0·764 m³
1 pint	=4 gills	=0·568 litres
1 quart	=2 pints	=1·136 litres
1 gallon	=8 pints	=4·546 litres
1 pint	=20 fl oz	=568·3 cm³

WEIGHT *Avoirdupois*

1 ounce	=437·5 grains	=28·35 gm
1 pound	=16 oz	=0·453 kg
1 stone	=14 lb	=6·350 kg
1 hundred-weight	=112 lb	=50·80 kg
1 ton	=20 cwt	=1·016 tonnes

Metric Measures and Equivalents

LENGTH

1 millimetre (mm)	=0·039 in
1 metre (m) =1000 mm	=1·093 yds
1 kilo- =1000 m metre(km)	=0·621 mile
1 metre =3·28 ft	=0·55 fathoms

SURFACE AREA

1 sq cm =100 mm² (cm²)	=0·155 sq in
1 sq metre =10,000 cm² (m²)	=1·196 sq yds
1 are (a) =100 m²	=119·6 sq yds
1 hectare =100 ares (ha)	=2·471 acres
1 sq km =100 hectares (km²)	=0·386 sq mile

CAPACITY

1 cu cm (cm³)	=0·061 cu in
1 cu deci- =1000 cm³ metre (dm³)	=0·035 cu ft
1 cu metre =1000 dm³ (m³)	=1·308 cu yds
1 litre (l) =1 dm³	=0·220 gallon

WEIGHT

1 gramme =1000 mg (g)	=0·035 oz
1 kilo- =1000 g gramme (kg)	=2·204 lb
1 tonne (t) =1000 kg	=0·984 ton

US Measures where different from Imperial

CAPACITY

1 pint	=4 gills	=0·473 litres
1 quart	=2 pints	=0·946 litres
1 gallon	=4 quarts	=3·785 litres
1 gallon	=231 cu in	=0·134 cu ft
1 US gallon	=0·833 Imperial gallon	
1 Imp gallon	=1·201 US gallons.	

WEIGHT

1 short ton =2000 lb	=907 kg

Table 17

Conversion Tables

LENGTH

millimetres	mm or inches	inches	kilometres	km or statute miles	statute miles
25·4	1	0·04	1·61	1	0·62
50·8	2	0·08	3·22	2	1·24
76·2	3	0·12	4·83	3	1·86
101·6	4	0·16	6·44	4	2·49
127·0	5	0·20	8·05	5	3·11
152·4	6	0·24	9·66	6	3·73
177·8	7	0·28	11·27	7	4·35
203·2	8	0·32	12·88	8	4·97
228·6	9	0·35	14·48	9	5·59
254·0	10	0·39	16·09	10	6·21
508·0	20	0·79	32·19	20	12·43
762·0	30	1·18	48·28	30	18·64
1016	40	1·58	64·37	40	24·86
1270	50	1·97	80·47	50	31·07
1524	60	2·36	96·56	60	37·28
1778	70	2·76	112·7	70	43·50
2032	80	3·15	128·7	80	49·71
2286	90	3·54	144·8	90	55·92
2540	100	3·94	160·9	100	62·14

kilometres	km or naut. miles	naut. miles	metres	m or feet	feet
1·85	1	0·54	0·30	1	3·28
3·70	2	1·08	0·61	2	6·56
5·55	3	1·62	0·91	3	9·84
7·40	4	2·16	1·22	4	13·12
9·25	5	2·70	1·52	5	16·40
11·10	6	3·24	1·83	6	19·68
12·95	7	3·78	2·13	7	22·96
14·80	8	4·32	2·44	8	26·25
16·65	9	4·86	2·74	9	29·53
18·53	10	5·40	3·05	10	32·81
37·0	20	10·8	6·10	20	65·62
55·5	30	16·2	9·14	30	98·43
74·0	40	21·6	12·19	40	131·23
92·5	50	27·0	15·24	50	164·04
111·0	60	32·4	18·29	60	196·85
129·5	70	37·8	21·34	70	229·66
148·0	80	43·2	24·38	80	262·47
166·5	90	48·6	27·43	90	295·28
185·3	100	54·00	30·48	100	328·10

kilogrammes	kg or pounds	pounds	litres	litres or Imp. gallons	gallons
	WEIGHT			VOLUME	
0·45	1	2·20	4·55	1	0·22
0·91	2	4·41	9·09	2	0·44
1·36	3	6·61	13·64	3	0·66
1·81	4	8·82	18·18	4	0·88
2·27	5	11·02	22·73	5	1·10
2·72	6	13·23	27·28	6	1·32
3·18	7	15·43	31·82	7	1·54
3·63	8	17·64	36·37	8	1·76
4·08	9	19·84	40·91	9	1·98
4·54	10	22·05	45·46	10	2·20
9·07	20	44·09	90·92	20	4·40
13·61	30	66·14	136·4	30	6·60
18·14	40	88·19	181·8	40	8·80
22·68	50	110·2	227·3	50	11·00
27·22	60	132·3	272·8	60	13·20
31·75	70	154·3	318·2	70	15·40
36·29	80	176·4	363·7	80	17·60
40·82	90	198·4	409·1	90	19·80
45·36	100	220·5	454·6	100	22·00

For Temperature and Barometric Pressure Conversions see p. 211–12

Table 18

Some Useful Approximations

LENGTH

2 inches	= 5 centimetres
11 yards	= 10 metres
8 stat. miles	= 7 nautical miles
5 stat. miles	= 8 kilometres

SPEED

1 knot	= 0·5 metres/sec.
	= 1·7 ft/sec.
	= 1·15 st. miles/hr
7 knots	= 8 st. miles/hr

AREA

6 sq yards	= 5 sq metres
3 sq miles	= 8 sq kilometres
5 acres	= 2 hectares

CAPACITY

1 pint	= 0·57 litres
1·76 pints	= 1 litre
3·5 pints	= 2 litres
5 pints	= 6 US pints
7 pints	= 4 litres
7 quarts	= 8 litres
2 gallons	= 9 litres
4 US gallons	= 15 litres
5 gallons (Imp)	= 6 US gallons

WEIGHT

3 avoirdupois ounces	= 85 grams
35 ounces	= 1 kilogram
11 pounds	= 5 kilograms

OIL OR TYRE PRESSURES

Pounds per Square Inch	Kilogrammes per Square Centimetre
20	1·40
22	1·54
24	1·68
26	1·82
28	1·96
30	2·10
32	2·24
34	2·38
36	2·53
38	2·67
40	2·80

Table 19
Trigonometrical Tables and Conversion, Degrees to Radians

Radian	Degree	Tangent	Sine	Cosine
0·0000	0	0·0000	0·0000	1·0000
0·0175	1	0·0175	0·0175	0·9998
0·0349	2	0·0349	0·0349	0·9994
0·0524	3	0·0524	0·0523	0·9986
0·0698	4	0·0699	0·0698	0·9976
0·0873	5	0·0875	0·0872	0·9962
0·1047	6	0·1051	0·1045	0·9945
0·1222	7	0·1228	0·1219	0·9925
0·1396	8	0·1405	0·1392	0·9903
0·1571	9	0·1584	0·1564	0·9877
0·1745	10	0·1763	0·1736	0·9848
0·1920	11	0·1944	0·1908	0·9816
0·2094	12	0·2126	0·2079	0·9781
0·2269	13	0·2309	0·2250	0·9744
0·2443	14	0·2493	0·2419	0·9703
0·2618	15	0·2679	0·2588	0·9659
0·2793	16	0·2867	0·2756	0·9613
0·2967	17	0·3057	0·2924	0·9563
0·3142	18	0·3249	0·3090	0·9511
0·3316	19	0·3443	0·3256	0·9455
0·3491	20	0·3640	0·3420	0·9397
0·3665	21	0·3839	0·3584	0·9336
0·3840	22	0·4040	0·3746	0·9272
0·4014	23	0·4245	0·3907	0·9205
0·4189	24	0·4452	0·4067	0·9135
0·4363	25	0·4663	0·4226	0·9063
0·4538	26	0·4877	0·4384	0·8988
0·4712	27	0·5095	0·4540	0·8910
0·4887	28	0·5317	0·4695	0·8829
0·5061	29	0·5543	0·4848	0·8746
0·5236	30	0·5774	0·5000	0·8660
0·5411	31	0·6009	0·5150	0·8572
0·5585	32	0·6249	0·5299	0·8480
0·5760	33	0·6494	0·5446	0·8387
0·5934	34	0·6745	0·5592	0·8290
0·6109	35	0·7002	0·5736	0·8192
0·6283	36	0·7265	0·5878	0·8090
0·6458	37	0·7536	0·6018	0·7986
0·6632	38	0·7813	0·6157	0·7880
0·6807	39	0·8098	0·6293	0·7771
0·6981	40	0·8391	0·6428	0·7660
0·7156	41	0·8693	0·6561	0·7547
0·7330	42	0·9004	0·6691	0·7431
0·7505	43	0·9325	0·6820	0·7314
0·7679	44	0·9657	0·6947	0·7193
0·7854	45	1·0000	0·7071	0·7071

Radian	Degree	Tangent	Sine	Cosine
0·7854	45	1·0000	0·7071	0·7071
0·8029	46	1·0355	0·7193	0·6947
0·8203	47	1·0724	0·7314	0·6820
0·8378	48	1·1106	0·7431	0·6691
0·8552	49	1·1504	0·7547	0·6561
0·8727	50	1·1918	0·7660	0·6428
0·8901	51	1·2349	0·7771	0·6293
0·9076	52	1·2799	0·7880	0·6157
0·9250	53	1·3270	0·7986	0·6018
0·9425	54	1·3764	0·8090	0·5878
0·9599	55	1·4281	0·8192	0·5736
0·9774	56	1·4826	0·8290	0·5592
0·9948	57	1·5399	0·8387	0·5446
1·0123	58	1·6003	0·8480	0·5299
1·0297	59	1·6643	0·8572	0·5150
1·0472	60	1·7321	0·8660	0·5000
1·0647	61	1·8040	0·8746	0·4848
1·0821	62	1·8807	0·8829	0·4695
1·0996	63	1·9626	0·8910	0·4540
1·1170	64	2·0503	0·8988	0·4384
1·1345	65	2·1445	0·9063	0·4226
1·1519	66	2·2460	0·9135	0·4067
1·1694	67	2·3559	0·9205	0·3907
1·1868	68	2·4751	0·9272	0·3746
1·2043	69	2·6051	0·9336	0·3584
1·2217	70	2·7475	0·9397	0·3420
1·2392	71	2·9042	0·9455	0·3256
1·2566	72	3·0777	0·9511	0·3090
1·2741	73	3·2709	0·9563	0·2924
1·2915	74	3·4874	0·9613	0·2756
1·3090	75	3·7321	0·9659	0·2588
1·3265	76	4·0108	0·9703	0·2419
1·3439	77	4·3315	0·9744	0·2250
1·3614	78	4·7046	0·9781	0·2079
1·3788	79	5·1446	0·9816	0·1908
1·3963	80	5·6713	0·9848	0·1736
1·4137	81	6·3138	0·9877	0·1564
1·4312	82	7·1154	0·9903	0·1392
1·4486	83	8·1443	0·9925	0·1219
1·4661	84	9·5144	0·9945	0·1045
1·4835	85	11·43	0·9962	0·0872
1·5010	86	14·30	0·9976	0·0698
1·5184	87	19·08	0·9986	0·0523
1·5359	88	28·64	0·9994	0·0349
1·5533	89	57·29	0·9998	0·0175
1·5708	90	∞	1·0000	0·0000

Table 20

Average Densities and Specific Gravities of Materials

	DENSITY lb per cu ft	DENSITY kg per litre	SPECIFIC GRAVITY
METALS			
Aluminium alloys	170	2·7	
Brass	530	8·4	
Bronze	545	8·6	
Copper	550	8·8	
Iron (cast)	450	7·2	
Lead	711	11·4	
Steel	490	7·8	
TIMBER			
Ash	43	0·68	
Elm (English)	42	0·67	
Elm (Rock)	44	0·70	
Iroko	40	0·64	
Mahogany	34–44	0·55–0·70	
Oak	45	0·72	
Pitch pine	41	0·65	
Pine (yellow)	34	0·55	
Spruce	28	0·45	
Teak	41	0·65	
VARIOUS			
Fresh Water	62·5	1·00	
Sea Water	64	1·03	
Petrol (Gasoline)	44	0·70	
Diesel Fuel (Gas Oil)	50	0·80	
Paraffin (Kerosene)	50	0·80	

1 Imperial gallon = 4·55 litres = 0·17 cu ft = 1·2 US galls = 10 lb of fresh water.

11

Coastal Navigation

Navigation has been broadly defined as the art of finding a ship's position at sea, and of safely conducting her from one position to another.

Coastal navigation in general concerns passages mainly within sight of land, though many of its principles apply equally to short passages offshore.

Pilotage is the art of manoeuvring a ship in restricted or tortuous waters, and in the vicinity of such hazards as rocks and shoals.

A good navigator never trusts implicitly a single source of information. He constantly cross-checks several sources, each against the others, so that if an error is made it soon becomes evident, and possibly dangerous situations avoided.

A good navigator will also know how to use different sources of information conjointly; positions of varying accuracy may be obtained by crossing a shore or radio bearing with a depth sounding, a course and distance run from a known position with a single bearing or depth, even, in suitable circumstances, from a line of depth soundings.

Chiefly, a good navigator will know the degree of precision he may attribute to each and every element of his work and will take this into account in deciding on the action most appropriate to the safe conduct of his ship.

There is no room whatsoever for unjustified optimism or wishful thinking in navigating a small craft; it is a serious but infinitely satisfying and rewarding art.

This book does not attempt to teach navigation. The world's bookstores and libraries have countless excellent specialist books on this subject; some of these are listed on p. 298.

Some technical colleges and institutions run courses in navigation, and so do the better sailing schools, some of which offer correspondence courses for people not within easy reach of the sea. But, having learnt the theory, the best way to become a really proficient navigator is to understudy an experienced skipper as often as possible in actual sea conditions. And then to practise and practise for as many years as one goes to sea.

NAVIGATION: SOME DEFINITIONS

Bearing   The angle between the local meridian and the direction of an object whose bearing it is, measured clockwise from North. 'True' bearing if from geographical North, 'Magnetic' bearing if from the magnetic meridian.

Cocked Hat   The triangle formed at the intersection of three lines of bearing drawn on a chart. The smaller the cocked hat, the more accurate the position thus determined.

Course   See 'Heading' and 'Track'.

Current   Strictly a unidirectional flow of water, separate from the tidal stream, such as that caused by the fresh water of a river entering a tidal estuary, but see also 'Tidal Stream'.

Dead Reckoning   The summation of courses steered and distances run, without regard to the effect of tides on a boat's position. (And see 'Estimated Position').

Departure   A point, either a landmark or a seamark, whose position is accurately known, used as a reference point for plotting subsequent tracks.

Deviation   The difference between a compass reading

and the actual magnetic direction. The error is caused by iron in the vicinity of the compass and it changes with a boat's magnetic heading.

Distance The Distance Run is the number of nautical miles the boat has travelled through the water as recorded by the patent log without regard to the effect of tidal streams or leeway. The Distance Made Good takes those effects into account, and is the actual distance travelled over the ground.

Estimated Position A boat's position at sea as determined from Dead Reckoning but corrected for the influence of tidal streams and leeway.

Fix The determination of a boat's position at sea by reference to the bearings of landmarks; visual fix from landmarks seen on shore, radio fix from radio beacons.

Heading The actual direction a boat is pointing. This may be different from the direction sailed over the ground on account of tidal streams and leeway.

Height of Tide The depth of water at any time above chart datum. See p. 197.

Knot A speed of one nautical mile per hour.

Landmark Any shore object conspicuous from seaward which is suitable for taking bearings as an aid to fixing position.

Latitude, Parallel of An imaginary line round the earth which joins all points of the same angular distance north or south of the equator. One degree of latitude is equal to 60 nautical miles in length, so one minute is one mile.

Leading Marks Two beacons (or other natural or man-made objects) so positioned that a boat sailing with them in line will be led clear of dangerous obstructions.

Leeway The sideways movement of a boat through the water due to the pressure of the wind on her weather side. Varies with the direction of the wind; often about 5 degrees in a sailing boat beating to windward, very variable in motor craft.

Longitude, Meridian of An imaginary line drawn from pole to pole at right angles to the equator. The Prime Meridian passes also through the old Observatory at Greenwich; other longitudes are measured by their angular distance east or west of the Greenwich Meridian. The length of a degree of longitude varies from zero at the poles to 60 nautical miles at the equator; it is therefore not used to measure distances at sea.

Mean Level of the tide. The height of water above chart datum above and below which the tides oscillate. See p. 195ff.

Mercator's Projection A method of representing the features of a spherical earth on a flat chart, on which the meridians of longitude are drawn parallel to each other and at right angles to the parallels of latitude. All charts likely to be used in a small craft are drawn on Mercator's Projection. NOTE: Adjacent parallels of latitude are drawn at different distances apart in different latitudes, so that the distance scale varies from the top to the bottom of a chart.

Mile A nautical or sea mile is equal to the length of one minute of latitude, approximately 6,080 feet. For all practical purposes in navigation it is taken as 2,000 yards.

Neap Tide See 'Spring Tide' and p. 194.

Position Line A single line of bearing drawn from a landmark or radio beacon. The boat from which the bearing was taken must lie somewhere along this line. The intersection of two or three position lines fixes the position of the boat unambiguously.

Range of the tide The amount the sea level ranges up and down between Low Water and High Water. It is greatest at Spring Tides and least at Neap Tides. See p. 194.

Rhumb Line A straight line drawn between two points on a Mercator's chart. It is not strictly the shortest distance between those points unless they lie north and south of each other, but over comparatively short distances in middle and low latitudes the differences may be ignored.

Rise of the tide. See p. 197.

Running Fix A fix obtained from a single landmark. See p. 165.

Set The effect of the tidal stream or current on the track of a boat.

Soundings The actual depth of water at any time and place, and the result of adding the rise of the tide at that instant to the charted depth at that place.

Spring Tide When the Sun and the Moon are on the same side of the earth they are said to be in 'conjunction' and when they are on opposite sides they are in 'opposition'. In both of these conditions the Sun and Moon act jointly to increase the height of what are then known as Spring Tides. They occur every fortnight, shortly after New Moon and Full Moon, and are in no way connected with the season of Spring. Neap Tides occur when the Sun and Moon are in 'quadrature' (90 degrees apart), halfway between the two Spring Tides in any four weeks. The rise and fall of the tides are then smallest, and tidal streams run most weakly. The Spring Tides with the greatest range usually occur about the time of the Equinoxes (about 21 March and 23 September).

Tidal Stream The horizontal flow of tidal water over the bottom of the sea. Its rate varies from hour to hour. from place to place and with Spring and Neap Tides. Tidal rates are measured in knots. (Known in the U.S. as tidal currents.)

Tides The vertical motion of the sea's surface. See 'Spring' and 'Neap Tide'.

Track Made Good Sometimes known as 'course made good', the actual path of a boat over the ground, and the result of combining the boat's speed and direction through the water, the effect of the tidal streams and the amount of leeway experienced.

Transit Two beacons, landmarks or other objects in line. See 'Leading Marks'.

Variation, Magnetic The angle between the direction of True North and the direction of the local magnetic meridian. A compass needle unaffected by deviation (q.v.) points along the local magnetic meridian. Variation is independent of the heading of the boat, but changes from place to place on the Earth's surface.

NAVIGATING EQUIPMENT

Good navigation depends far more on the ability of the navigator than the quantity and cost of instruments at his disposal. A small boat used exclusively for local day-sailing might be adequately equipped with no more than a steering compass and a lead and line.

More ambitious cruising requires more equipment; how much should be carried will depend on the size of the boat, the nature of her intended cruises and still on the skill of the navigator.

Basically, one needs equipment to measure direction, distance, time and depth of water. The equipment chosen may be simple or sophisticated, but should never exceed the ability of the navigator to use it at sea.

A five-tonner used for weekend coastal cruising and the occasional overnight cross-channel passage in the hands of a reasonably competent amateur navigator needs a good **steering compass** whose deviation has been checked and recorded in a deviation table if it exceeds the odd degree or so. A **hand bearing-compass** will be needed for fixing position off the coast.

She will also need a **patent log** (rotator and line pattern or electrical equivalent) to measure distance sailed through the water. A **lead and line** will give depth of water;

nowadays **depth sounders** are small and inexpensive and can be accommodated in most cruising boats. It's still a good idea to have a lead and line as a standby; batteries run down and electronics are not infallible.

One assumes that there will be at least one reliable **watch** or **cabin clock** on board; a **stop-watch** will be found useful for timing the flashes of buoys and lighthouses and the rotation rate of the patent log, but a sweep second hand on any watch or clock will do the same job.

Paperwork follows us even to sea. Maritime **charts** are vital to show the positions of places and dangers and to enable the navigator to plot the progress of the boat. Charts come on various scales; passage charts on a small scale and showing both the point of departure and intended destination are needed for planning a voyage; coastal charts on a larger scale but covering the same route will enable the navigator to sail a safe course and plot his position at all times. Harbour plans on a large scale enable one to enter what may be tricky anchorages and select a safe and convenient berth; these may often be found in pilot books published for yachtsmen.

A **log book** is essential. This may be a specially-designed yachtman's log book or merely a school notebook suitably ruled in columns for recording times, courses, distances, fixes and other navigating data. Navigation without a log book is like running a business without an account book: you soon get lost.

The other paperwork includes **tide tables** to give the times and height of High Water at various places on the cruise, **tidal atlases** to show the speed and direction of tidal streams. While these can be bought separately, most small-boat navigators find it more convenient to buy a **nautical almanac** (such as Reed's) which gives not only tidal data but also a great wealth of other useful information and knowledge.

Pilot books are available which help to amplify the information given on the charts and tidal atlases; government publications are very detailed but tend, naturally, to cater for the needs of bigger ships, whereas yachtsmen's pilot books are compiled with the small boat in mind. Those by Adlard Coles are deservedly popular in Europe. See 'Book List' on p. 298.

A **chart table** is required on which to spread out the chart in use and plot position lines; if possible it should measure at least 28 by 22 inches (715 by 560 mm) to take a folded chart. A table 30 by 27 inches (760 by 685 mm) is better. This could be the existing cabin table in a very small boat but a chart table dedicated to the exclusive use of the navigator when on passage can often be devised; it might be arranged to hinge down over the foot of a bunk when in use and fold away against a bulkhead or the side of the boat at other times. An **amber light** is a great help on night passages; it permits the navigator to use the chart without spoiling his dark-adaptation for when he comes on deck again.

The chartboard instruments are quite simple; a **parallel rule** (Captain Field's or roller pattern, or perhaps a Douglas protractor) is needed to lay off courses, and a **pair of dividers** to measure distances on the chart. A **soft pencil** with a really sharp point draws lines on the chart and an **eraser** rubs them out when finished with. A **magnifying glass** or **illuminated chart reader** helps to decipher the fine detail.

The remaining equipment needed by a serious navigator consists of a good pair of **binoculars** (the optimum power for use at sea has been found to be 7×50) and an **aneroid barometer** to keep track of the weather. This should have a range from about 950 to 1,050 millibars.

Since **direction-finding radio** receivers are comparatively inexpensive and anyway a **radio** is needed to receive weather forecasts, many small cruising boats are equipped to use the navigation facilities offered by coastal radio beacons. The use of a DF radio is described on p. 219.

With the foregoing equipment and an adequate knowledge of its use a navigator might take his boat almost anywhere in coastal waters. A **sextant** and **chronometer** are needed only for ocean passages of considerable length, though fun to use at any time. Many sophisticated instruments are available to get the maximum performance out of ocean racing yachts, but their navigators will know about these already and they will not be described here.

CHARTS AND CHARTWORK

Maritime charts are prepared and published by the Hydrographer of the Navy in Britain, by the U.S. Defense Mapping Agency in Washington, by the Canadian Hydrographic Service in Ottawa and by equivalent authorities in other countries. They are generally available from official chart agents in most major shipping ports.

Simplified yachtsmen's charts based on official publications are prepared and published by Stanford and by Imray Norie in Britain. In the U.S. Socony Mobil's Cruising Guides and the Standard Oil Company's Southern Guide to Florida and the Gulf Coast are deservedly popular with small-boat owners. These charts may be obtained from yacht chandlers and marinas.

The official charts are used exclusively by professional navigators because they carry more detail and can be periodically corrected when changes have occurred in coastlines, depths, buoyage and in the many other points of detail which may, if wrongly interpreted, lead to disaster.

These charts are corrected by reference to a document known as **Notices to Mariners**, published weekly in Britain by the Hydrographer of the Navy, in the U.S. by the Defense Mapping Agency jointly with the U.S. Coast

Guard. Copies of these Notices may be obtained from chart agents and, in Britain, from Custom Houses.

Not all Notices to Mariners contain information relevant to the limited number of charts normally owned by yachtsmen, for they have to cover thousands of charts applicable to the whole world. But they are indexed each week to show which charts are affected by the current issue; it is the work of seconds to establish whether one's own charts are affected.

Take good care of charts. Not only are they rather expensive (or very cheap, depending on how you look at them) but their fine detail is easily confused or obscured by dirty marks, and you could be misled into dangerous situations.

Erase all pencil work when you have finished with a chart (or at least before you use it again). Old courses and bearings can be mistaken for current ones with potentially serious results.

If you can possibly avoid folding charts, do so, because the more folds there are, the more areas there will be which are difficult to interpret.

Use a soft pencil (B or 2B) kept really sharp for chartwork. A soft eraser will then remove old or erroneous work without trace. It's worth keeping at least one spare pencil locked up and out of general use.

Chart Symbols

The symbols used to denote various features of charts carry a vast amount of information for those familiar with them. From them an experienced navigator can build up a mental picture of what to expect when he reaches an unfamiliar coastline.

Its appearance, outlying rocks and shoals, navigable channels, buoys, seamarks and landmarks, the depth and nature of the sea bed, harbours and sheltered anchorages, virtually everything one might need to know for safe navigation will be found on the charts coded in the appropriate symbols. Some of the more important of these will be found in Figs. 28 and 29. The complete list of symbols used on British charts is given in Admiralty Booklet 5011. The corresponding U.S. publication is National Ocean Survey Chart No. 1.

	Light buoy	BR BW RW	Chequered
Bell	Bell buoy	W	White
Gong	Gong buoy	B	Black
Whis	Whistle buoy	R	Red
	Can buoy, Cylindrical buoy	Y	Yellow
	Conical buoy, Nun buoy	G	Green
	Spherical buoy	Gy	Grey
etc.	Spar buoy, floating beacon	Bl	Blue
	Pillar buoy Lighthouse buoy		Amber
	Spindle buoy		Orange
etc.	Buoy with topmark	etc.	Beacons
	Light buoy with topmark	Bn Bn	
	Barrel buoy, Ton buoy	Bn Bn Tower Tower	Beacon tower
R B G G G G	Light-float		
	Wreck buoy	etc.	Topmarks
	Mooring buoy		Stake; Perch
RY RY	Practice area buoy		Radar reflector
BW RW BR	Horizontal stripes or bands	Target	Range targets, markers
RW BR BW	Vertical stripes		

28a Chart Symbols: Buoys and Beacons

☆	Position of important light		
*	Position of minor light	VI	Violet
Lt	Light	Bl	Blue
Lt Ho	Lighthouse	G	Green
☆ Aero	Aero light	Or	Orange
☆	Aeromarine light	R	Red
☆	Lighted beacon	W	White
	Light-vessel		
Lt V	Light-vessel		
F	Fixed		
Occ	Occulting		
Fl	Flashing		
Iso	Isophase		
Qk Fl	Quick flashing		
Int Qk Fl	Interrupted quick flashing		
Alt	Alternating		
GpOcc	Group occulting		
GpFl	Group flashing		
F Fl	Fixed and flashing		
F Gp Fl	Fixed and group flashing		
Mo(A)	Morse code light (with flashes grouped as in letter A)		

28b Chart Symbols: Lights

BUOYAGE SYSTEMS

One ought to be able to decide, from a momentary glimpse of a buoy, which side of it to sail to avoid the danger it marks. The shape and colour make this possible. There are however numerous different systems in general use in various parts of the world. In 1976 the International Association of Lighthouse Authorities agreed to rationalize the existing systems into two new systems. As it will take several years to introduce them worldwide, the most commonly used present systems and also the future systems are described in this book.

Present Systems (1976)

In European waters the Lateral and Cardinal systems are both found, and in North America a different lateral system.

Lateral systems depend on the principle that buoys recognised as Port Hand Buoys shall be left to port by craft proceeding in the direction of the main flood tidal stream and Starboard Hand Buoys of course are left to starboard.

160

(4)	Rock which does not cover (with elevation above MHWS)
(4) Dries 1.2m *(12)	Rock which covers and uncovers (with elevation above chart datum)
(12)	Rock awash at the level of chart datum
R	Sunken rock with 2 metres or less water over it at chart datum, or
Wk	Wreck showing any portion of hull or super-structure at the level of chart datum
(Masts) (mast 3m) (Funnel) (Mast dries 2.1m)	Wreck of which the masts only are visible
	Wreck over which the exact depth of water is unknown but is thought to be 28 metres or less, and which is considered dangerous to surface navigation
7₃ Wk	Wreck over which the depth has been obtained by sounding, but not by wire sweep
	Wreck over which the exact depth is unknown but thought to be more than 28 metres
Foul	The remains of a wreck, or other foul area, no longer dangerous to surface navigation but to be avoided by vessels anchoring trawling, etc.
7₃ * 9₁	Limiting danger line

Eddies

Overfalls and tide-rips

Breakers

BASED ON ADMIRALTY CHART 5011

ABBREVIATIONS:

Bk	Bank
Sh	Shoal
Rf	Reef
Le	Ledge
Obstn	Obstruction
Wk	Wreck
dr	Dries
cov	Covers
uncov	Uncovers
(repd)	Reported
discolrd	Discoloured
(PA)	Position approximate
(PD)	Position doubtful
(ED)	Existance doubtful
posn	Position
Unexamd	Unexamined

29 Chart Symbols: Dangers

The opposite applies when proceeding against the direction of the main flood stream.

The direction of the main flood is obviously upstream in any tidal river or estuary; it is not so obvious in the open sea. See Appendix A, p. 288, which also shows the alternative shapes and top marks for lateral-system buoys.

The **Cardinal system** of buoys is used in Europe in places where the direction of the main flood stream cannot be unambiguously defined. In this system the buoys and their top marks indicate that craft should pass to the north, south, east or west of the buoy as appropriate. See Appendix A, p. 291.

By night, when one cannot see the shape, colour or top mark of a buoy, a uniform system of flashing lights is used to identify buoys. Not all buoys are lit, but buoys of major importance have a unique characteristic flashing code which differentiates them from others in the same vicinity. See Fig. 30.

Future Systems

Beginning in 1977, a Combined Cardinal and Lateral System will be progressively introduced into the waters of Europe, Africa, India, Australia and most of Asia. The buoys of this new System 'A' are illustrated in Appendix A, pp. 292–3.

Note that after the introduction of System 'A' to British waters, the Conventional Buoyage Direction (formerly known as the Direction of the Main Flood Stream) is reversed along the whole East Coast from the Thames Estuary to the Shetlands and also through the North Channel between Scotland and Ireland. See Appendix A.

System 'B' will eventually apply to the North and South American Continents, the Caribbean and to parts of Asia.

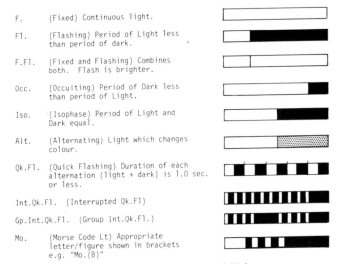

F.	(Fixed) Continuous light.
Fl.	(Flashing) Period of Light less than period of dark.
F.Fl.	(Fixed and Flashing) Combines both. Flash is brighter.
Occ.	(Occulting) Period of Dark less than period of Light.
Iso.	(Isophase) Period of Light and Dark equal.
Alt.	(Alternating) Light which changes colour.
Qk.Fl.	(Quick Flashing) Duration of each alternation (light + dark) is 1.0 sec. or less.
Int.Qk.Fl.	(Interrupted Qk.Fl)
Gp.Int.Qk.Fl.	(Group Int.Qk.Fl.)
Mo.	(Morse Code Lt) Appropriate letter/figure shown in brackets e.g. "Mo.(B)"

30 Flashing Codes, Buoys and Lights

POSITION FIXING

A boat's position at sea is indicated in terms of **latitude** and **longitude** when out of sight of land and by **range** and **bearing** from a known landmark towards the vessel when in coastal waters.

A **Position line** is a single line of latitude or longitude or a bearing on a landmark or radio beacon, or a dipping distance from a light on the horizon, or a sounding. No one of these alone defines a boat's position unambiguously, because one knows only that she is at some point along that line.

A **Fix** is obtained at the intersection of two or more position lines in any combination, the observations being made simultaneously or as nearly so as possible.

Taking Bearings

Identify positively the landmarks of which bearings are to be taken, both on the shore and on the chart. Three bearings about 60 degrees apart will give maximum accuracy.

Use the hand bearing-compass in a position where it is least likely to be affected by deviation due to the proximity of iron. Take the bearings in the order which reads the one most nearly abeam last; its bearing is changing more rapidly than the others. Note the time in the log to the nearest minute.

Plot the reciprocals (add or subtract 180 degrees, the answer is self-evident from the chart rose) of each bearing from the landmarks on the chart; if they intersect at the same point the fix is good, but if they result in a triangle ('cocked hat') whose sides are more than a quarter of a mile long on the scale of the chart, the bearings include at least one wrong one and all three should be taken again.

If only two landmarks are available, they should ideally be about 90 degrees apart; the further one departs from this optimum the less accurate the fix. A pair of bearings less than 30 degrees or more than 150 degrees apart is not reliable, and any two-bearing fix should be regarded with caution in the absence of a third.

Doubling the Angle on the Bow

If only one identifiable landmark is visible, its bearing should be taken when it is well ahead on one bow or the other. The angle between the landmark and the bow should be calculated by subtracting it from the direction of the ship's head (or vice versa), allowing for deviation of the steering compass. Read the mileage on the patent log, note the time, and be careful to stay on the same compass course.

Keep taking bearings of the landmark until the angle on the bow is double its original value. Read the log again, and note the time. Assuming little or no tide, the boat will be on the position line of the second bearing and the same distance from the landmark as the difference between the two log readings.

If however the tidal stream has been running substantially from ahead or astern, its effect must be subtracted from or added to the distance sailed through the water as given by the log. This will give the distance sailed over the ground, and this distance is now the same as the distance away from the landmark.

Any variation of speed during the run between the two bearings will not affect the accuracy of this method, but the effect of a cross tide or any change in course will invalidate the result. It is possible to plot on the chart the effect of a tidal stream setting across the boat's course; in this case the length of the track (resultant of course sailed and tidal set) will be the distance off the landmark at the time of the second bearing.

Four-point Bearing

A useful special case of doubling the angle on the bow may be used to determine the distance off a headland. Read the log and note the time when the headland bears 45 degrees on one bow or the other. When the headland is exactly on the beam (90 degrees) read the log again and note the time. Making allowance if necessary for tidal stream, the distance sailed over the ground between the times of the two bearings will be the distance off the headland at the time it is abeam.

Running Fix

A fix can be obtained from two position lines taken on the same landmark at different times. Take the first bearing, note the log reading and time as for doubling the angle on the bow. When the bearing has changed about 90 degrees, take the second bearing and note again the log reading and time.

On the chart, plot the ship's course and the tidal set to determine the track from any convenient point on the first position line. Through the Estimated Position at the end of the run, draw another position line parallel with the first. This is known as a Transferred Position Line. Where it intersects the second position line taken at the end of the run fixes the ship's position at that time.

Running Fix by Radio

The same technique can be adopted using radio beacon bearings instead of compass bearings. The resulting fix should however be used with caution, as radio bearings are not as accurate as visual ones.

Position Fixing by Depth

A depth sounding taken at the same time as any of the above fixing methods may help to establish confidence in the fix. But if the echo sounder gives a depth noticeably different from that charted for the position (allowing for the height of the tide) something is seriously wrong and the fix should be discounted.

Where the sea bed has contours unique to the area in which the boat is known to be, depth soundings alone can give a reasonably accurate position fix. If for instance one expects to cross a small 5 fathom patch in an area which is generally over 10 fathoms deep, the echo sounder will show when this occurs. But if there are several 5 fathom patches charted within a few miles, the method is not unambiguous and should not be used.

A depth sounding combined with a single visual or radio bearing may give a reasonable fix, but examine the chart closely in the vicinity of the line of bearing and its extension; there may be other positions showing the same depth. If however any second position showing the same depth is out of visible range of the land and you have just taken a visual bearing, this second possible position may confidently be discarded. But not so with radio bearings.

Estimating Position by Shipping and Air Lanes

This isn't position fixing at all. If a well-known cross-channel ferry is encountered at sea, you are probably but not necessarily on a position line between her two terminal ports. She may have been diverted for some reason unknown to you. So don't use this for anything except to tell your crew smugly 'Spot on track'. And even then keep a mental reservation.

People have been fooled by lightships on course to or from their normal stations but at the moment many miles from them. Look for her anchor ball; if it's not there she is probably under way.

Angle and Distance Judging

Table 21 gives distance run through the water for a given time and speed.

The following approximations are useful when complete precision of measurement for position fixing is not essential.

With the hand held at arm's length:
Full span, thumb tip to little finger tip = about 20°
Width of closed fist = about 10°
Closed fist with extended thumb = about 15°
Thumb's width = about 3°
Little finger width = about 2°

A rough check of the bearings of headlands, other shipping, etc. is possible if you know the angles between dead-ahead and the shrouds and various guardrail stanchions as seen from the normal steering position in the cockpit. This obviously varies with different boats.

The angles between the horizon and the masthead or crosstrees give a rough measurement of elevation for locating stars and planets when sailing at night.

A relaxed way of steering at night is to put the boat on

Table 21

Time, Speed and Distance

KNOTS

Min.	1	2	3	4	5	6	7	8	9	10
2		0·1	0·1	0·2	0·2	0·2	0·2	0·3	0·3	0·3
4		0·1	0·2	0·3	0·3	0·4	0·5	0·5	0·6	0·7
6		0·2	0·3	0·4	0·5	0·6	0·7	0·8	0·9	1·0
8	0·1	0·3	0·4	0·6	0·7	0·8	0·9	1·0	1·2	1·3
10	0·2	0·3	0·5	0·7	0·8	1·0	1·2	1·3	1·5	1·7
12	0·2	0·4	0·6	0·8	1·0	1·2	1·4	1·6	1·8	2·0
14	0·2	0·5	0·7	1·0	1·2	1·4	1·6	1·9	2·1	2·3
16	0·3	0·5	0·8	1·1	1·3	1·6	1·9	2·1	2·4	2·7
18	0·3	0·6	0·9	1·2	1·5	1·8	2·1	2·4	2·7	3·0
20	0·3	0·7	1·0	1·4	1·7	2·0	2·3	2·7	3·0	3·3
22	0·4	0·7	1·1	1·5	1·8	2·2	2·6	2·9	3·3	3·7
24	0·4	0·8	1·2	1·6	2·0	2·4	2·8	3·2	3·6	4·0
26	0·4	0·9	1·3	1·8	2·2	2·6	3·0	3·5	3·9	4·3
28	0·5	0·9	1·4	1·9	2·3	2·8	3·3	3·7	4·2	4·7
30	0·5	1·0	1·5	2·0	2·5	3·0	3·5	4·0	4·5	5·0
32	0·5	1·1	1·6	2·2	2·7	3·2	3·7	4·3	4·8	5·3
34	0·6	1·1	1·7	2·3	2·9	3·4	4·0	4·5	5·1	5·7
36	0·6	1·2	1·8	2·4	3·0	3·6	4·2	4·8	5·4	6·0
38	0·6	1·3	1·9	2·6	3·2	3·8	4·4	5·0	5·7	6·3
40	0·7	1·3	2·0	2·7	3·3	4·0	4·7	5·3	6·0	6·7
42	0·7	1·4	2·1	2·8	3·5	4·2	4·9	5·6	6·3	7·0
44	0·7	1·5	2·2	3·0	3·7	4·4	5·1	5·9	6·6	7·3
46	0·8	1·5	2·3	3·1	3·8	4·6	5·4	6·1	6·9	7·7
48	0·8	1·6	2·4	3·2	4·0	4·8	5·6	6·4	7·2	8·0
50	0·8	1·7	2·5	3·4	4·2	5·0	5·8	6·7	7·5	8·3
52	0·9	1·7	2·6	3·5	4·3	5·2	6·1	6·9	7·8	8·7
54	0·9	1·8	2·7	3·6	4·5	5·4	6·3	7·2	8·1	9·0
56	0·9	1·9	2·8	3·8	4·7	5·6	6·5	7·5	8·4	9·3
58	1·0	1·9	2·9	3·9	4·8	5·8	6·8	7·7	8·7	9·7
60	1·0	2·0	3·0	4·0	5·0	6·0	7·0	8·0	9·0	10·0

Miles Run Through Water
(Correct For Tidal Stream or Current)

course by compass and note which star lies at the end of the crosstrees; sail to keep the star in that position but remember that the star will move 15 degrees every hour and you must adjust for this movement.

To establish whether you are on a collision course with another vessel, take a series of bearings on her with the hand bearing-compass. If the bearing remains constant, you are on a collision course. The other boat will pass astern if the bearing draws aft, or ahead of you if the bearing draws forward.

Distances at sea are difficult to judge without considerable practice. In good visibility short distances are often over-estimated and longer ones under-estimated.

A large buoy is just visible at 2 miles ⎤ but not colour
A small buoy is just visible at 1½ miles ⎦ or shape

The shape of a small buoy is dis-
    cernible at   — 1 mile

The colour and markings of a large
    buoy are discernible at   — 1 mile

A man is distinguishable but his limbs
    are not at   — 1 mile

A moving man begins to take shape at—800 yards (750 metres)

A man's legs and a rower's arms
    show at   —400 yards (350 metres)

Faces are distinguishable at   —250 yards (230 metres)

Table 22 shows the distance of the sea horizon in good visibility.

Table 22

Distance of the Sea Horizon

			Eye height				
5	6	7	8	9	10	feet	above sea level
1·5	1·8	2·1	2·4	2·7	3·0	metres	
2·6	2·8	3·0	3·2	3·4	3·6	miles	

Horizon distance

		Eye height				
12	14	16	18	20	feet	above sea level
3·6	4·2	4·8	5·4	6·0	metres	
4·0	4·3	4·6	4·9	5·1	miles	

Horizon distance

Light Dipping Distances

Approximate distance away from a lighthouse can be estimated at night by noting when the light appears above (or disappears below) the horizon.

This method should be used with caution if there is any sea running, as the height of the eye is not constant.

The height of the light above Mean H W Spring Tide level is given on the charts and in the almanacs.

Table 23 applies to an eye height of 5 feet (1·5 metres) above sea level:

Table 23
Light Dipping Distances

		Light height			
50	60	70	80	90	feet
15	18	21	24	27	metres
10·7	11·5	12·3	13·0	13·5	miles

Dipping distance

		Light height			
100	120	140	160	180	feet
30	36	42	48	54	metres
14·0	15·0	16·0	17·0	18·0	miles

Dipping distance

		Light height			
200	225	250	300	400	feet
60	68	75	90	120	metres
18·8	20·0	21·0	22·5	25·5	miles

Dipping distance

Rule of Thumb

The original 'rule of thumb' was probably the principle adopted by shipmasters that they would never allow their vessels to approach a danger nearer than the distance which corresponded to a thumb's width on the chart in current use. Thus, they could navigate closer to dangers on a large-scale chart with plenty of detail than would be prudent on a small-scale chart with less. It's still a good principle.

The Dutchman's Log

A boat's speed may be estimated in the absence of a patent log by timing how long the boat takes to pass a floating object.

Two persons are needed, one stands in the bows and the other right aft. The distance between them must be known in advance.

The man in the bows throws a small piece of wood into the water ahead and to one side of the bow. When it passes the bow at right angles to the boat's track he calls 'NOW' and the man at the stern starts a stop-watch.

When the piece of wood passes the stern at right angles the stop-watch is stopped, and the speed calculated from the time elapsed for the boat to travel one length.

One knot is one nautical mile per hour, i.e. 6,080 feet in 3,600 seconds. Table 24 gives a few speeds for typical lengths of boat, but the principle applies to any speed and length.

Table 24

Boat's Speed by Dutchman's Log

| Speed in knots | Distance in feet | | | |
	15	20	25	30
	Time in seconds			
1	8·9	11·8	14·8	17·8
2	4·5	5·9	7·4	8·9
3	3·0	3·9	4·9	5·9
4	2·2	3·0	3·7	4·4
5	1·8	2·4	3·0	3·6

Latitude and Longitude without a Sextant

Given a nautical almanac, **latitude** may be determined

approximately from the duration of daylight.

Note the exact time when the upper limb (top edge) of the sun crosses the horizon at sunrise, and again at sunset. From these times calculate the duration of daylight.

From the almanac, in the sunrise and sunset tables for the day, find two tabulated latitudes for which the duration of daylight is slightly longer in one case and shorter in the other than the duration for your own case. In Reed's Almanac these two latitudes are two degrees apart in latitudes above 50 degrees.

A simple interpolation will give your own latitude to half a degree or better, depending on the time of year. At the equinoxes (about March 21 and September 23) and for a week or so on either side, the change of duration of daylight is too small for the method to be used with any confidence.

The period between sunset and sunrise may be used if this is more convenient; the method of working is the same.

Not for short-distance day sailing, but good enough to find the English Channel or the New England coast if you've lost track of your dead reckoning after a couple of weeks at sea.

Longitude can also be found approximately if you have a radio with which to receive time signals. This enables you to have an accurate knowledge of Greenwich Mean Time.

Note the exact time (in GMT) when the Sun's upper limb crosses the horizon at sunrise.

From the almanac, find the tabulated time of sunrise for the latitude you have already determined by the above method. This time will be for the longitude of the Greenwich meridian.

The difference between these two times is your longitude in terms of time. Convert it to an angle, 4 minutes of time being equal to one degree of longitude and one hour to 15 degrees.

When your local time of sunrise is earlier than the tabulated GMT, your longitude is east of Greenwich; when it is later your longitude is west. Remember the jingle: '*Longitude East, Greenwich least; longitude West, Greenwich best*'.

NAVIGATING IN FOG

Sailing in fog by day is more difficult than in clear weather by night; at least you can see the lights on the shore and other ships in the latter case.

Sailing in fog at night is quite eerie but needn't lead to disaster if certain measures are taken.

Fog at sea can take any form from a mistiness which reduces visibility to a mile, to a cold wet pea soup through which you can't see the other end of the boat.

Perhaps the most important thing you can do is to know exactly where you were when the fog descended and to keep a careful reckoning of your track thereafter. If there are fog banks about, try to get a fix before entering one and at any other time when you're in the clear. Remember that depth soundings may be as useful as shore bearings.

In no circumstances attempt to close an unknown coastline; it's risky even if you know it as well as the back of your hand. Keep well at sea, and if possible out of the shipping lanes. This may mean a diversion from your intended plans, but that's better than losing your boat and perhaps your life.

If you have a crew member to spare, post him right forward as a look-out in the eyes of the boat away from the noises and distractions of the cockpit. He'll see and hear things before the afterguard, but don't leave him there too long before relieving him or he'll imagine things which aren't there.

In a power craft or any in which the motor is running, shut it down at intervals and listen for the engines or foghorns of other shipping. Sound travels in a deceptive way in fog, and even if the sounds heard are astern, they might still come from a ship which is overtaking you. Soundless areas are not unknown; you may enter or emerge from one quite quickly.

A good and well-sited radar reflector (at least 12 inches corner to corner, and preferably 18 inches) can be a great comfort, but don't let it lull you into a sense of false security; most ships carry radar, but not all, and you've no guarantee that you've been spotted.

Lung-operated foghorns may have been all very well in the days before power-driven ships but it is doubtful whether one would be heard above the ambient noise on the bridge of a merchant ship or even by a look-out in the bows. Those modern aerosol foghorns are quite cheap and effective. A lung-powered horn may be operated by the bellows used to inflate rubber dinghies.

The fog signals made by shipping are easily recognised and distinguished from those from lighthouses. Rule 35 of the International Regulations for Preventing Collisions at Sea gives them in detail; broadly the requirements are that power craft (including sailing boats while motoring) shall sound a prolonged blast at intervals of not more than two minutes when making way through the water. When stopped and not making way, two prolonged blasts with a two-second gap between them must be made at intervals of not more than two minutes.

Sailing boats must sound at intervals of not more than two minutes three blasts in succession, namely one prolonged followed by two short blasts. (Dah-dit-dit).

The characteristics of the sound signals made by foghorns and diaphones located at lighthouses and lightships make them easy to recognise, e.g. a regular blast every 25 seconds, or two blasts every minute. The nautical almanacs print the relevant details for each installation, and you can time them with a stop-watch as you might a flashing buoy.

If your knowledge of meteorology is such that you can confidently recognise advection fog forming as the wind blows on to a coastline, you can sometimes find an anchorage or harbour free from fog in the lee of a headland in which you can shelter until the fog at sea disperses. But you also have to be very confident of your position at sea and the accuracy of your reckoning.

Some harbours have a fog signal on the pier head, and you may be able to grope your way in cautiously along a safe line of bearing, provided that there are no outlying rocks or other dangers. Post a man forward with instructions to point in the direction of the sound every time he hears it.

If you are caught out in the fog when fishing from a small boat without a compass, there is a risk that you'll go round in circles when you think you are rowing for the shore. First, establish the direction of the land by listening for traffic noises, dogs barking or other shore sounds. Then rig up a fishing rod and line pointing dead astern over the transom and pull for the shore. Any deviation from a straight course will be shown by the deflection of the line to one side or the other. Take a pocket compass next time.

On some foggy nights at sea the fog layer may be thin enough for the stars still to be visible. Learn to recognise the Pole Star; it's always in the North, and you'll be able to set a course by it for the shore with sufficient accuracy to get you there and to prevent the boat from going round aimlessly in circles. See p. 188.

Cliff Echo Pilotage

The distance from a cliff may be determined when expecting a landfall or coasting in fog or on a very dark night by sounding the fog signal and noting on a stop-watch the interval in seconds before the echo returns.

The distance off in cables (200 yards, 180 metres) will be nine tenths of the time elapsed in seconds. So for most purposes an interval of one second indicates a distance of 200 yards.

As small-craft fog signals are not very powerful the presence of an echo at all suggests increasing the distance off with all haste unless one is very familiar with the coast-line and certain of the boat's position.

When coasting by this method a check on estimated position may be given if the echoes suddenly cease, indicating the edge of an inlet, estuary or bay.

The use of a depth sounder in conjunction with cliff echoes gives added confidence, but if there are outlying rocks or headlands in the vicinity it will be safer to get out into deeper water and chase the contours with depth sounder alone.

In any event, check the range of your fog signal's echoing ability in clear weather before attempting cliff echo pilotage; it may be insufficient to keep you a safe distance off.

FINDING DIRECTION WITHOUT A COMPASS

When the sun is shining, the direction of North can be found by pointing the hour hand of a watch at the sun. An imaginary line bisecting the angle between the hour hand and 12 o'clock on the dial gives the North-South line to within a few degrees. In the northern hemisphere the extension of the bisector line in the direction one is looking gives South, and North is 180 degrees away behind the observer's back. Don't forget to allow for the added hour when Summer Time is kept.

In overcast conditions, it is sometimes possible to apply

the same principle by poising the tip of a knife-blade vertically on the thumb nail. The blade will cast a dim shadow which varies in width as the knife is rotated. When the shadow is of minimum width or disappears altogether the breadth of the blade is aligned with the sun. The hour hand of a watch is then pointed in the same direction and the North–South line found as above. This method should be used with caution; if the sun is obscured by a heavy cloud but the sky is bright to the east or west it could be misleading.

Neither of these methods will work in thick fog, but it is still possible to steer a moderately straight course without a compass in calm weather by streaming a line astern from a fishing rod. The line will stay dead astern if a straight course is steered, but will deflect to one side or the other when the course is altered.

On a clear night there's always the Pole Star; learn to recognise it and use it to indicate True North. You can steer a reasonably accurate course in any required direction by keeping an appropriate part of the boat (such as a shroud or guard rail stanchion) aligned with Polaris.

THE MAGNETIC COMPASS

Compass Deviation

This compass error is caused by the presence of iron in the vicinity of the compass. Unlike magnetic variation it changes with the heading of the boat.

A small craft with a long iron keel, a heavy motor and a compass located low down in the cockpit may suffer serious deviation; a similar boat with a lead keel and no motor may suffer none, until someone puts down a steel bucket, a tool or a tinplate beer-can within a few inches of the compass.

Deviation can be minimized, perhaps eliminated, by

careful siting of the compass. The further it can be located from heavy iron or steel objects the less the deviation. Most heavy items are located low down in a boat; if a compass is three feet above the engine and it can be moved one foot higher the deviating force will be almost halved.

If a boat's compass suffers from serious deviation which resiting fails to eliminate or reduce to a degree or so, it is necessary to 'swing' the compass so that the error is known on all headings. Steel-hulled craft may need the services of a professional compass adjuster, who will neutralise the effect by fitting small magnets around the compass.

Skippers and owners of small craft can easily swing their own compasses by the method given in the following paragraphs.

How to Swing a Compass

Accurate navigation requires a knowledge of deviation on all headings; if the maximum error is greater than 5 degrees a professional compass adjuster will reduce the error with small magnets.

When the error is less than about 5 degrees it is sufficient to 'swing' the compass and to prepare a deviation table. This is quite easily done with the aid of a home-made pelorus constructed as shown in Fig. 31.

The base of the pelorus should be attached firmly to the cabin top with its centre line accurately aligned with the fore-and-aft line of the boat. A piece of twine stretched from the base of the mast to the centre of the transom will help to get the alignment right.

To carry out the swing, you need two assistants, one to tow the boat's bow round with a dinghy, the other to operate the pelorus.

Before beginning, ensure that all ironwork is in its usual sea-going position; no buckets in the cockpit nor pocket knives within a few inches of the compass.

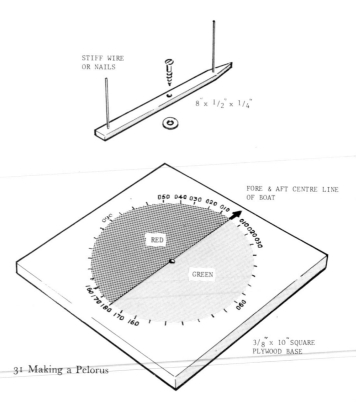

STIFF WIRE
OR NAILS

8″ x 1/2″ x 1/4″

FORE & AFT CENTRE LINE
OF BOAT

050 040 030 020 010

030

010 020 030

RED

GREEN

060

160 170 180 170 160

3/8″ x 10″ SQUARE
PLYWOOD BASE

31 Making a Pelorus

Choose a spot where the boat may be towed round on various headings without changing her position more than a few yards, perhaps at anchor or near a buoy, and at slack water. It should also be possible to sight a prominent landmark (a factory chimney or church tower) from at least five miles distance.

A table should have been drawn up in advance like that on page 182 and the pelorus operator briefed on how to fill it in.

He should keep the two sighting pins on the pointer aligned with the chosen landmark, and be ready to read the bearing from the scale and record it in the table.

When all is ready, turn the boat's head until the steering compass reads 000°, and call 'ON'. At that instant the pelorus man must call out his bearing of the landmark, e.g. 'GREEN 040' and then record it in the table.

A similar procedure is adopted for the other seven directions, NE, East, SE, South, SW, West and NW.

The table can then be completed at leisure, the deviation curve plotted and a 'Course to Steer' table drawn up from it for future use. See example below; Fig. 32 and Tables 25 and 26.

In a small boat where the compass is perforce nearer the motor than might be desirable, a second compass swing with the motor running will establish whether this causes any further deviation. If there is any significant difference (say 2 degrees or more on any heading) a separate 'Course to Steer' table should be drawn up for use when motoring.

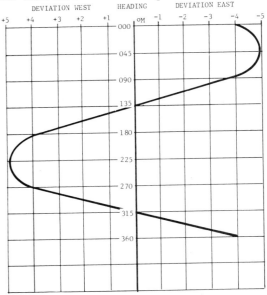

32 Yacht 'Lodestone': Deviation Curve

The deviation curve should be reasonably symmetrical, so that the 'plusses' added together are equal to the 'minuses' within a degree or two. Should this not be so, it is likely that the lubber line of the steering compass is not aligned accurately with the centre line of the boat. The whole compass mounting should then be turned through an angle equal to half the difference between the 'plusses' and the 'minuses' until the deviation curve is symmetrical.

The prudent navigator loses no opportunity to check the deviation of his compass; this can be done whenever the boat is sailing along a transit whose direction is known or can be determined from the chart.

Table 25

Yacht 'Lodestone'.   Compass Swing.   Date:

A		B	C	D	E
Boat's Heading °M	Diagram	Bearing by Pelorus	Magnetic Bearing	Actual Mag. Bearing	Compass Deviation
N 000		Green 036	036	040	−4
NE 045		Red 010	035	040	−5
E 090		Red 054	036	040	−4
SE 135		Red 095	040	040	0
S 180		Red 136	044	040	+4
SW 225		(Astern) 180	045	040	+5
W 270		Green 134	044	040	+4
NW 315		Green 085	040	040	0

/ = Landmark bearing   Total 320

↗ = Boat's heading

Divide by 8:   040   = Actual Mag. Bearing

Column A is the compass reading when you call 'On'.
Column B is the pelorus reading at the same instant.

Column C is the sum or difference between Columns A and B; inspection of the diagram decides which.

Column D is the average of all the readings in Column C.

Column E is Column D subtracted from Column C.

Table 26

Yacht 'Lodestone': Course to Steer

To Achieve Magnetic Course	Steer Compass Course	To Achieve Magnetic Course	Steer Compass Course
000	356	180	184
010	006	190	194
020	016	200	204
030	025	210	215
040	035	220	225
050	045	230	235
060	055	240	244
070	066	250	254
080	076	260	264
090	086	270	274
100	097	280	283
110	108	290	292
120	119	300	301
130	130	310	310
140	140	320	320
150	151	330	329
160	162	340	338
170	173	350	347
180	184	360	356

(These numbers are extracted from the deviation curve to the nearest degree)

Using a Sextant

Nothing magic or occult about the mariner's sextant; it merely measures angles like a protractor but much more accurately.

Some of the traditional methods of determining one's position at sea by means of celestial bodies and the sextant may indeed suggest a black art, but these have been bypassed by simplified modern methods and astronomical tables so that anyone who can add and subtract numbers can confidently attempt celestial navigation.

This book does not attempt to teach the subject; there are many excellent books which do so clearly and concisely; see booklist on p. 298.

While a professional navigator's sextant is an expensive and extremely precise instrument, several cheaper versions are now available for yachtsmen. They are naturally not so precise but are quite adequate for most purposes, and their principle of use is no different from that of a professional's instrument.

A sextant can measure angles in both the vertical and the horizontal planes. By measuring the horizontal angles between three landmarks while coasting a very accurate fix may be obtained, more precise than from compass bearings.

The 'distance off' may be obtained by measuring the angular height of the lantern of a lighthouse above High Water mark and reading the distance from Table 27.

It is of course necessary to know the actual height of the lantern; this for most lighthouses is shown on the charts and in nautical almanacs.

By taking a compass bearing of the lighthouse at the same time, a fix may be obtained in terms of range and bearing.

Celestial observations are made by measuring the angle

Table 27

Distance off by Vertical Sextant Angle

HEIGHT OF TOWER ABOVE HWL		DISTANCE OFF, NAUTICAL MILES					
feet	metres	0·5	1·0	1·5	2·0	2·5	3·0
50	15	0° 56′	0° 28′	0° 19′	0° 14′	0° 11′	0° 09′
65	20	1° 14′	0° 38′	0° 25′	0° 19′	0° 15′	0° 12′
80	25	1° 32′	0° 47′	0° 31′	0° 24′	0° 18′	0° 15′
100	30	1° 53′	0° 57′	0° 38′	0° 28′	0° 23′	0° 19′
115	35	2° 10′	1° 05′	0° 43′	0° 33′	0° 26′	0° 22′
130	40	2° 27′	1° 14′	0° 49′	0° 37′	0° 29′	0° 24′
150	45	2° 48′	1° 22′	0° 56′	0° 41′	0° 33′	0° 27′
165	50	3° 05′	1° 32′	1° 01′	0° 46′	0° 37′	0° 31′
245	75	4° 40′	2° 20′	1° 33′	1° 10′	0° 56′	0° 46′
330	100	6° 10′	3° 05′	2° 03′	1° 32′	1° 14′	1° 01′

between the horizon and the Sun, Moon, planet or star observed. A very simple way of determining latitude is by Meridian Altitude of the Sun. The angular distance of the Sun above the horizon is measured at local noon (not noon by clock time; the almanac gives the difference for the date of the observation). A small correction is applied (Sun Altitude Total Correction: almanac again).

The result is subtracted from 90 degrees to give Zenith Distance; to this is added the Sun's Declination for the date and time of observation (in Greenwich Mean Time; almanac yet again).

The answer is your latitude . . . if as is likely it happens to be Summer in the hemisphere in which the observation is taken. Better read one of those books before trying it in Winter.

Star Sights: when the night sky is full of stars you can't

see the horizon to measure altitudes from. So the celestial navigator takes his star sights at twilight, morning or evening, when the horizon and some bright stars are visible.

Using a sextant in a small boat bouncing in a seaway requires skill which can only come with practice. Stance is important; legs and feet must be firmly planted so that the trunk can bend in the opposite direction to the boat's motion, keeping the sextant aligned with the horizon and the Sun or star, and swinging it pendulum-fashion to establish the true vertical.

If possible, a series of three or five sights should be taken, timed at roughly equal intervals of about 30 seconds; any obviously inconsistent sights must be rejected and the remaining good ones averaged. Time-keeping needs an assistant who can be trusted to read a stop-watch and record it accurately when you call 'Stop', i.e. when you are satisfied that the sextant really is showing the true altitude of the Sun or star.

But there's more to celestial navigation than just this; get one of the recommended books and study the subject in greater detail.

Care of the Sextant

Even the cheapest plastic sextant is a delicate precision instrument; it must be looked after carefully if its readings are to have any meaning. Mechanical distortion due to a very slight blow will cause big errors. Handle it with great care and stow it away in its case somewhere dry where damage is least probable.

Don't let the idle curious play with it; some day it may help to save your life and ship.

The sextant should be kept clean; wipe it dry with a clean handkerchief when it has been wetted by rain or spray.

Periodically lubricate the rack and worm with light oil and wipe off the surplus; the movement of the worm must be completely smooth.

Don't leave a sextant in the sun when not in use, and never handle the mirrors, except when cleaning them.

Adjusting the Sextant

The more expensive and precise the sextant, the more facilities there will be for correcting various errors. Unless you have considerable experience with sextants, it is best to leave all the corrections except one to a nautical instrument adjuster.

The exception is Index Error, which is the difference between the angle actually measured and what is read from the arc and micrometer drum. This is fairly simple to reduce, often difficult to eliminate altogether. No matter; if you know what the error is you can allow for it in calculations. Up to three or four minutes of arc is tolerable.

First determine the Index Error by setting the index to zero and looking at a horizontal line (perhaps a rooftop) at least two miles away. If the direct and reflected images are exactly in line, there is no Index Error.

If one line is displaced above the other, adjust the micrometer drum until there is no break in the alignment. The micrometer reading is then the Index error, 'minus' if the reading is 'on the arc' (on the side of zero towards 90 degrees), 'plus' if 'off the arc' (on the side away from 90 degrees).

Leave well alone if the Index Error is less than three or four minutes of arc in either direction. If greater, adjust the screw on the horizon mirror until the error falls within that limit.

Check the error again and note it in the log or on a slip of paper pasted in the sextant case. Never miss an opportunity to recheck the Index Error, ideally before or after every sight taken.

FINDING THE POLE STAR

The Pole Star (Polaris) is very nearly exactly over the North Pole; its direction at any time may therefore be taken as True North for all purposes except precise celestial navigation.

It is the bright star at the end of the 'handle' of the constellation Little Dipper (or Little Bear, or Ursa Minor). See Fig. 33.

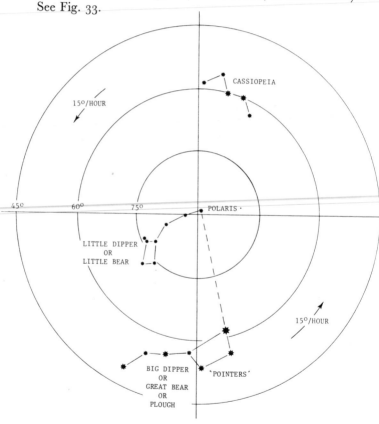

33 Finding the Pole Star

On the side of the Big Dipper (or Great Bear, Ursa Major or the Plough) remote from the 'handle' two bright stars are aligned with the Pole Star; these are the 'Pointers', Merak and Dubhe. Once you can recognise the Big Dipper they are the easiest way of finding Polaris.

The two Dippers have occasionally been confused, especially if cloud covers one or the other. The Big Dipper has its 'handle' bent 'downwards' (presumably due to the bigger dip it takes) whereas the 'handle' of the Little Dipper is bent 'upwards' (not having been bent down by little dips).

The relative positions of Polaris and the two Dippers do not change from the pattern in Fig. 33, but the Dippers appear to revolve (as do the other stars) around a fixed Pole Star as the night wears on.

12

The Rule of the Road

Called colloquially 'The Rule of the Road', the International Regulations for Preventing Collisions at Sea cover far more than merely the rules for steering and sailing.

The latest version of the Regulations (the '1972' rules) contains 38 Rules and 4 Annexes. The full text is published in Britain in a Stationery Office booklet. The rules of greatest importance to small craft are summarised below, but ignorance of the other rules is no excuse if their infringement causes a collision or other incident. This summary is considerably simplified, and a wise skipper will become familiar with the full version.

Bear in mind that local harbour authorities have power to enact local rules which are not part of the International Regulations; these usually refer to light and sound signals and details may be found in the Pilot Books.

LIGHTS

Between sunset and sunrise the correct lights must be shown: red to port, green to starboard and a white sternlight for craft under sail; the same plus a white masthead light for power craft and sailing craft while under power.

(Rules 23 and 25)

The lights of craft more than 12 metres (40 feet) but less than 20 metres (65 feet) long should be visible at least three miles (masthead), two miles (side lights) and two miles (stern light). *(Rule 22b)*

The lights of craft less than 12 metres (40 feet) long should be visible at least two miles (side lights one mile).

(Rule 22c)

Dinghies whether under oars or sail are excused the foregoing provided that they carry a powerful torch (or lantern) which can show a white light in time to prevent a collision. *(Rule 25)*

An anchor light, white and visible all round the horizon, is required by small craft at anchor. (This rule is usually honoured in the breach by yachts moored with others in yachting harbours, but is most advisable for craft anchored in bays or estuaries overnight). *(Rule 30)*

White flares or a signalling lamp are useful for attracting the attention of an approaching vessel which may be thought not to have seen the lights of a small craft. (Rule 36) (But remember it's often easier for a small yacht to alter course herself in good time to avoid the need for a firework display. A good radar reflector also helps).

Annex 1 to the Regulations gives positioning and technical details of lights and shapes, including required luminous intensities for the specified ranges of visibility. These have been converted into lamp wattages in the section on boat electrics, see p. 112.

Sailing craft of less than 12 metres (40 feet) in length may carry their lights in a combined lantern at the mast head (Rule 25). This system saves current and gives good visibility, but some patterns of lantern fail to give an adequately sharp boundary between adjacent coloured sectors and should be avoided.

An option open to sailing craft carrying normal separate side lights (but not a masthead lantern) is the carriage of two extra lights, red over green and one metre apart and visible all round the horizon (Rule 25c). Since these lights are to be carried at or near the masthead, it is difficult to see how they are to be mounted in practice to achieve all-round visibility when the sails are hoisted.

STEERING AND SAILING RULES

Two sailing craft meeting, with a risk of colliding:

The one with the wind on the port side keeps out of the way of the other. If both have the wind on the same side, the one to windward keeps out of the other's way.

(*Rule 12*)

Two power craft meeting end on or nearly so, with a risk of collision:

Both alter course to starboard.   (*Rule 14*)

Two power craft crossing, with a risk of collision:

The one with the other on her starboard side keeps out of the way.   (*Rule 15*)

A sailing craft and a power craft meeting with a risk of collision:

In general, the power vessel will keep out of the way of the sailing craft, but this may not be possible for a large ship in a narrow channel or for fishing vessels while actually engaged in fishing. In these circumstances the sailing craft must take early positive action to keep out of the way of the power craft, and be seen to do so.

(*Rule 18*)

Whenever one vessel is required to keep out of the way of another, the other must maintain her course and speed unaltered; to do otherwise confuses the situation.

(*Rule 17*)

'Giving-way' craft should alter course and speed early and in such a manner as to avoid crossing ahead of the 'stand-on' craft.   (*Rule 16*)

Any overtaking craft, power or sail, must keep out of the way of the craft being overtaken.   (*Rule 13*)

All craft should keep to the starboard side of any narrow channel.   (*Rule 9*)

SOUND SIGNALS

A power craft taking action to avoid any other craft must indicate her intentions by a sound signal from her whistle or siren:

> One short blast: I am altering course to starboard.
> Two short blasts: I am altering course to port.
> Three short blasts: My engines are going astern.

> A short blast is of about one second's duration. (*Rule 34*)

If a 'stand-on' power craft is in doubt whether a 'giving-way' craft is taking sufficient action to avoid a collision, she may sound at least five short and rapid blasts to show her doubt. (*Rule 34*)

No sound signals are prescribed by the rules for sailing craft in good visibility, but a sailing craft proceeding under motor becomes a power craft and must conform with the above rules.

In fog or restricted visibility various additional sound signals are required of sailing and power craft. Power craft making way through the water must sound one prolonged blast (4 to 6 seconds duration) at intervals of not more than two minutes. Sailing craft must sound three blasts in succession: one prolonged followed by two short blasts (dah-dit-dit) at intervals of not more than two minutes.

Note. It cannot be over-emphasised that the above is an extreme simplification of the complete Rules; there are many exceptions and exemptions all of which are important in particular circumstances or for particular boats. The complete Rules should be studied and learnt by all serious skippers and owners.

13

Tides, Currents and Tidal Streams

Tides are the vertical movement and tidal streams (currents in the U.S.) are the horizontal movement of the sea. Both are caused by the gravitational pull of the Moon and the Sun upon the oceans; the Moon being much closer to the earth offers about twice the pull of the Sun and is thus the stronger influence.

When the relative positions of the Sun and Moon with respect to the earth are such that their pulls are in the same direction, their combined effect is greatest and the resulting tides are highest; this happens every fortnight just after Full Moon and New Moon and the tides are known as **Spring Tides.**

When the positions of the Moon and Sun are such that their gravitational pulls are at right angles to each other, their combined effect is least and we get lower High Waters, known as **Neap Tides.** These occur at the First and Last Quarters of the Moon, midway between any two Spring Tides.

As the earth rotates daily on its axis, the waters raised by the combined pull of the Moon and Sun tend to follow that attraction rather than the rotation of the earth and two tidal waves are generated, one on each side of the earth, which move at a different speed from the earth's rotation. It is these two tidal waves which cause in general two High Waters and two Low Waters every twenty-four hours or so.

In practice, many factors like the obstruction caused to the tidal waves by large land masses result in variations from the ideal situation depicted above; there is for instance a lag of about thirty-six hours between Full or New Moon and highest Spring Tides in the English Channel.

All this is taken care of in the tide tables, but it is useful to remember that the interval between High Water and Low Water is on average about $6\frac{1}{2}$ hours and that to-morrow's tide times will be about fifty minutes later than today's.

While the tide tables are based on observation of local tidal effects over many years, they can only be approximate. Weather conditions can have a noticeable effect on the heights of tides and the strengths of streams and currents. A prolonged period of high atmospheric pressure can depress the mean level of the sea and cause lower High and Low Waters. Conversely stormy (low pressure) conditions can raise them. A strong wind blowing persistently in one direction for several days can change the rate of currents and of tidal streams. Tidal predictions therefore relate to average weather conditions, and in all tidal calculations a margin of safety should be included.

MAKING TIDAL CALCULATIONS

To calculate the height of the tide at various times and in different localities, a knowledge of tidal terms is necessary. Fig. 34 defines these.

The time and height of High Water on any particular day are tabulated directly for Standard Ports (i.e. most major ports) in various nautical almanacs. To obtain the same information for Secondary Ports, a simple correction is applied to the time and height at the nearest Standard Port; this correction is also given in the almanacs under the heading Tidal Differences. The same table gives the Mean

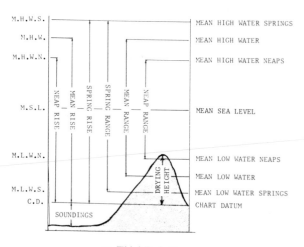

34 Tidal Definitions

Level and the Duration of Mean Rise for Secondary Ports; these figures are required to calculate the height of the tide at any time other than High Water.

To calculate the time and height of Low Water, the time is obtained by subtracting the Duration of Mean Rise from the time of High Water; subtracting the tabulated height at High Water from TWICE the Mean Level gives the height at Low Water.

The **Range** of the tide for the day is the difference between the heights of High and Low Water, and the **Rise** is the height above chart datum at any High Water. At Spring Tides, the Range is approximately equal to the Rise and is the difference between the depth at High Water Spring Tides (MHWS) and the level of the chart datum.

At Neap Tides, the range is calculated by doubling the difference between the depth at Mean High Water Neap Tides (MHWN) and chart datum and then subtracting the Spring Rise as determined above. On days intermediate between Spring and Neap Tides, the range and rise may be interpolated.

Chart datum is an arbitrary level to which all other heights and depths are referred. It is decided by international agreement and is quoted on all charts. Usually it is at a level which rarely (if ever) dries at Low Water.

The drying heights of rocks and banks as shown on charts will therefore often be greater than observation would suggest, even at the lowest Spring Tides.

To estimate the height of the tide at any time between Low Water and High Water Tables 28 and 29 may be used. In Britain, as in the rest of Europe, tide tables give heights in metric units and Table 28 should be used. Its values are approximate but are adequate for normal use.

Table 28

Fall or Rise of Tide in Metres

Range for the day in metres	At end of 1st hour	2nd hour	3rd hour	4th hour	5th hour	6th hour
1	0·1	0·3	0·5	0·8	0·9	1·0
2	0·2	0·5	1·0	1·5	1·8	2·0
3	0·2	0·8	1·5	2·3	2·7	3·0
4	0·3	1·0	2·0	3·0	3·6	4·0
5	0·4	1·3	2·5	3·8	4·6	5·0
6	0·5	1·5	3·0	4·5	5·5	6·0
7	0·6	1·8	3·5	5·3	6·4	7·0
8	0·6	2·0	4·0	6·0	7·4	8·0
9	0·7	2·3	4·5	6·8	8·3	9·0
10	0·8	2·5	5·0	7·5	9·2	10·0

In North America and elsewhere heights are still given in feet and Table 29 should be used. The old 'Rule-of-Twelfths' may be used for a quick approximation; this says that the tide will rise (or fall) one twelfth of the day's range in the first hour after Low (or High) Water, two twelfths in the second hour, three twelfths in the third hour, three twelfths in the fourth hour, two twelfths in the fifth hour and the remaining one twelfth in the sixth hour.

Think of the rule as 1—2—3—3—2—1. It applies equally of course to metric tides but the mental arithmetic is not so easy as with feet.

Table 29

Fall or Rise of Tide in Feet

Range for the day in feet	At end of 1st hour	2nd hour	3rd hour	4th hour	5th hour	6th hour
4	0·3	1·0	2·0	3·0	3·7	4·0
6	0·4	1·5	3·0	4·5	5·6	6·0
8	0·5	2·0	4·0	6·0	7·5	8·0
10	0·7	2·5	5·0	7·5	9·3	10·0
12	0·8	3·0	6·0	9·0	11·1	12·0
14	0·9	3·5	7·0	10·5	13·0	14·0
16	1·0	4·0	8·0	12·0	14·8	16·0
18	1·2	4·5	9·0	13·5	16·7	18·0
20	1·4	5·0	10·0	15·0	18·6	20·0
22	1·5	5·5	11·0	16·5	20·4	22·0
24	1·6	6·0	12·0	18·0	22·3	24·0
26	1·7	6·5	13·0	19·5	24·2	26·0
28	1·8	7·0	14·0	21·0	26·0	28·0
30	2·0	7·5	15·0	22·5	28·1	30·0

TIDAL STREAMS AND CURRENTS

A knowledge of the speed and direction of the tidal stream or current is most important to the small-boat skipper, since he will make no progress whatsoever if he sails westward at four knots against a four-knot east-going tide. But by 'working the tide' and using it to best advantage the four-knot boat will actually make eight knots over the ground if the same westward passage is made when the tidal stream is west-going.

The speed and direction of tidal streams may be found sufficiently accurately for most purposes from the tidal atlases and more accurately from the charts. Both of these sources show the rate of the stream for every hour from the time of High Water at a quoted Standard Port to the next High Water; this rate varies in general in accordance with the 'Rule of Twelfths' but there may be local anomalies.

It should be noted in particular that the time of slack water at a headland is not necessarily the time of High or Low Water at a nearby port. The tidal atlases and charts quote two tidal stream rates, that for Spring Tides and a lower rate for Neap Tides; the rates for 'in-between' tides may be estimated with sufficient accuracy by interpolation.

The direction of a tidal stream in coastal waters depends on the configuration of the coastline. Along a straight stretch of coast tidal streams are often rectilinear; the flood tide may be east-going and the ebb west-going. But behind prominent headlands and in large bays the stream may be rotatory; during the twelve-hour tidal cycle the stream will run through 360 degrees. In these conditions the careful navigator will ensure that his boat is not set inshore into danger by a rotatory tide.

Tidal streams or currents usually run most strongly off prominent headlands, often forming tidal races which are well avoided in bad weather. In these areas tide rips or overfalls may be caused which may be hazardous to small craft and uncomfortable to larger vessels. The charts show these overfalls by a series of wavy lines.

Eddies sometimes occur along the shores of bays when the stream offshore is running in the other direction; by taking advantage of an inshore eddy a foul tide may be turned into a fair one.

Non-tidal currents should not be confused with tidal streams and currents; they do not change direction with the tide-raising forces of the Moon and Sun though their rates may vary with changing meteorological conditions. The Gulf Stream is an example of a big-scale non-tidal current, and the outflow of fresh water from a large river produces a small-scale constant-direction current which, when added to the oscillatory tidal stream in an estuary, may result in the ebb tide running faster than the flood.

14
Weather

A good **aneroid barometer** is by far the most useful instrument for weather forecasting at sea. It should have a range of 950 to 1050 millibars (28 to 31 inches): barometers with a larger range do not show small changes of pressure distinctly enough. Mercury barometers are not a practical proposition in small boats; they are too large and are subject to 'pumping' due to the motion of the boat in a seaway.

Make a habit of keeping an eye on the barometer; it may give warning of approaching bad weather before the next broadcast weather forecast.

The calibration should be checked and corrected occasionally (see p. 210 on barometer adjustment). But it is the CHANGE of reading which matters rather than the actual reading at any time.

A **hygrometer** can be useful in weather forecasting; increasing humidity gives an indication of approaching rain. The wet-and-dry bulb hygrometer is best suited to small craft but it may be difficult to locate. Ideally it should be above deck, as the moisture content of the cabin may be quite unlike that of the outside atmosphere. But it must be out of the direct rays of the sun and away from the heat of the engine.

Anemometers are sometimes fitted to the mastheads of the more expensively equipped yachts. They may help the ocean-racing fraternity but most skippers don't need an instrument to tell them when the wind is too strong for the sail they are carrying. A portable hand-held anemometer is however helpful when it comes to logging the wind strength; it's very easy to over-estimate it in a small craft.

Wind direction is a different matter; it's difficult to sail the best course to windward without an indicator of the apparent wind direction. A burgee at the masthead and tell-tale ribbons on the shrouds and backstay are all that is needed.

CLOUD TYPES

If you can identify cloud types there's a lot to be learnt about the weather from them.

For convenience, clouds are first classified by the height of their bases; low cloud from ground level to 6500 feet, medium cloud from 6500 to 23,000 feet (25,000 feet in the tropics) and high cloud from 16,500 to 45,000 feet (20,000 to 60,000 feet in the tropics). See Fig. 35.

High cloud may be Cirrus (Ci), Cirrostratus (Cs) and Cirrocumulus (Cc) types.

Medium cloud may be Altocumulus (Ac) or Altostratus (As).

Low cloud may be Nimbostratus (Ns), Cumulus (Cu), Cumulonimbus (Cb), Stratocumulus (Sc) or Stratus (St).

Cirrus cloud ('Mare's tails') is wispy or feathery in appearance; consisting of very thin ice particles, it leaves no shadow. If followed by cirrocumulus and cirrostratus, it foretells a change in the weather.

Cirrocumulus ('Mackerel sky') reminds one of fish scales.

Cirrostratus is a formless sheet of frozen cloud of greasy appearance which may cause a halo round the sun or moon.

Altocumulus consists of rounded masses of white or grey

45,000 FT.

CIRRUS HIGH CLOUDS

CIRROSTRATUS CIRROCUMULUS

ANVILTOP

23,000 FT.

MIDDLE CLOUDS

ALTOSTRATUS

ALTOCUMULUS

6,500 FT.

LOW CLOUDS

STRATOCUMULUS

CUMULONIMBUS

CUMULUS

STRATUS

NIMBOSTRATUS

35 Cloud Types

lumpy cloud, sometimes flattened at the base and fibrous.
Altostratus is a grey sheet through which the sun may
be seen indistinctly, but it does not form a halo. It may
thicken to become nimbostratus.

Nimbostratus is a dark grey sheet of wet and ragged
appearance. Rain or snow may fall from it over a wide area.

Cumulus is dense white billowy cloud, dome-shaped on
top and usually flattened at the base.

Cumulonimbus builds up from a low base to a great
towering height, often topped with an anvil or plume.
This is a thunderstorm cloud; there may be heavy rain,
hail and strong winds beneath it.

Stratocumulus is a layer of cloud with a flattish base
but with rounded masses above. Due to this variable thickness the underside has light and dark grey patches.

Stratus is a low grey layer of formless sheet cloud usually
associated with drizzle; it may reach down to sea or ground
level and is then called fog.

Different types of cloud may appear at the same time
at different heights or at the same height in different parts
of the sky. A skilled observer may deduce from the pattern
the probable weather in the immediate future, perhaps up
to 24 hours.

This needs however some knowledge of meteorology
beyond the scope of this book; many excellent books are
available on weather forecasting for amateurs and yachtsmen, see book list, p. 299.

Some weather signs are given in the following section;
it is good practice to decide first for yourself what you
think the weather will do before listening to the broadcast
weather forecasts. With enough experience you may
eventually be able sometimes to beat the experts at their
own game, at least for your local area.

Readers in the Southern Hemisphere will probably know
that their weather patterns rotate in the opposite sense to

those in the Northern Hemisphere. In other respects the information in this chapter applies to both hemispheres.

Approaching Bad Weather

Clouds: Feathery Cirrus ('mares' tails') at high altitude, followed by Cirrocumulus ('mackerel sky') and then by greasy-looking Cirrostratus, covering the sky and forming a halo round the sun or moon. Finally low Stratus, rain and poor visibility mark arrival of depression. See Fig. 36.

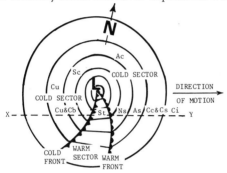

TYPICAL DEPRESSION IN PLAN

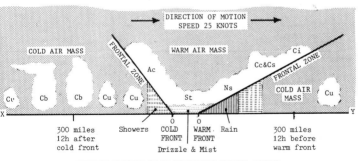

VERTICAL SECTION XY OF DEPRESSION FRONTAL SYSTEM

36 Typical Depression (Northern Hemisphere)

Barometer: Sharp fall or rise; a change of 5 millibars in three hours will bring strong winds if not gales.

Wind: Backing from a westerly direction towards South or South-east, then veering South-west or West as visibility decreases. (In Southern Hemisphere, veering from West to North-west or North, then backing to West or North-west.)

Improving Weather

Clouds: Low Stratus breaking up and giving way to billowing Cumulonimbus.

Barometer: Slow and steady rise.

Wind: Veers to West or North-west as cold front passes and visibility improves. (Backs to West or South-west in Southern Hemisphere.)

Weather Set Fair

Clouds: Small fleecy Cumulus, or none; Cirrus dissolving.

Barometer: High (1020 mb or over) and steady or rising slowly.

Wind: Light easterly or north-easterly.

WAVES AND SWELL

Waves are caused by the passage of the wind over the surface of the sea; the stronger the wind the bigger the waves, and the Beaufort Scale, Table 30, shows the probable and maximum heights for a given wind strength. These figures are valid for the open sea; an off-shore wind will result in smaller and steeper waves near the coast.

Waves travel in the same direction as the wind, but may continue for some time in the same direction after the wind direction has shifted. Waves breaking on a shore or on a shallow patch will be higher than they would be in deeper water in the same wind strength.

The **height** of a wave is the vertical distance between the crest and the trough. The **period** is the time elapsed between the passage of consecutive crests past a given point; this is related to its **speed,** which for a simple wave in deep water is about 3·1 times the period, (speed in knots, period in seconds).

The wave **length** is the horizontal distance between successive crests; wavelength in metres is usually about 1·5 times the square of the period in seconds. Although period, length and speed are related, height is not and may change without affecting the other measurements. There is however a limit to height in relation to length; this limit is reached when the height becomes 7 or 8 per cent of the length.

In practice, a wave rarely resembles the theoretical ideal above; it is a combination of a number of waves which have different lengths and speeds; this accounts for the apparent random motion of waves.

Waves tend to travel in groups with patches of relatively calm water between them; these groups usually travel at about half the speed of the individual waves forming them. **Swell** is the after-effect of stormy weather, perhaps hundreds of miles from the location where it is experienced. It has a very long wavelength, and is most noticeable when local conditions are calm. Its height should be taken into account when sailing over shallow bars as one might bump the bottom in a trough in a place where sufficient water would exist were there no swell.

The height of swell may be estimated before crossing the bar by noting its rise and fall on nearby rocks. Swell and wind-driven waves may be present at the same time in any location at sea.

Shallow-water waves behave quite differently from those in the open sea; their speed is reduced and height increased and their direction may change to bring them parallel

Table 30

Beaufort Wind Scale

To convert knots to metres/sec. divide by 2.

Beaufort Scale Number	Description and limit of wind speed in knots	Sea Criterion	Probable Height of Waves in metres*	Probable Maximum Wave Height in metres*
0	Calm Less than 1	Sea like a mirror.	—	—
1	Light air 1–3	Ripples with the appearance of scales are formed but without foam crests.	0·1	0·1
2	Light breeze 4–6	Small wavelets, still short but more pronounced, crests have a glassy appearance and do not break.	0·2	0·3
3	Gentle breeze 7–10	Large wavelets. Crests begin to break. Foam of glassy appearance. Perhaps scattered white horses.	0·6	1
4	Moderate breeze 11–16	Small waves, becoming longer; fairly frequent white horses.	1	1·5
5	Fresh breeze 17–21	Moderate waves, taking a more pronounced long form; many white horses are formed. (Chance of some spray).	2	2·5
6	Strong breeze 22–27	Large waves begin to form; the white foam crests are more extensive everywhere.	3	4

		waves begins to be blown in streaks along the direction of the wind.	4	5·5
8	Gale 34–40	Moderately high waves of greater length; edges of crests break into spindrift. The foam is blown in well marked streaks along the direction of the wind.	5·5	7·5
9	Strong gale 41–47	High waves. Dense streaks of foam along the direction of the wind. Sea begins to roll. Spray may affect visibility.	7	10
10	Storm 48–55	Very high waves with long overhanging crests. The resulting foam in great patches is blown in dense white streaks along the direction of the wind. On the whole the surface of the sea takes a white appearance. The rolling of the sea becomes heavy and shocklike. Visibility affected.	9	12·5
11	Violent Storm 56–63	Exceptionally high waves. (Small and medium-sized ships might be for a time lost to view behind the waves). The sea is completely covered with long white patches of foam lying along the direction of the wind. Everywhere the edges of the wave crests are blown into froth. Visibility affected.	11·5	16
12	Hurricane 64 and over	The air is filled with foam and spray. Sea completely white with driving spray; visibility very seriously affected.	14	?

*In the open sea.

with the shore. They break when their height becomes greater than 7 or 8 per cent of the wavelength. Shallow water in this context may be considered as being less deep than about half a wavelength.

Waves have the greatest impact on small craft where they break or form confused patterns. Over shoals and harbour bars waves tend to break into surf and should be avoided if possible even if there is known to be an adequate depth of water.

When approaching a sea wall waves may meet the reflections of earlier waves and pile up to double their normal height. This may make an oblique entry into a harbour difficult, but if the entrance is reasonably wide a boat may find a track at right angles to the wall comparatively free from high waves.

Where the tide runs fast off a headland with an outlying submerged ridge the water becomes turbulent, causing a short steep wave pattern known as an **overfall**. Such areas are well avoided, especially when the wind is blowing in the opposite direction to the tidal stream.

A similar effect may be found in channels with a rocky bottom when the tide runs fast; not only overfalls but also powerful eddies may occur, making it difficult to steer a course.

Overfalls and rough water may sometimes be found where two currents meet, particularly where the ebb from an estuary meets a strong coastal tide.

BAROMETER ADJUSTMENT

The calibration of aneroid barometers should be checked every season and whenever their readings are suspect.

Most aneroids have an adjusting screw accessible through a hole in the rear of the case. This resets the pointer in a manner similar to an old-fashioned pocket watch.

A telephone request to the nearest Met. Office will obtain a sea-level pressure at the time of request. This will be in millibars.

Barometers calibrated in millibars should be reset to this figure without delay. The conversion table, Table 31, can be used to obtain the equivalent in inches of mercury for instruments so calibrated.

Table 31

Pressure Conversion:
Millibars to Inches

mb	in	mb	in	mb	in	mb	in
950	28·05	976	28·82	1002	29·59	1028	30·36
951	28·08	977	28·85	1003	29·62	1029	30·39
952	28·11	978	28·88	1004	29·65	1030	30·42
953	28·14	979	28·91	1005	29·68	1031	30·45
954	28·17	980	28·94	1006	29·71	1032	30·47
955	28·20	981	28·97	1007	29·74	1033	30·50
956	28·23	982	29·00	1008	29·77	1034	30·53
957	28·26	983	29·03	1009	29·80	1035	30·56
958	28·29	984	29·06	1010	29·83	1036	30·59
959	28·32	985	29·09	1011	29·85	1037	30·62
960	28·35	986	29·12	1012	29·88	1038	30·65
961	28·38	987	29·15	1013	29·91	1039	30·68
962	28·41	988	29·18	1014	29·94	1040	30·71
963	28·44	989	29·21	1015	29·97	1041	30·74
964	28·47	990	29·23	1016	30·00	1042	30·77
965	28·50	991	29·26	1017	30·03	1043	30·80
966	28·53	992	29·29	1018	30·06	1044	30·83
967	28·56	993	29·32	1019	30·09	1045	30·86
968	28·59	994	29·35	1020	30·12	1046	30·89
969	28·61	995	29·38	1021	30·15	1047	30·92
970	28·64	996	29·41	1022	30·18	1048	30·95
971	28·67	997	29·44	1023	30·21	1049	30·98
972	28·70	998	29·47	1024	30·24	1050	31·01
973	28·73	999	29·50	1025	30·27		
974	28·76	1000	29·53	1026	30·30		
975	28·79	1001	29·56	1027	30·33		

1 mb = 0·0295 in of mercury

TEMPERATURE

The formulae for converting Celsius to Fahrenheit thermometer readings are given below. See Table 32, though, for quick reference.

Table 32

Temperature Conversion:
Celsius to Fahrenheit

°C	°F	°C	°F	°C	°F
40	104	20	68	0	32
39	102	19	66	—1	30
38	100	18	64	—2	28
37	99	17	63	—3	27
36	97	16	61	—4	25
35	95	15	59	—5	23
34	93	14	57	—6	21
33	91	13	55	—7	19
32	90	12	54	—8	18
31	88	11	52	—9	16
30	86	10	50	—10	14
29	84	9	48	—11	12
28	82	8	46	—12	10
27	81	7	45	—13	9
26	79	6	43	—14	7
25	77	5	41	—15	5
24	75	4	39	—16	3
23	73	3	37	—17	1
22	72	2	36	—18	0
21	70	1	34	—19	—2

To convert Celsius to Fahrenheit:

$$°F = \frac{9 \times °C}{5} + 32$$

To convert Fahrenheit to Celsius:

$$°C = \frac{5(°F - 32)}{9}$$

In temperate latitudes this jingle may help:
    Five, fifteen and twentyone,
    Winter, spring and summer sun!

WEATHER FORECASTS FOR YACHTS AND SHIPPING

Radio transmissions of weather forecasts for professional seamen are also of great value to skippers of small craft, particularly those which include a synopsis of the pattern of high and low pressure areas and fronts.

The forecasts are made for large areas of the sea and therefore can only provide a general picture of likely weather in each area. By following changes in the synoptic pattern and making his own observations the yachtsman can often make very accurate predictions of the weather in his immediate vicinity.

The Meteorological Office provides weather information for vessels in the English Channel, the North Sea, the Irish Sea and the eastern North Atlantic. This information is most easily available to yachtsmen by means of BBC radio broadcasts or by telephoning the nearest weather station or forecasting centre ashore. The following extracts from a Met Office leaflet are published with the permission of the Controller of Her Majesty's Stationery Office.

SHIPPING FORECASTS

BBC Radio 2

Weather bulletins for shipping are broadcast on BBC Radio 2 on 200 kHz (1500 m) at the times shown below:

Monday-Saturday	*Sunday*
(Clocktime)	(Clocktime)
0033–0038	0033–0038
0633–0638	0633–0638
1355–1400	1155–1200
1755–1800	1755–1800

Contents of broadcasts

The broadcasts will consist of the following items and will be broadcast in the order shown:

(i) A statement of the gale warnings in force at the time of issue of the forecasts.

(ii) A general synopsis giving the situation in so far as it affects the area within the next 24 hours, with information as to expected changes within that period.

(iii) Forecasts for the next 24 hours for each coastal sea area, giving wind speed and direction, weather and visibility. The areas will be given in a fixed order (see below). When appropriate, contiguous sea areas may be grouped together. (See Fig. 37.)

(iv) The latest reports from a selection of the following stations will be broadcast in this order, the number of stations depending on the time available: Tiree, Sule Skerry, Bell Rock, *Dowsing*, *Galloper* and *Varne* lightvessels, Royal Sovereign Light tower, Portland Bill, Scilly/St. Mary's, Valentia, Ronaldsway, Malin Head and Jersey (not yet included in all shipping forecasts). The elements given will be wind direction

(compass points) and speed (Beaufort force), present weather (including 'past hour' weather), visibility and, if available, sea-level pressure and tendency in qualitative terms.

The words 'wind', 'force', 'millibar' and 'visibility' have been omitted from weather bulletins broadcast by the BBC. This is to enable the forecast to be given in a clearer and more concise form in the time available.

Gale Warnings

Gale warnings are broadcast on BBC Radio 2 as soon as possible after receipt and are repeated at the following hour, e.g. a warning received at 1520 will be broadcast as soon as possible and will be repeated at 1600. A summary of gale warnings in operation is issued on Radios 1 and 2 at 0530 Monday–Saturday and as part of the shipping bulletin at 0630 on Radio 2 on Sunday.

FORECASTS FOR INSHORE WATERS

BBC Radio 4

Forecasts for inshore waters (up to 12 miles offshore) of England and Wales 'until 1800 tomorrow' are broadcast at the end of the English and Welsh Radio 4 programmes. The forecast of wind, weather and visibility is followed by the 2200 reports of wind direction (compass points) and speed (Beaufort force), present weather, visibility and, if available, sea-level pressure and tendency in qualitative terms from the following stations: Acklington (nr. New-castle), Gorleston (nr. Yarmouth), Manston (nr. Rams-gate), Portland Bill, Scilly/St. Mary's, Mumbles (nr. Swansea), Aberporth (Cardigan Bay) and Ronaldsway (Isle of Man).

At the end of the Northern Ireland Radio 4 programme a similar forecast for Northern Ireland inshore waters is given with 2200 reports from Kilkeel (Co. Down), Killough (Co. Down), Malin Head, Machrihanish (Kintyre), Ronaldsway (Isle of Man), Valley (nr. Holyhead) and Orlock Head (nr. Bangor, Northern Ireland).

The forecast for Scottish inshore waters is given towards the end of the Scottish Radio 4 programme with the 2200 reports from the following stations: Machrihanish (Kintyre), Tiree, Stornoway, Wick, Aberdeen (Dyce) and Leuchars.

Details of precise times and frequencies are published in the *Radio Times*.

BBC Radio 3

A forecast for inshore waters of Great Britain is given daily on BBC Radio 3, at 0655 Monday to Friday and at 0755 on Saturday and Sunday.

WEATHER FORECASTS: EUROPEAN MAINLAND COASTAL STATIONS

The BBC Radio 2 Shipping Forecasts on 200 kHz are usually received at adequate strength on a normal yacht radio anywhere between the southwest coast of Norway and the north coast of Spain, including the western Baltic Sea. It may however be convenient at times to use local forecasts broadcast from continental coastal stations when sailing in foreign waters.

Many of these forecasts are broadcast on the 'trawler' band or on HF ('short') wavelengths, but some yacht radios are equipped to receive these broadcasts. Since the frequencies and times of transmission tend to vary, these details should be looked up in the current Reed's Almanac. There is often a choice of frequencies for each station; on one of these the broadcast may be in English.

In addition to the above, local forecasts and gale warnings are given by certain French broadcasting stations, but always in French. They cover the areas 20 miles to seaward from specified sections of the French coast, and in that respect are akin to the BBC forecasts for inshore waters. Table 33 shows the stations, their radio frequencies and the times of these weather broadcasts.

Table 33

French Radio Stations for Weather Forecasts

Sea Area	Stations	Frequency (kHz)	Times (GMT)
Belgian frontier to	Paris	1070	
Cherbourg	Lille	1376	0615
Cherbourg to	Quimerc'	1403	1130
R. Loire	Rennes	710	1815
R. Loire to	Limoges	791	(1830 Sundays)
Spanish frontier	Bordeaux	1205	

Also, in English:

Channel Islands	Jersey Radio	1657·5	0645, 1245 1845, 2245

The French long-wave station France Inter (164 kHz) broadcasts sea-area weather forecasts ('Service Mer') something like the BBC Radio Two shipping forecasts. These broadcasts are timed for the first natural break after 0810, 1300 and 1850 GMT and may be useful when you've missed the BBC's transmission.

15

Radio Aids to Navigation

A large number of radio beacons is installed in lighthouses and lightships around the coastlines of the world. Because of their strategic locations they provide a simple method of obtaining a series of position lines for coastal navigation at no cost to the user and with inexpensive equipment.

Coastal radio beacons operate on various frequencies in the band 285–315 (325 in U.S.) kilohertz (kilocycles per second). The transmitting frequencies of individual beacons are occasionally changed for operational reasons so they are not recorded here. Nautical almanacs give up-to-date frequencies, call signs and nominal ranges.

Beacons are often grouped geographically, with up to six using the same frequency in the same sea area; they transmit in turn each for one minute and thus permit several position lines to be obtained without the need for retuning the DF receiver.

The bearing of a radio beacon (or its reciprocal 180° away) is obtained with an accuracy of about 2 degrees when the DF loop is rotated to the zero-signal or 'null' position. It should be evident from the boat's dead-reckoning position or from bearings from other radio beacons whether the bearing obtained is direct or a reciprocal.

The accuracy of a bearing depends on the direction from which the beacon transmission is received. No correction is needed for bearings from the North to South, the maximum correction (called 'half-convergency') to bearings from the East or West.

In practice the comparatively limited range (average 100 miles) of most beacons means that the correction is very small in middle and lower latitudes but in higher latitudes and when the range of the beacon is over 100 miles it should not be ignored.

Table 34 gives the half-convergency corrections needed; Mid. Lat. is half the sum of the latitudes of the boat and the radio beacon, and D. Long. is the difference between their longitudes. The correction should be made towards the equator, i.e. added to easterly bearings, subtracted from westerly bearings in the Northern hemisphere, the opposite in the Southern hemisphere.

Table 34

Half-convergency Corrections

Mid. Lat.	D. Long			
	$2°$	$4°$	$6°$	$8°$
$52°$	I	2	2	3
$54°$	I	2	2	3
$56°$	I	2	3	4
$58°$	I	2	3	4
$60°$	I	2	3	4

Aeronautical radio beacons (200–400 kHz) may be useful in certain conditions for providing position lines. They operate continuously on similar frequencies to coastal beacons; the exact frequencies are given in the almanacs with their identifying call signs.

Aero. beacons on islands and on the coast are particularly useful for approaches, but bearings from beacons sited inland are always suspect due to refraction at the coastline.

Low-powered marker beacons with a range of 10 miles are used to indicate the positions of certain harbours and inlets in the U.S.

The nominal range quoted for any radio beacon is normally the maximum one might expect in good conditions with a very sensitive receiver well above the waterline of a ship. The effective range with a less sensitive receiver sited low down in a small yacht may be less than half the nominal range. It sometimes helps in fine weather to operate the DF receiver on the cabin top; the height thus gained can noticeably increase sensitivity.

Radio bearings should always be used with caution; they should not be relied upon unless a clear and sharp 'null' has been obtained.

The compass error must be accurately known before radio bearings may be plotted on the chart. (See p. 178.)

Bearings in daytime from a radio beacon farther than about 50 miles distant are suspect, as a small error makes a big difference to the position obtained.

Bearings from a distance greater than about 25 miles by night are suspect due to the effect of the sky wave. This is most noticeable at sunset and sunrise and for an hour on either side; the 'null' will lose its sharpness and the signal may fade out and back periodically.

Never use a radio bearing from a beacon sited obliquely along the coast line from the boat's position; it may be incorrect due to coastal refraction.

Similarly, a bearing from a beacon sited the other side of high land may be refracted and unreliable.

It is normally bad practice to 'home' on a radio beacon in poor visibility; you may hit the land or the lightship on which it is located before you see it. But if the contours of the sea bed are suitable and the depth sounder is used continuously it is possible to 'home' safely and break off the approach at a predetermined depth of water, proceeding thence by dead reckoning.

CONSOL

This useful radio aid to position-finding in Western European waters is available to any boat equipped with a receiver capable of tuning to frequencies between 250 and 320 kilohertz. A direction-finding loop is not needed.

Three Consol beacons transmit continuously a coded signal of 60 Morse 'dots' and 'dashes'. The exact number of dots and dashes changes with the bearing from each beacon.

A Consol chart (Admiralty or from Imray Laurie Norie and Wilson) is needed to convert the coded signals into lines of bearing.

To use the system, the receiver is tuned to a Consol beacon and the beacon first identified by its call sign. (See Table 35 for call-signs and frequencies).

After the call-sign the beacon transmits the 60 dots and dashes, e.g. 40 dots followed by 20 dashes, or 35 dashes followed by 25 dots.

At the transition from dots to dashes (or vice versa) there is a short period during which it is difficult to decide whether dots or dashes are being transmitted. This is called the 'equisignal'.

To clarify this, one counts the number of characters clearly heard before and after the equisignal, e.g. 38 dots—equisignal—18 dashes. To make a total of 60, the equisignal must thus contain 4 characters, and these can be divided equally into 2 dots and 2 dashes, making a correct Consol count of 40 dots and 20 dashes.

The Consol charts show lines of bearing from each beacon labelled with various combinations of dots and dashes, permitting one to select (or interpolate) one's own position line.

Table 35

Consol Beacons

STATION. LAT. & LONG.	CALL SIGN	FREQUENCY KHZ
Ploneis (Brittany) 48°01′ N 4°13′ W	F R Q	257
Covers from 033 to 179 and 213 to 359° True.		
Stavanger (Norway) 58°37′ N 5°38′ E	L E C	319
Covers from 350 to 140 and 170 to 320° True.		
Lugo (Spain) 43°15′ N 7°29′ W	L G	285
Covers from 019 to 157 and 199 to 337° True.		

The Consol beacon at Bush Mills in Northern Ireland was closed down in September 1976, but there has been no indication that any other Consol station will cease transmission in the known future.

Since there are several position lines from each beacon with the same combination of dots and dashes, the system is not unambiguous, but they are sufficiently far apart to be distinguished by reference to the boat's dead reckoning position.

By obtaining two or more position lines from that number of different Consol beacons, or by crossing a single position line with one from a coastal radio beacon or with a sounding, an approximate fix may be plotted.

NOTE: Consol is essentially a long-range beacon system; in daytime its maximum range is about 1200 miles and by night 1500. It should not be used within about 25 miles from a beacon or for coastal navigation or landfalls.

RADAR REFLECTORS

Most shipping is fitted with radar nowadays, but a small yacht or power craft is not a good echoing target and may not be 'seen' by the radar until it is quite close, especially in bad weather.

Radar reflectors if properly chosen and fitted enhance the echoes of small craft and add substantially to their safety at night or in fog.

Bearing in mind that ships cannot alter course instantaneously to avoid an obstruction or other vessel, and that large ships may need to alter course a mile or more away from what may be a collision position, any small craft which may be at sea at night or in fog should carry a radar reflector capable of making her visible as far as possible.

Experiments have shown that reflectors measuring less than 12 inches (30 cm) along the angles are of little use; 18 inches (45 cm) is a better size, and it should be hoisted as high as possible, say a minimum of 15 feet (5 metres) above the waterline.

It is important that the reflector should be correctly suspended from the centre of one side and not from an apex; only this position gives the maximum reflection.

When not in use radar reflectors should be kept in a flat box which prevents the metal sheets from becoming bent; a distorted reflector has its echoing power seriously reduced.

Contrary to popular belief, metal masts do not make good radar reflectors; their reflection pattern is broken up in such a manner as to give only a small echo to a ship's radar.

CONVERTING RADIO FREQUENCIES TO WAVELENGTHS

Table 36, overleaf, is a ready reference for converting radio frequencies in kHz into wavelengths in metres. To convert any radio frequency into wavelength or vice versa, other than those tabulated, divide it into 300,000.

Table 36

Converting Radio Frequencies
to Wavelengths

RADIO BEACON BAND				BROADCAST BAND	
FRE-QUENCY (kHz)	WAVE-LENGTH (m)	FRE-QUENCY (kHz)	WAVE-LENGTH (m)	FRE-QUENCY (kHz)	WAVE-LENGTH (m)
200	1500	305	984	550	545
285	1053	306	980	600	500
286	1049	307	977	650	462
287	1045	308	974	700	429
288	1042	309	971	750	400
289	1038	310	968	800	375
290	1034	311	965	850	353
291	1031	312	962	900	333
292	1027	313	958	950	316
293	1024	314	955	1000	300
294	1020	315	952	1050	286
295	1017	316	949	1100	273
296	1014	317	946	1150	261
297	1010	318	943	1200	250
298	1007	319	940	1250	240
299	1003	320	938	1300	231
300	1000	321	935	1350	222
301	997	322	932	1400	214
302	993	323	929	1450	207
303	990	324	926	1500	200
304	987	325	923		

16

Signalling at Sea

Communication between yachts and other vessels or the shore is by visual signalling, sound signalling or by radio.

Visual signalling comprises communication by flags of the International Code of Signals or by flashing Morse Code by means of a lamp. Semaphore seems little used nowadays.

Sound signalling of certain single-letter International Code messages by fog-horn, whistle or siren is permissible. See pp. 229 and 295.

Radio communication may be by VHF radiotelephony, HF radiotelephony and HF or MF radiotelegraphy. Telegraphy is not usually appropriate to small craft. See p. 233 on radiotelephony.

The International Code is published in a number of languages, (in English by HM Stationery Office and the U.S. Government) and signals have the same meaning in all languages, thus avoiding language difficulties.

A knowledge of the Code flags and the Morse code is extremely useful as well as interesting to small-boat skippers. The flags are shown in colour in Appendix B, p. 294, and Morse code is shown on p. 229.

FLAG SIGNALS

Single-letter flag signals are those in most common use or concerned with urgent messages. See list in Appendix B, p. 295.

Single-letter flags complemented by one or more numeral pendants have specific meanings allocated in the Code book; these meanings are not necessarily similar to those of single flags alone.

Two-letter flag signals carry the bulk of routine messages; complemented by one numeral pendant the message is made more specific. The Code book contains all these.

Three-letter flag signals concern medical matters; they always begin with 'M', and are used when advice is sought or given in the event of sickness or accident on board.

Four-letter flag signals indicate the nationality and identity of a vessel. They are used as the vessel's call-sign. Only nationally-registered craft may be allocated a four-letter call-sign, but any vessel may spell out her name in full to indicate her identity.

The foregoing notes on flag signals apply equally to Morse code signalling by lamp or by radiotelephony when communicating with a craft or shore station in which English is not understood.

In flag signalling the three '**substitute**' flags are used to avoid the need to carry several sets of code flags. The First Substitute repeats the uppermost flag in a hoist, the Second and Third Substitutes repeat the second and third flags down.

The phonetic alphabet has been agreed internationally to avoid confusion which may arise from different pronunciations in foreign languages. The English letter A hailed over a distance or spoken over a poor radio link may sound like E to another speaker of English, while a Frenchman understands it as I. So we call it ALFA.

The complete list of phonetic letters and numbers is given on the next page.

(The code flags are reproduced in colour in
Appendix B, p. 294)

LETTER	CODE WORD	PRONOUNCED	MORSE CODE
A	Alfa	**AL** FAH	•—
B	Bravo	**BRAH** VOH	—•••
C	Charlie	**CHAR** LEE	—•—•
D	Delta	**DELL** TAH	—••
E	Echo	**ECK** OH	•
F	Foxtrot	**FOKS** TROT	••—•
G	Golf	GOLF	——•
H	Hotel	HOH **TELL**	••••
I	India	**IN** DEE AH	••
J	Juliett	**JEW** LEE **ETT**	•———
K	Kilo	**KEY** LOH	—•—
L	Lima	**LEE** MAH	•—••
M	Mike	MIKE	——
N	November	NO **VEM** BER	—•
O	Oscar	**OSS** CAH	———
P	Papa	PAH **PAH**	•——•
Q	Quebec	KEH **BECK**	——•—
R	Romeo	**ROW** ME OH	•—•
S	Sierra	SEE **AIR** RAH	•••
T	Tango	**TANG** GO	—
U	Uniform	**YOU** NEE FORM	••—
V	Victor	**VIK** TAH	•••—
W	Whiskey	**WISS** KEY	•——
X	X-ray	**ECKS** RAY	—••—
Y	Yankee	**YANG** KEY	—•——
Z	Zulu	**ZOO** LOO	——••

NUMERAL	CODE WORD	PRONOUNCED	MORSE CODE
0	Nadazero	NAH–DAH–ZAY–ROH	—————
1	Unaone	OO–NAH–WUN	•————
2	Bissotwo	BEES–SOH–TOO	••———
3	Terrathree	TAY–RAH–TREE	•••——
4	Kartefour	KAR–TAY–FOWER	••••—
5	Pantafive	PAN-TAH–FIVE	•••••
6	Soxisix	SOK–SEE–SIX	—••••
7	Setteseven	SAY–TAY–SEVEN	——•••
8	Oktoeight	OK–TOH–AIT	———••
9	Novenine	NO–VAY–NINER	————•
Decimal point	Decimal	DAY–SEE–MAL	(*Spell out in full*)
Full stop (period)	Stop	STOP	(*Spell out in full*)

Flag Etiquette

A national maritime ensign flown on a staff at the stern of a vessel indicates her country of ownership or registration. It may be flown with or without the burgee of a recognised yacht club at the masthead (but see below).

It is usual to hoist it when going on board or at 8 a.m., and to lower it at sunset or when the boat is being left for more than a few hours. This tells other craft whether the owner is on board or not.

The **Red Ensign** may be flown in all craft of British ownership; Australian and New Zealand yachts wear the Red Ensign 'defaced' with six and four white stars respectively. The U.S. yacht ensign has the usual red and white stripes and a foul anchor surrounded by 13 white stars on a blue background. Canadian yachts wear the national ensign, a red—white—red tricolour with a red maple leaf in the centre.

The **Blue Ensign** may be flown only by British owners who have a Ministry of Defence Warrant to do so. This Warrant may be obtained through certain yacht clubs; it cannot be had by direct application.

When the Blue Ensign is flown, the burgee of the yacht club through which the Warrant was obtained must always be at the masthead.

It is customary to hoist and lower the Blue Ensign at the same times as are indicated above for Red Ensigns. A Blue Ensign (or for that matter a Red Ensign) left up after sunset is a disgrace to a smart craft.

The **White Ensign** is reserved exclusively for ships of the Royal Navy and for members of the Royal Yacht Squadron.

The British Union Flag has no place in privately-owned small craft; it is used only by Royalty and the Royal Navy.

A **triangular burgee** is worn at the masthead to indicate that the owner is on board (or in the near vicinity). It may be flown in home waters with or without the appropriate ensign. It may also indicate a yacht or sailing club of which the owner is a member.

A **swallow-tailed broad pendant** at the masthead indicates that the craft wearing it is carrying a Flag Officer of a yacht or sailing club.

Burgees are customarily hoisted on coming on board and lowered when the owner leaves for more than a few hours. Opinions differ whether they should also be lowered at sunset with the ensign or left flying overnight. Economy suggests they should be lowered, as they serve no useful purpose after dark.

A **rectangular flag** at the masthead indicates that the boat wearing it is actually engaged in racing. Since it is good manners for craft not racing to avoid hampering the racing craft, it must be bad manners not to lower it when racing is over.

A pleasant custom of seamen when in foreign waters is to hoist the ensign of the country visited. This courtesy ensign is normally flown in yachts from a signal halyard on the starboard crosstrees, or lashed to a starboard shroud as high as possible. Be careful to use the maritime ensign of the country visited (foreign vessels visiting the UK fly the Red Ensign); take advice ashore if necessary because the wrong ensign is discourteous and may cause offence.

Dipping the ensign in salute to warships, to Flag Officers of one's yacht or sailing club and to isolated yachts on the high seas is still a courteous practice which gives pleasure all round. The ensign should be lowered half way down its staff well before passing the vessel to be saluted and kept there until the other craft acknowledges by lowering and raising her own ensign. The yacht's ensign is then hoisted 'close up', i.e. to the top of its staff.

The Quarantine Flag

International Code flag Q is hoisted when a craft first enters foreign territorial waters from another country. Strictly it indicates that the vessel is 'healthy' and carries no infectious disease, but it is also taken to mean that Customs clearance is desired.

After entering harbour it should be worn until Customs officers have been on board and given clearance. In some foreign ports it may be customary for the skipper to visit the Custom House if no officer arrives within a reasonable period. The Q flag should be lowered on the skipper's return.

The same procedure should be observed when returning home from foreign waters.

The fact that a yacht carries no dutiable stores does not absolve her skipper from flying the Q flag and obtaining clearance.

DISTRESS SIGNALS

The International Regulations for Preventing Collision at Sea (1972) authorise 14 types of signal from vessels in distress. Not all of these are appropriate to yachts and small craft but one or more of the following selection might be used in anything from a rowing dinghy upwards.

Continuous sounding of the fog signal.

The Morse Code signal SOS ($\cdots$ $-$$-$$-$ $\cdots$) by signal lamp, electric torch or foghorn.

A 'Mayday' signal if the boat has a VHF or HF radio transmitter.

Hoisting a square flag with a ball above or below (the Q flag or a duster with a spherical anchor buoy or fender or even the galley kettle.)

A **red** parachute flare or hand flare, or an **orange** smoke signal.

Slowly raising and lowering the outstretched arms.

Clearly, the method used will depend on the size of the boat and whether she is within sight or earshot of land or of a potential rescuer. A shirt attached to an oar will attract attention to a dinghy close inshore but washing drying in the rigging of a five-tonner will probably not.

A fog signal, a torch and a square flag should be already available in any estuary cruiser or larger boat, but pyrotechnic flares are inexpensive and very effective and well worth the small space they occupy.

A sealed waterproof can with a number of red and white flares is a good investment; the white flares might be needed to draw attention to one's whereabouts on a dark or foggy night at sea. Many pyrotechnics are supplied ready packed in waterproof plastic wrappings.

Red parachute flares are more expensive but well worth having in a boat making a cross-Channel or longer passage; they burn for half a minute and might be seen 20 miles away by night and over 5 miles by day.

Because distress flares are so rarely used, they are often stowed in an inaccessible, perhaps forgotten, place. Keep them handy to the cockpit or in the wheelhouse, check their condition from time to time and become familiar with the firing instructions.

Pyrotechnics are marked with a life-expiry date; when this date arrives you can practise using them, perhaps on a firework night, but do it well inland to avoid calling out the rescue services needlessly.

RADIO COMMUNICATIONS

Small-ship radio telephones are compact and reasonably economical in their use of electrical energy; they provide a simple and effective means of communicating with the shore and other craft on occasions of routine and emergency.

233

They must however be used in a disciplined manner; for this reason most countries require the licensing of the equipment and its operators.

VHF radio telephones are extremely simple to use, but their range is normally limited by the horizon. The antenna should be fitted as high as possible to maximize the range.

HF radio telephones have a greater range (up to 150 miles) but are somewhat more difficult to operate. The antenna might be an insulated standing backstay in a sailing yacht or a whip-antenna on the bridge of a power craft.

Both types can communicate on a number of channels, i.e. radio frequencies. Channel selection in VHF sets is by push-button. In HF sets either by push-button or manually. The channels are numbered.

These channels may not be used at random; a specific purpose is allocated to each. Use of the wrong channel will at best merely fail to establish communication, at worst it may interfere with the operation of the emergency services.

Communication from ship to shore is first established on the 'calling' frequency by calling the name of the wanted shore station three times followed by the name or call-sign of the ship three times. When the shore station answers it will offer a choice of frequencies or channels on which subsequent operations should be conducted.

Having acknowledged this '. . . Roger, Channel 27 (or whatever)' the ship transfers to that channel and calls again as before. The message may then be passed.

To make the most effective use of radio telephony, the ship must be in a position to receive calls as well as to initiate them. This means that a 'listening watch' must be kept on the calling frequency. This is normally done by loudspeaker.

This enables the ship not only to receive calls addressed to herself, but also to intercept possible distress calls from other craft in the vicinity, or to relay such (or any other) calls when the calling vessel may be failing to contact a shore station.

The permutations and combinations of frequencies and channels in use internationally are too many to be given here; various national reference books detail them and certain nautical almanacs print selections.

The phonetic alphabet (p. 229) should always be used in spelling out words, call signs or numbers. If a language problem exists the groups of letters and numerals from the International Code of Signals (p. 295) may be used; they mean the same thing in any language.

Even if no radio transmitter is carried, useful signals may be received on the HF band of many direction-finding receivers, provided that they are connected to a suitable antenna (insulated backstay or whip, as before). Many coast radio stations broadcast weather forecasts and gale warnings for their local sea areas. These are often more up-to-date and specific than the shipping weather forecasts broadcast by long-wave transmitters. See Chapter 14 on weather.

A FEW USEFUL FRENCH WORDS

ENGLISH	FRENCH	PRONOUNCED
Aground	Echoué	Ay-shoo-ay
Anchor (an)	Ancre	Ahn-kr
Anchor (to)	Ancrer	Ahn-kray
Anchor, Foul	L'ancre surjalé	Lahn-kr sir-zhah-lay
Anchorage	Mouillage	Moo-yazh
Beacon	Balise	Ba-leez
Boat	Bateau	Ba-toh
Buoy	Bouée	Boo-ay
Cast off	Dégager	Day-gah-zhay
Chandler	Fournisseur de marine	Foor-nee-ser de(r) mah-reen
Chart	Carte marine	Kart mah-reen
Club (yacht)	Club nautique	Klub noh-teek
	Cercle nautique	Sehr-kl noh-teek

235

ENGLISH	FRENCH	PRONOUNCED
Customs	Douane	Dwan
Diesel fuel	Fuel-oil domestique	Fuel-wahl daw-mes-teek
	Gas-oil	Gahz-wahl
Dinghy	Youyou	Yoo-yoo
Engine	Moteur	Maw-terr
Ensign	Pavillon	Pa-vee-ohn
Fender	Défense	Day-fahns
Flag, Quarantine	Fanion	Fahn-yohn
Fresh water	Eau douce	Oh doos
	Eau potable	Oh paw-tabl
Gas	Gaz	Gahz
Harbourmaster	Capitaine de port	Ka-pee-ten de(r) pawr
Jetty	Jetée	Zhe(r)-tay
Landing place	Cale	Kahl
Lie alongside . . .	S'amarrer le long de . . .	Sa-mah-ray le(r) lohn de(r)
Lights	Feux	Fe(r)
Make fast	Amarrer	A-mah-ray
Meth. spirit	Alcool à brûler	Al-kawl ah brew-lay
Mooring (a)	Corps mort	Kawr mawr
Moor (to)	Amarrer	A-mah-ray
Motor	Moteur	Maw-terr
Nylon	Nylon	Nee-lohn
Paraffin	Pétrole raffiné	Pay-trol rah-fee-nay
Petrol	Essence	Eh-sahns
Rope	Cordage	Kawr-dazh
Sail (a)	Voile	Vwahl
Slipway	Cale de halage	Kahl de(r) ah-lazh
Sparking plug	Bougie	Boo-zhee
Terylene	Tergal	Ter-gahl
Tide	Marée	Mah-ray
Tow (to)	Remorquer	Re(r)-mawr-kay
Weather forecast	Météo	May-tay-oh

ENGLISH	FRENCH	PRONOUNCED
One	Un	E(r)n
Two	Deux	De(r)
Three	Trois	Trwa
Four	Quatre	Katr
Five	Cinq	Sank
Six	Six	See
Seven	Sept	Set
Eight	Huit	Weet
Nine	Neuf	Nerf
Ten	Dix	Dee
Twenty	Vingt	Van(k)
Thirty	Trente	Trahnt
Forty	Quarante	Ka-rahnt
Fifty	Cinquante	Sank-ahnt
Sixty	Soixante	Swa-sahnt
Seventy	Soixante-dix	Swa-sahnt-dee
Eighty	Quatre-vingts	Katr-van(k)
Ninety	Quatre-vingt-dix	Katr-van(k)-dee
Hundred	Cent	Sahn

Yacht Handling and Boatwork

This chapter does not attempt to instruct in the elementary principles of sailing and power craft handling. Rather, it discusses some events which happen at sea and suggests seamanlike methods of dealing with them.

BERTHING, MOORING, ANCHOR-WORK

(For Anchors, Cables and
Mooring see also Chapter 7.)

Berthing Alongside a Jetty or Another Boat (Docking)

Don't attempt to moor alongside another boat which is much smaller than your own. You may damage it by squeezing against the wall.

If you berth alongside a much bigger craft than your own, be ready to let a larger boat arriving later berth between you and the big craft, or you may yourself be damaged by squeezing.

Generally, a ballasted-keel sailing boat will not happily lie alongside a shallow-draft motor cruiser with much top-hamper. Like with like is a good rule. But if you berth a sailing boat alongside another, always look aloft to make sure that cross-trees and rigging will not tangle when they roll.

At least four ropes are needed. Two should be of the same size as the anchor warp and the same length as the boat. These make the bow and stern warps. The other two, for use as springs, should also be the boat's length and about half the diameter of the anchor warp. See Chapter 4 for rope sizes.

Short breast ropes may also be needed to keep the boat close to the quay or neighbouring yacht. See Fig. 38.

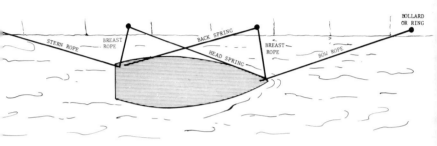

38 Mooring Alongside

Tend the warps with the rise and fall of the tide; don't go ashore at High Water leaving the ropes taut or you may get an unpleasant surprise later. Long ropes cause least trouble.

If there are already lines from other boats on a quayside bollard to which you wish to make fast, put the eye of your own line under and through the others (Fig. 39). It will then be possible to release any boat first without disturbing the others.

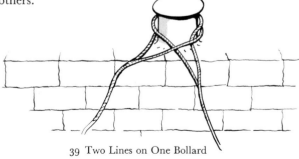

39 Two Lines on One Bollard

239

Picking up a Strange Mooring

Misunderstandings are frequent over the use of private moorings. A harbour may have a number of permanent moorings laid, of which some are the property of the harbour authority and some laid at their own expense by private owners. A proportion of those laid by the harbour authority may have been rented out for the season to private owners, and some may be reserved for visiting craft, usually on payment of a fee.

Nobody has a right to pick up any mooring other than his own though most owners are reasonable about this and do not object to the temporary occupation of their moorings by other craft. But 'temporary' means until the Harbourmaster has been consulted and his advice taken, shifting berth if necessary.

In no circumstances should a boat be left unattended on a 'temporary' mooring; someone competent should be left on board to shift berth in the event of the owner's return.

Should an owner return to find his mooring occupied, he can either tie up alongside, take up an adjacent mooring (if there is one) or move the visiting boat to another mooring. In the last event however he is responsible that he does so in a seamanlike manner and causes no damage. Needless to say, it would be the height of irresponsibility to leave the visiting boat insecurely moored.

In picking up any mooring, one should be assured of its adequacy for the boat to be moored. Many owners prudently paint the name and tonnage of their boats on the pick-up buoy, so that a light-weight mooring for a 2-ton dayboat isn't dragged by a 25-ton ketch. Moorings are often grouped; those for heavier and deep-draught boats on the outer trots and those for smaller craft in shallower water further inshore. See pp. 86 ff.

Mooring a Cable Each Way

In a crowded harbour or narrow waterway there may be insufficient room to swing comfortably at anchor. You can restrict your own swinging room by using two anchors; this is known as 'mooring a cable each way'.

This can be achieved by letting out twice as much anchor chain as you will eventually need, drawing it out to its full scope, then dropping the kedge anchor on its warp underfoot, finally hauling in the redundant half of the anchor chain so that your boat is 'middled' between the two anchors.

The anchor chain and kedge warp should be lashed together by such a distance from the bow fairlead that the boat can swing unhindered with the tide. See Fig. 40.

In law, no boat is considered to be properly moored unless she is anchored in this manner.

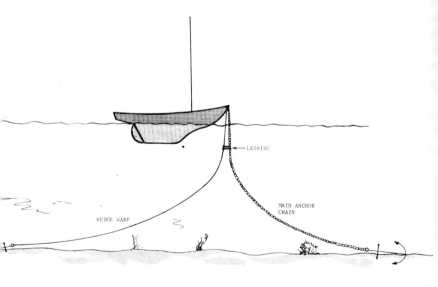

40 Mooring a Cable Each Way

Dragging Anchor

Anchors don't drag except in a strong wind or tide. The first sign of dragging may be a rumbling sound from below. If you haven't done it already, take bearings of several objects on the shore and note if they are changing. Two convenient objects in transit on the beam will appear to move apart if the anchor really is dragging (or of course if the boat is swinging with the change of tide.)

The remedy is to let out more anchor chain beyond the original amount which should have been at least 3 times the depth of water. Remember that if you anchored with that much chain at Low Water it will be insufficient at High Tide.

If you use a nylon rope anchor warp it may not help to let out more rope unless it is weighted to lie along the bottom. A convenient way of doing this is to suspend a heavy weight from a shackle round the anchor warp and lower it with a second rope until it touches the sea bed. The weight should be of about 5 pounds for a 20-foot boat to 15 pounds for a 30-footer.

In extreme cases it may be necessary to lay out a second anchor ahead; this might be done from the dinghy but if wind and tide are strong it would be better to motor up to a position a few yards on either side of the first anchor and to drop the second underfoot, then allowing the boat to fall back to her original position and adjusting the tension on the second anchor until it is about equal with that on the first.

If none of these measures succeed, there's nothing for it but to weigh anchor and to look for a more sheltered anchorage.

Laying Out a Kedge Anchor

A kedge may be needed to haul a boat off which has run aground, or perhaps to moor to two anchors when swinging room is very limited. Since kedges are normally used with rope warps, 2 or 3 fathoms of chain should always be kept shackled on to improve holding.

Before rowing out to lay the kedge from a dinghy, good preparatory work can simplify the task greatly. The kedge should be suspended over the dinghy transom with a bight of rope attached to the centre thwart, so that one end can be released to allow the anchor to drop. You can't row properly while paying out the warp and trying to keep the kedge in position with your feet, especially in a tideway.

The kedge warp should be coiled down on the bottom of the dinghy on top of the chain, free from kinks and free to run as you row away from the yacht, to which the free end should be made fast inboard. It's a waste of time and energy to attempt to tow the warp through the water while someone uncoils it on deck. Much easier to pay it out as you row.

Row away in the required direction; often someone on board the yacht may be in a better position to judge this, and he should make some appropriate signals to show when you've got it right. When all the warp has been paid out, release one end of the rope which secures the kedge over the transom and the job is done, except for hauling the warp taut until the anchor 'bites'.

You can't do this with an outboard motor on the dinghy transom, and don't be tempted merely to throw the kedge over the side of the dinghy unless it's a very light one indeed, in which case it may not be of much help. Nor can you hope to save dinghy work by throwing the kedge overboard from the yacht; it won't go far enough for the warp to lie along the sea bed and so permit the anchor to take a strain.

Recovering a Foul Anchor

Anchors sometimes get caught beneath mooring chains, power cables or other underwater obstructions. If a tripping line has been attached to the anchor it will in most cases free it; it's therefore wise to use one in a harbour known to have chains and cables everywhere.

If there is no tripping line, or it fails to work, be prepared for some hard and wet labour, and perhaps a prolonged stay of several hours, maybe a tide or two.

Unless the water is very clear, you will not yet know what has fouled the anchor. Begin by winching in the anchor chain as far as possible; a 'handy-billy' or other block-and-tackle arrangement will help if the boat has no anchor winch.

This, after much hard work, will bring a mooring chain or power cable to or near the surface. Pass a rope round it, from the dinghy and with the aid of a boathook if necessary, and make both ends fast inboard.

Slacken the anchor chain so that the rope takes the weight of the mooring chain. The anchor will then fall free and may be hoisted inboard. When you are ready to leave, let go one end of the rope and allow the mooring chain to fall to the bottom. You're free!

If however it has not been possible to bring the chain within reach to pass a rope around it, try again at dead Low Water. You might then be able to lift it the shorter distance and get the rope in position as above.

In the event that hoisting the anchor chain merely pulls the bows of the boat down without apparently lifting the obstruction from the bottom, the anchor is probably fouled under a rock or very heavy piece of wreckage. There is a chance that it may be cleared by pulling on the chain from the opposite direction from that in which it is normally lying, probably with the tide.

This means slackening out all the chain you have and motoring upstream to its limit, and then going astern at full power in an attempt to dislodge the fouled anchor. If you do so, it will certainly dig in again, but with any luck clear of the obstruction and you will be able to raise it normally.

244

If all else fails, you're stuck with having to slip the anchor chain from its inboard end, having first attached a buoy and line so that it can later be recovered by a diver. Another good reason for never having less than two anchors on board.

All this work is made more difficult if there's a strong tide running; best to make your attempt at slack water, especially at Low Tide.

CLEARING A ROPE FROM THE PROPELLER

If the boat is in restricted waters, drop the anchor immediately to avoid being driven ashore or into other craft.

If, as is probable, the rope is from your own craft, try unwinding it by putting the gear lever into reverse and turning the engine over slowly by hand (with the ignition or fuel turned off) while someone else hauls on the inboard end of the rope. It may be necessary to wind alternately astern and ahead a fraction of a turn at a time to un-jam the rope initially, while still maintaining a strain on the inboard end.

If the rope's end is not inboard, someone must go over the side and attach another rope to it which may be hauled on as above.

A good underwater swimmer may be able to free the rope, but if the above methods have failed he will probably need a sharp knife to cut it free. In any case attach a line to him; if there is a swell he may hit his head on the bottom of the boat and need help.

Failing all else, the boat will have to be beached either on legs or alongside a wall and the rope removed at low water.

In heavily polluted waters it may be a large plastic bag or similar debris which has fouled the propeller; a rope should be attached to any free area of material by a rolling hitch and hauled on as above.

TOWING OTHER BOATS

Towing a dinghy from a larger boat: best done with two painters, one from each quarter of the towing boat to a ring low down on the bow of the dinghy. The painters should be twice as long as the dinghy plus sufficient to ensure that when the towing boat is on a wavecrest the dinghy is on the next wavecrest astern.

A weight such as the dinghy anchor in the stern will lift the bow of the dinghy and make her easier to tow and less liable to sheer about wildly. But be sure all loose gear is securely lashed down; in a confused sea the dinghy could capsize and you'll lose the lot. This applies particularly to oars and rowlocks.

Towing a larger boat from a dinghy: the main problem is always to keep the tow rope taut and to avoid snatching. Adding weight to the dinghy by carrying a passenger, a heavy anchor or some other substantial weight will minimize snatching. The passenger might also help to row.

If the dinghy has an outboard motor it is often best to lash the dinghy alongside and to steer the combination by the larger boat's rudder. The dinghy should be secured about level with the shrouds with springs and fenders and the main tow line led from the quarter of the dinghy to well aft in the larger boat.

Towing any boat from one of similar size: a lot of damage can be caused to both boats if this is not done carefully. Best to use the anchor chain of the towed boat for towing any significant distance. Pay out at least two boat's lengths of chain and attach the free end to the towing boat with a rope which can be easily slipped in an emergency. The chain will minimize snatching and will avoid the risk of fouling the propeller when the towed boat surges forward.

Towing will be easiest when the length of the tow is such that both boats are simultaneously on wave crests.

When one heavy boat is towing another in a seaway there will be very heavy loads on both boats; the towing chain or rope should be made fast to substantial fittings at both ends, such as the sheet horse in the towing boat. Ordinary deck cleats are unlikely to withstand the strain.

Never tow any boat faster than her natural maximum speed; not only does the load become much larger and put a greater strain on fittings, tow line and the clutch and gearbox of the towing boat's engine, but the towed boat is also liable to sheer about uncontrollably. More towed boats have been lost through excessive towing speeds than for any other reason.

Towing another boat when under sail: most difficult when beating to windward, as the weight of the tow often prevents the towing boat from going about. Rig a pair of control lines from about the shrouds on each side of the towing boat to a point on the tow line one boat's length astern. When going about slacken one control line and haul in on the other to help the boat round.

BEACHING A DINGHY IN SURF

Consider first whether this might be foolhardy; all depends on the size of the waves, the skill of the crew and the size of the dinghy. If in doubt, don't do it.

It is vital to keep the boat at right angles to the breakers at all times; broadside on she will broach-to and capsize.

If possible, select a landing spot which is comparatively sheltered, perhaps under the lee of a cliff, rock or pier. But never attempt to land on a rocky shore when there are breakers or a big swell.

It's often advisable to cover the last few yards to the

shore stern first, as the bow of the dinghy will rise more readily than the stern to the oncoming waves, and as the last wave sweeps the boat on to the beach, you can control its speed and direction by pulling hard on the oars.

A good method of keeping bows-on to the waves is to drop a dinghy anchor before getting into the worst of the surf and then to pay out a long line slowly, keeping a tension on the line.

You can't do any of these tricks with an outboard motor, because when you lift it prior to beaching you will have lost all directional control at the time you need it most.

Incidentally, never consider running any boat ashore during a gale and swimming for it when she hits. The bitter experience of centuries has shown it to be suicidal.

BAD-WEATHER SAILING

Anyone can get caught out in a blow, especially on a long passage.

Astute passage planning can avoid or minimize the discomfort; if the weather is unsettled plan the route so that a diversion to a sheltered anchorage is always possible.

Understand at least the basics of weather forecasting and take note of the warnings given by the sky and the barometer.

Listen to the radio Weather Forecasts for Shipping, not only for your own sea area but also for the adjacent ones; heavy weather moves fast and may reach your area before the next forecast is due.

When the wind begins to perk up get into oilskins before the spray starts to fly, with a sweater underneath and a strip of towelling worn like a scarf round the neck.

Secure all loose gear on deck and in the cabin.

Anyone prone to seasickness should take his favourite pill before the symptoms of sickness are evident.

Don't wait too long before shortening sail. As soon as the boat begins to feel pressed change down to a smaller foresail and reef the mainsail. Little speed will be lost as the wind strength increases, and if a further reduction of sail becomes necessary it will be easier to achieve.

Consider whether you should carry on, turn back or divert for shelter. The decision will be influenced by the distance to go (or return), the wind strength and direction, the likelihood of a long or short blow, and of course the size of the boat and the strength of her crew.

It doesn't follow that the nearest land is necessarily the best place to aim for; if it should be a dead lee shore without shelter it will be more dangerous than helpful.

The best shelter to make for will be a harbour in the lee of a headland or island.

If you decide to stay at sea, a change of course may be advisable to avoid approaching the land too closely. It's always safer in deep water.

Given plenty of sea-room, the least uncomfortable course will be down-wind, but consider whether this will put you on a lee shore before the gale has blown itself out.

Sailing down-wind with the wind slightly on one quarter or the other will minimize the risk of gybing 'all standing' (and perhaps dismasting) when the boat corkscrews in a big following sea. Towing the kedge warp astern in a great bight will help to keep her steady.

The helmsman must be very alert to avoid broaching-to in these conditions; he should be relieved before he becomes too tired to react quickly.

If a long run down-wind is expected it may be better to lower the mainsail completely and run under two goose-winged foresails hanked on the same stay, but this should not be attempted in restricted waters where it may be necessary to alter course by more than a few degrees.

In bad weather nobody may feel like preparing or eating

food, but this is the time when hot food and drink are most important to keep morale high. A hot stew from canned ingredients is most easily prepared and provides the necessary nourishment.

Keep regular watches at the helm and on deck and insist that those off watch should rest, even if it is daytime. Fatigue is a destroyer of morale, and a tired man at the helm could endanger the boat and her crew. Four hours on watch and two hours at the helm are quite enough, and the watchkeepers should be relieved promptly.

Lifelines and safety harnesses are more essential than ever during bad weather, especially by night in a short-handed boat with only one man on deck. If he should get swept overboard his chances of being found are virtually nil.

RUNNING AGROUND

Running aground may cause no more trouble than a short delay if the tide is rising and has some way to go before High Water. You'll float off again when the tide lifts the boat off the bottom.

But the rising tide may push the boat further on the mud. Sailing boats should lower all sails immediately, start the motor and attempt to reverse away in the direction from which the boat went on. Some craft with fin keels may be persuaded to pivot about them and come off the mud if the foresail is lowered, the mainsheet hauled in and all spare bodies on board sent right forward to reduce draught.

If these tactics are unsuccessful, the kedge anchor should be laid out from the dinghy as far as possible dead astern. See p. 242. Hauling on the kedge warp may bring the boat into deeper water. Failing this, the warp should be hauled taut and made fast at the after end of the boat to prevent her from being driven further on by the rising tide. She will in due course float and may then be hauled off into deeper water.

On a falling tide you might try all the above, but you have to move quickly as the water level is getting lower every minute, making the task progressively more difficult.

If you haven't refloated after a few minutes on a falling tide, resign yourself to waiting for the flood. She'll refloat at about the same time AFTER Low Water as she went on BEFORE it.

Shallow-draft and bilge-keel craft will probably sit comfortably on the bottom as the tide recedes. Deep-draught and fin-keel boats however will heel at what may be a considerable angle if left high and dry. Loose gear such as books and crockery should be stowed in lockers or drawers if they are likely to fall out of their normal stowages, and fuel cocks turned off to avoid flooding when in an abnormal position. The same may apply to galley and heads seacocks. If in doubt turn them off. And give a thought to the danger of spilled battery acid.

It may be possible in a deep-draught boat which carries beaching legs to rig them before the boat heels too far. This is fine on a hard sandy bottom, but on soft mud it may be better to let the keel sink in and keep the boat upright that way. Before rigging the legs prod around with the boathook to see whether the bottom is hard or soft and whether there are any rocks which might prevent the legs from keeping the boat upright.

Lay out the kedge anchor towards deeper water and secure the warp aft; it will prevent the boat being driven further on by the rising tide and will help to pull her off when there's enough water.

COLLISION

If a boat collides with another or with any obstruction to sea room, the first priority is saving life. Someone may have fallen or been knocked overboard or injured by the impact.

Throw him a line or a lifebuoy; if he appears to be unconscious someone will have to go in after him. See section on 'Man Overboard', p. 257.

Next priority is saving the boat. Most small craft can take hard knocks, and if the damage is above the waterline it may be that nothing needs doing immediately. But have a quick look at the other boat; she may be in worse shape than yours, and need your help.

The damage may be on or below the waterline, in which case you may have to move quickly to prevent her from sinking. Stuff something in the hole, a towel or a cushion, preferably from the outside, to minimize the ingress of water. A big hole or a long split may need a bunk mattress to cover it; lash it in position with lines passed right round the hull and hauled taut.

An alternative way of dealing with a big hole is to pass a sail under the boat in such a way as to cover the hole, hauling it taut and securing it to the guard rails. This may be the only way of dealing with damage low down caused by striking a submerged rock.

You then have to decide whether you can make harbour or whether the boat should be beached on the nearest suitable shore for repairs.

The lowest priority in dealing with an incident of this nature is to quibble about whose fault it was. See the section on insurance, p. 49.

FIRE

Fire at sea is the hazard most feared by mariners, and the professional seaman instinctively does all he can to avoid it.

Read about fire-fighting in the section on safety (pp. 44–8). Hope that you may never need to use this information but always be prepared to deal with a conflagration in the galley or engine room.

Hull

Holes in the hull or deck: see p. 37.

Broken skin fittings: keep a number of tapered wooden plugs on board, at least one for each size of skin fitting. Hammered in (from the outside if possible) they will keep water out until the fitting can be replaced.

Steering Gear

Broken tiller: put it in splints by lashing on any suitable strips of wood or metal with seizing wire.

Lost tiller: you may have to sacrifice a dinghy oar or boat hook.

Broken or lost rudder: most sailing craft can be kept on a desired course by trimming the sails and adjusting the sheets minutely to make small alterations of course. This needs practice in advance. If you can trim your boat to sail a required course without using the rudder, you have learnt a lot about the subtleties of sail trimming.

Twin-screw power craft can be manoeuvred by judicious manipulation of the throttles. This too is worth practising in advance in the open sea. In some circumstances single-screw craft can be handled without a rudder over a short distance by going slow ahead and giving an occasional kick astern to turn her in the required direction. This probably won't work if there's any wind; you'll have to rig a jury rudder or get a tow home.

Jury rudders: steering oars were used in ancient craft before rudders were invented; a dinghy oar may still be used as a rudder in most small craft. A single oar lashed loosely to the bottom of the standing backstay of a sailing craft can be quite effective.

If there is no standing backstay or other suitable way of

lashing a steering oar over the stern, the boat hook or another oar might be lashed vertically to the rudder gudgeons to act as a pivot to which the steering oar may be lashed.

If none of these remedies is feasible, two oars can be used, one on each side of the boat and lashed as far aft as possible. In this case the oars must be dipped into and removed from the water alternatively, as may be required by the change of course desired. Two steersmen may be needed to operate this system.

Standing Rigging

Instant action is needed to avoid dismasting.

If a **shroud** or its rigging screw parts, put the boat about immediately on the other tack to put the load on the opposite good shroud. Make good the broken shroud with bulldog grips if necessary and a lanyard made from strong rope. See section on dismasting, p. 255.

If a **forestay** or its rigging screw parts while beating or reaching, turn on to a run immediately to put the load on the backstay. Repair as for a broken shroud, or use the spinnaker halyard as a temporary forestay.

If a **backstay** or its rigging screw parts while running, turn on to a beat immediately to put the load on the forestay and shrouds. Repair as for a broken shroud, or use the topping lift (if strong enough) as a temporary backstay.

Running Rigging

The spinnaker halyard can often do the job of a broken fore or jib halyard, and (if you've had the foresight to make it strong enough) the topping lift can do the same for a broken main halyard.

Foresail and jib sheets usually break where they pass through deck blocks. Put the boat about on the other tack or gybe and repair or replace at leisure.

If a sheet breaks so that it is completely detached from the clew of the sail it is usually better (if the wind has any strength) to lower the sail while repairs are made. Even if the repairer isn't knocked overboard by the flogging of the sail, his spectacles are almost certain to be.

Broken Boom

Often the simplest way of dealing with this is to remove the boom completely and use the sail loose-footed. This may mean modifying the sheeting arrangements temporarily so that the foot of the sail is pulled outwards as well as downwards.

If the gears of a roller-reefing mechanism are stripped of their teeth, the boom can still be rotated for reefing purposes by attaching a rope to the tack fitting and winding it around the boom for at least as many turns as you wish to put in the reefed sail. The free end of the rope should be knotted tightly to the boom downhaul fitting when the requisite number of turns have been put in the sail. Alternatively a block-and-tackle arrangement may be used to haul the rope taut and prevent the sail from unwinding.

If the swivel at the outboard end of the boom has broken, the mainsheet may be reattached by fitting the mainsheet block to the boom end by means of a strop. A light lashing will prevent the strop from moving when not under load.

Dismasted

Dismasting: if you have sea room, first get the sails inboard and below deck. This gives easier access to the rest of the shambles and may prevent further damage.

Resist the Ancient Mariner's impulse to chop things away with an axe; it will probably do more harm than good in a modern craft.

Try to get everything inboard. You may need every shackle, rigging screw and inch of rope and wire you can lay your hands on.

If drifting toward shore or other danger, drop your anchor on a good scope; it will find bottom as you come into shallower water. Don't try to use the engine until you are certain that none of the rigging can foul the propeller.

Coil down the halyards, remove the sheets and stow them below and tidy things up as much as possible.

Sit down with a pipe and a glass and calmly work out the best course of action. Forget any idea of being home for tea.

Can you motor home, or to a nearer convenient port? What is the weather like now? Will it improve or deteriorate?

If you rig a jury mast, you will be able to sail downwind, to some extent across it but never to windward. With the wind expected, will you be able to make port or will you be blown further to seaward? Will you finish up on a lee shore without the ability to claw off it?

There can be no omnibus answer to all these questions; every case will be different, but if you are beyond easy motoring distance from port a good compromise is to sail as far as possible and to conserve fuel for entering harbour and avoiding rocks and other obstructions.

To rig a jury mast, choose the broken length which is more advantageous. If the fracture is in the middle of the mast, the upper section is better because it already has standing and running rigging attached.

Cut the mast off clean just above the fracture (if using the upper section) or just below it if using the lower. Modify the new heel so that it will fit the old step (if stepped on deck) or so that it can be located on deck by chocks or some other means if originally stepped through the deck.

Measure the new length of the shrouds and make new eyes in them at the appropriate positions by clamping the wire to itself by bulldog grips or by lashing with seizing wire. Attach these eyes to the shroud rigging screws by several turns of a strong lanyard.

Estimate the lengths of the new forestay and backstay; make similar eyes and attach a lanyard to each, ready to secure the mast when it has been erected.

Unless the mast is a very heavy one, two people should be able to get it upright and one to hold it there while the other makes fast the fore- and backstays.

A heavier mast can be erected by lashing the spinnaker pole or main boom to the foot, leading the forestay (or a halyard) to the other end of the boom and hauling down on it.

The shortened shrouds if of about the right length will prevent the mast from falling over sideways while it is being erected in a fore-and-aft direction.

The lanyards can then be adjusted for length, taking the strain temporarily on a halyard if it is necessary to remake any of the eyes in a different position in a shroud or stay.

Some means of preventing the heel of the mast from moving must be devised, such as wire-lashing it to the original step or surrounding it by wooden chocks nailed to the deck.

With this rig it should be possible to set a small foresail and blow down wind with adequate steerage way. You are unlikely to be able to set a mainsail, but in favourable conditions a second foresail might be hoisted on the main halyard and boomed out with the spinnaker pole or a boat hook.

MAN OVERBOARD

Better avoided if at all possible, but accidents will happen in the best-regulated boats and families.

Before it happens, you should have satisfied yourself that the boat is so laid out and equipped that it is difficult to fall overboard and as easy as possible to retrieve the victim.

Read Denny Desoutter's *Small-Boat Skipper's Safety Book* (Hollis & Carter) on guardrails, lifelines, safety harnesses, lifebuoys and all the other equipment and methods used to prevent anyone from going overboard and to get him back if nevertheless it happens.

The following notes summarize a subject which should be studied in depth by all responsible skippers.

Assuming the boat is under way (it's obviously easier when the boat is moored or anchored), the vital actions are:

to keep the chap afloat,
not to lose sight of him, and
to get the boat back to where he is as soon as possible.

Whether you're at the helm or elsewhere on deck, throw a lifebuoy immediately (this may be difficult if the lifebuoys are lashed neatly to the guardrails) and yell 'Man Overboard' to alert anyone else on board.

Detail the first person to arrive to do nothing but keep the victim in sight, so that he can be pointed out instantaneously irrespective of any manoeuvres the boat may make.

Man overboard from craft under sail: the best way to sail back to pick the chap up depends on whether you are running, reaching or beating; the standard gybing manœuvre is not always the quickest.

If running with the mainsail boomed out to port, a gybe is unnecessary if you turn the boat to starboard, harden in the sheets and when hard on the wind tack to return to the chap in the water. Turning to port in the same conditions makes a gybe and a tack necessary, and you may lose way in making the two manœuvres in quick succession.

The converse applies when running with the mainsail boomed out to starboard; turn to port and avoid the need to gybe.

On a reach or broad reach a gybe may be necessary, but

in many modern craft which turn quickly the alternative may be to turn into the wind and tack without putting the foresail over. In this hove-to condition it may be possible to return to the victim without further manœuvres.

On a beat the gybe may also be appropriate, but there is still the option of first bearing away into a reach and then tacking and heaving-to, as in the previous paragraph.

An afternoon spent practising these manœuvres to determine which applies best to your own boat may later prove to be well spent.

Man overboard from a power craft: the rules about throwing a lifebuoy and keeping the chap in sight still apply, but it's unlikely that stopping the boat and going astern will be as quick as turning through 270 degrees while keeping way on.

The turn may be to port or starboard, though single-screw craft turn more quickly in one direction that the other. It may be an advantage to turn in the direction which will put the sun astern when making the run up to the victim; the glare on the water may make it difficult to see him if the turn is made in the other direction.

If you should yourself be the man overboard (and this applies to any crew member) don't waste energy swimming after the yacht; you're unlikely to catch up with it. Save your efforts for keeping afloat until the boat comes back for you.

If you're alone with a capsized dinghy, don't swim for the shore unless it's obviously within easy reach. Stay with the boat; you're more likely to be seen and rescued that way.

SEARCH AND RESCUE

The Coastguard Service is responsible for commencing and co-ordinating search and rescue. Their work is greatly facilitated in Great Britain and Northern Ireland if they already have details of the yacht or small craft on Form CG66. (See p. 265).

The Coastguard will enlist the aid of lifeboats, other shipping in the vicinity, ships, aircraft and helicopters as may be most appropriate.

In most cases, the exact position of a distressed yacht is likely to be unknown to the rescue services, but the yacht can help in several ways. When a rescue vessel or aircraft is sighted (and this may be before the yacht has been sighted) further distress signals should be made. Orange smoke, red flares or the signal lamp will be most effective, as sound signals will not be heard by a rescue craft at a distance with her engines running, or by an aircraft. For distress signals see Chapter 16.

Identification from the air presents a real difficulty, and time may be wasted investigating other small craft in the vicinity. A boat with her name painted in large letters on a cockpit dodger is quickly identified even if she has exhausted her pyrotechnic flares. Such a dodger lashed flat on the deck will be of extra assistance.

It will help an approaching helicopter to know the direction of the surface wind; orange smoke flares will show this, and so will a long pennant or streamer flown from the masthead or rigging.

The mast of a sailing yacht will prevent the helicopter from making a rescue from directly overhead; it may be necessary for the crew to take to a dinghy or to jump into the water wearing lifejackets before they can be picked up. The dinghy should remain attached to the yacht by a line at least 100 feet long; a similar line should be used if the crew have to take to the water so that they do not drift apart or too far away from the yacht.

There is no need to take to the dinghy or the water if the distressed craft is a motor boat or dismasted yacht; the crew should remain on board whence they may be lifted off directly.

When towing, avoid sharp acceleration and braking. Brake earlier than you would without the trailer and take corners a little wider.

Remember the extra length of the trailer and its load when overtaking.

Balance the boat correctly on the trailer; if the load is too far aft the trailer will snake.

The pressure of the rear tyres of the towing car should be two or three psi above normal. Tyre pressures of an empty trailer should be 8–10 psi less than when loaded.

There is a knack to reversing; turn the rear of the car in the opposite direction to that in which the trailer is to turn.

Trailers towed by private cars in Britain (or light vans of less than 30 cwt. [1·5 tonnes] unladen weight) are subject to a speed limit of 50 mph. (80 km/hr) provided that:

> If fitted with brakes, the trailer's designed maximum weight (or actual laden weight) must not exceed the kerbside weight of the towing vehicle.
> If not fitted with brakes, the trailer's weight must not exceed 60 per cent of the towing vehicle's weight.
> The vehicle and the trailer must be marked with their weights.
> The trailer must have at the rear a plate of the pre-scribed pattern showing the number 50, as well as the registered number of the towing vehicle.
> Lights for the trailer (tail, stop and turn indicator) must duplicate those carried on the towing vehicle. Two reflective triangles are also required. (See

Dave Jenkins' *The Dinghy-Owner's Handbook* for full details.)

These regulations apply to the United Kingdom; if trailing elsewhere check the rules for the countries you'll pass through.

If the trailer is also used for launching the boat, its wheel bearings should not be immersed while still hot after the the journey. When cool, the bearings should be fully greased before immersion.

Salt water should be hosed off the trailer after launching or recovering the boat, or corrosion will be rapid.

18

Customs and Coastguard

CUSTOMS AND EXCISE, IMMIGRATION

Yachts sailing for and returning from overseas are subject in general to the same rules as other foreign-going ships. In Britain this includes passage to and from the Channel Islands and Eire.

British yachts are exempt from the licensing requirements of the Small Craft Regulations (1953) provided that they are used exclusively for pleasure purposes and without remuneration for the owner, whether he is on board or not.

A yacht hired or chartered is not regarded as being used exclusively for pleasure, and a licence should be obtained from the local Collector of Customs and Excise. There is no charge for this licence.

The Customs Office nearest to the place of departure should be notified of the date of intended departure. This is quite independent of any notification given to the Coastguard service for passage surveillance.

Duty-free stores may be shipped in bond in yachts sailing from the UK south of Brest or north of the River Elbe if prior application is made at the Custom House, where Customs Officers will advise on procedures and restrictions.

Yachts arriving from abroad should fly the yellow code flag Q (QQ if any contagious infection is suspected on board) until clearance has been given by a Customs Officer (and if necessary the Public Health Authority). See p. 232.

Dutiable stores (liquor, tobacco etc.) must all be declared

on the form provided by the Customs Officer by all members of the yacht's crew.

The Immigration Regulations require that the permission of an Immigration Officer must be obtained before any person not of local nationality is allowed to embark or disembark. The yacht's owner or master is responsible for obtaining this permission.

COASTGUARD

The Coastguard Service keeps a constant watch on shipping including yachts and small craft around the coastline. Certain selected Coastguard Stations are designated as Rescue Headquarters Stations.

Coastguard Stations are in communication with lifeboats, inshore rescue boats, helicopters and coast radio stations which can ask shipping in the vicinity of an incident to assist.

A most useful service rendered in Britain to yachtsmen by HM Coastguards is the surveillance of passages and local sailing. A white Card CG66A sent in at the beginning of a season will inform the Coastguard what your boat looks like, her performance, safety equipment, normal cruising area and similar relevant data.

A pink Card CG66B sent in before beginning a coastal passage will alert the Coastguards to keep an eye on your safety during that passage.

The two cards are illustrated here, Fig. 41; the service is absolutely free and the cards are postage prepaid. You can get them from yacht clubs, marinas, Harbourmasters and Coastguard Stations.

Having sent in a pink card, don't forget to inform the Coastguards of your arrival, delays, changes of plan, IMMEDIATELY. Failure to do this may result in the search and rescue services being alerted unnecessarily.

CG 66 A LOCAL SURVEILLANCE	Issuing Authority	Club or Association	Name of Craft
Type of Craft		Usual base, mooring and activity	
Length			
Colours: Hull Topsides Sail		Usual local operating area(s)	
Sail Number			
Special identification features		Is the following equipment carried? Anchor Lights Compass Life jackets	
Speed and endurance under power		Owners name address and telephone No.	
Life raft type and Serial No.			
Radio HF/MF VHF			
Distress signals			
		Date Signature	
For official use only			

41 Coastguard Forms CG66 A (White) and B (Pink)

CG 66B PASSAGE SURVEILLANCE	Issuing Authority	Master and Club or Association		Name of Craft	
Type of Craft		PASSAGE INFORMATION			
Length		PORT		Estimated Date and Time	
				Arrival	Departure
Colours: Hull Topsides Sail					
Sail Number					
Special identification features		Further Intentions			
Speed and endurance under power					
Life raft type and Serial No.		Name Address and Telephone number of Agent with whom duplicate has been lodged			
Radio HF/MF VHF					
Distress signals					
No. of persons on board		Date Signature			
For official use only					

For passages to and from France, a similar yacht passage report scheme is operated in conjunction with the French maritime authorities.

SHIP'S PAPERS

Although not mandatory in pleasure craft, certain documents ought to be carried on board, particularly during foreign cruises, when they may be called for by Customs or

Harbour Authorities. These include:

Certificate of Registry, which identifies the nationality, ownership and tonnages of the vessel. (But not all small craft are necessarily registered; any other documentary proof of ownership is usually acceptable.)

Insurance documents, showing extent of third-party coverage.

Warrant to fly a Blue Ensign (British craft only.)

Charter Party documents if the boat is hired from a person not on board.

Radio Telephony Licence (if an R/T set is carried.)

Customs Clearance Certificate from last port visited during a foreign cruise. (This and the following documents are mandatory.)

Victualling Bill (from Customs if dutiable stores are carried.)

Passeport de Bateau (Green Card) if visiting French ports. (Obtained from Douane at first French port visited.)

Ship's Log. This is of course an important document; it should carry not only navigational data but also details recorded at the time of any event which may have a subsequent bearing on safety at sea, legal action, insurance claims and the like. It is also a convenient place in which to record fuel and water embarked, and the names of crew-members joining or leaving during a cruise.

19

First Aid at Sea

Advice on this topic seems to range from far too little to far too much. While a yacht skipper should be prepared to deal with any injury or illness within reason, the amount of knowledge and equipment he should possess must vary with the size and nature of his boat and her crew and with the length of her voyages.

Most cruising is done within 12 hours' sail of the shore; 4 or 5 hours is even more common. You can sail a thousand miles or more in Europe or America without being a day's sail from medical assistance.

If something really serious happens on the high seas you can summon help from a bigger ship with the code flag W (I need medical assistance). With a radio telephone and the Medical Section of the International Code of Signals you can obtain advice anywhere in the world.

As for what you can do yourself, even professional medical advice tends to range from 'Do nothing' to 'Do more than many small boat skippers would be capable of'. These notes assume that the boat is a 5-tonner used for weekend coastal cruising and the occasional cross-Channel trip by a family consisting of two parents and two youngsters. They are based however on experience with various bunches of ocean racing toughs and with the opposite extreme.

The obvious must be said; a good skipper seeks to prevent accidents by constantly looking for potential causes and removing them before an accident happens. Sharp corners, projecting bolts and screws, trip-wires and the like are potentially more lethal than the same things ashore.

Crew training is equally important; a well-disciplined and fit crew is obviously more efficient and less accident-prone than a slap-happy gang. If nothing else, they'll learn to take a mild bonk on the bonce without screaming for an ambulance.

FIRST AID IN PRACTICE

Artificial respiration may be needed in cases of near-drowning or suffocation. The so-called **kiss of life** is simple and effective. See Fig. 42.

42 Artificial Respiration

Lay the patient on his back and clear away any obstructions from his mouth. He may have swallowed his tongue. The head should be pushed well back with the left hand on his forehead.

With the right hand on the chin, hold his mouth open. Pinch the nostrils with the thumb and forefinger of the left hand.

Take a deep breath, cover his open mouth with yours and inflate his lungs by blowing. Remove your mouth and pause while his lungs deflate.

Inflate his lungs repeatedly at your own breathing rate until he is breathing naturally, then turn him on his side in a prone position to recover.

You can alternatively inflate the lungs via the nostrils should there be injuries to the mouth.

In the case of small children, give very small gentle puffs.

Bleeding from superficial wounds is easily controlled by applying a dressing or pad of gauze held in position firmly with a bandage or by hand. Raise the bleeding limb or part of the body so that the heart has to pump uphill. If the dressing becomes saturated, don't remove it but put another on top. A large pad of cotton wool is very effective.

More severe and open cuts which might justify a few stitches were one ashore can be held together with 'Dumbell' or 'Butterfly' closures. Failing these, the gash may be kept closed by sticking a non-elastic zinc oxide plaster strip on each side, covering it with sterile gauze and drawing the edges together with a plaster strip on top of everything. Take care not to reopen the wound by stretching it.

Cleanliness is of course important; a dirty wound should be cleaned with Savlon or similar cream on a pad of cotton wool, and a little of the same cream applied to the subsequent dressing.

Broken bones must be treated with great care if they are to knit properly later. They must be made incapable of movement by bandaging a splint firmly to each side of the fracture. A sail batten cut to the right length may suit an arm or lower leg; alternatively a broken leg can be bandaged to the good one as a temporary measure. If a fracture has broken through the skin a sterile dressing must be applied before splinting. Obviously the victim must be taken ashore as soon as possible.

Bruises, see **Cuts.**

Burns are easily sustained in the galley or from hot exhaust pipes. Impregnated gauze such as tulle gras or sofra tulle is not only soothing but excludes air and so promotes healing. Apply it under a loose bandage; adhesive plasters will irritate. Serious burns should be treated thus and the victim taken ashore for professional treatment as soon as possible.

Concussion may arise from a hard blow on the head and may have serious consequences. Although he may be unwilling, the sufferer should be made to lie down and kept warm. If there is any sign of injury to the head, he must be taken ashore for examination and treatment.

Cuts and **bruises** are treated no differently afloat than they would be ashore. A supply of sterile dressings and bandages of various sizes should be kept in a watertight first-aid box readily accessible to everyone aboard in case of need. Adhesive plasters in cut sizes and in strip should be of waterproof type. Even these suffer when exposed to constant wetting, but they may be held in position with adhesive PVC tape. Incidentally, no harm comes from wetting a cut or abrasion with clean sea water.

Fractures, see **Broken bones.**

Scalds should be treated in the same manner as burns.

Seasickness: everyone has a favourite remedy; Avomine, Marzine, Hyoscine, Dramamine, etc. The main thing is not to wait until sickness happens but to take the remedy in advance when the possibility exists. The effect is not instantaneous. Watch out though for drowsiness. A severe case should be wrapped up warmly in a bunk with a bucket at hand and discouraged from coming on deck. He'll be of no use to himself or the watch on deck until he's had a chance to sleep it off. An old but well-tried remedy for a mild case is to keep the victim so busy that he doesn't have a chance to think about seasickness.

Shock may accompany concussion, broken bones or serious loss of blood. It is manifested by trembling, perspiration and a very pale countenance. The victim may collapse. If these symptoms are present, treatment is urgent and must commence as soon as copious bleeding has been dealt with and you are sure that the victim is breathing (see Artificial respiration).

The treatment of shock is largely psychological. The patient needs assurance that things are under control and that he is being competently looked after. He needs to feel that he is being made as comfortable as possible. An absence of panic and a few words of comfort are very important. Banish any hysterical friends or relatives to the upper deck, wrap him up warmly in his bunk (or in blankets if he can't be moved). If you are reasonably certain that he has no stomach injury or other possible cause of internal bleeding, a cup of warm (not hot) well-sweetened tea will help. But no alcohol.

A check on his pulse rate every fifteen minutes will show how he is getting on. It will initially be weak and well over the normal rate (about 36 beats per half-minute for most people) but should progressively strengthen and slow down as he responds to treatment. Failing this, he should be landed and taken to hospital quickly. This may be needed in any event for a serious injury, but the above treatment should be given in the meanwhile.

Strains and **sprains** are treated by strapping up the affected joint tightly with an elastic bandage and resting it for as long as possible. If this is not feasible, as with a strained back, the victim should lie flat in a hard bunk without cushions. If this gives no relief, he must be taken ashore for treatment.

Sunburn: you shouldn't let it happen, but not everybody is familiar with the high actinic value of sunshine at sea.

Treat with calomine lotion or Synalar cream, severe cases as for any other burn. Children are particularly susceptible to sunburn and the effects of ultra-violet light; their eyes may suffer badly from the double dose, direct and reflected from the sea.

CHECK LIST: FIRST-AID BOX

Assorted bandages and prepared dressings. Crepe bandage. Sterile gauze

Impregnated gauze (tulle gras, sofra tulle)

Lint and cotton wool

Adhesive plaster, roll and cut sizes, zinc oxide plaster roll. Butterfly closures.

Scissors, tweezers, eye-bath, thermometer, safety pins.

Dettol or other antiseptic

Vaseline

Avomine, Marzine, Hyoscine or Dramamine seasickness pills

Codeine or Aspirin; Alka Seltzer

Calamine lotion; sunburn cream

Savlon or similar antiseptic cream

Keep in an airtight and waterproof container to avoid deterioration of contents.

More ambitious skippers or those undertaking long sea passages might well invest in a copy of the *Ship Captain's Medical Guide* (HM Stationery Office). It covers about everything from chilblains to childbirth.

20

Own Ship's Data

This section is intended as a permanent record of data and dimensions relevant to your own boat. By completing it and up-dating when necessary you will have immediate access to her vital statistics without the need for re-measuring every time you want them.

OWN SHIP'S DATA

Name: _____

Owner: _____

Address: _____ Phone number:

_____ _____

_____

Dimensions: LOA in metres _____ LOA in feet _____

LWL ,, ,, _____ LWL ,, ,, _____

Beam ,, ,, _____ Beam ,, ,, _____

Draught ,, _____ Draught ,, _____

Tonnages: Gross Registered _____

Net Registered _____

Displacement _____

Thames Measurement _____

Registered Number: _____

Port of Registration: _____

Class: _____

Designed by: _____

Built by: _____

Year: _____

Sail Number: _____

Rig: _____

SAIL DIMENSIONS

SAIL	LUFF	LEACH	FOOT	AREA	MAKER	YEAR	MATERIAL
Main							
Mizen							
Genoa (1)							
,, (2)							
,, (3)							
Working Jib							
Staysail							
Spinnaker							
Storm Trysail							
Storm Jib							

OWN BOAT'S CONSTRUCTION

Hull Material: _____

Skin/Planking Material: _____

   Thickness: _____

Timbers (*Material*): _____

   Scantlings: _____

Frames (*Material*): _____

Fastenings: _____

Ballast Keel Material: _____

   Weight: _____

Internal Ballast: _____

   Weight: _____

   Stowage Plan, pp. 285 ff. _____

Deck Material: _____

   Thickness: _____

Main Mast Material: _____

   Height: _____

Mizen Mast Material: _____

   Height: _____

Main Boom Material: _____

   Length: _____

Mizen Boom Material: _____

   Length: _____

Spinnaker Boom Material: _____

   Length: _____

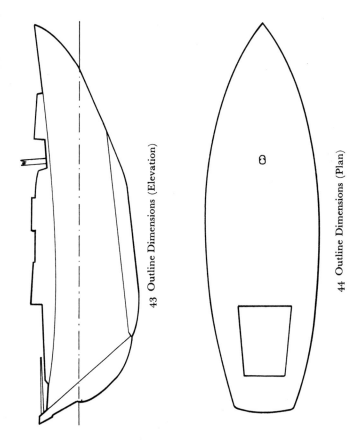

43 Outline Dimensions (Elevation)

44 Outline Dimensions (Plan)

RUNNING RIGGING

HALYARDS	LENGTH	DIAM.	MATERIAL	YEAR
Main				
Mizen				
Fore				
Jib				
Spinnaker				
Burgee				
Signal				
Topping Lift				

SHEETS

Main				
Mizen				
Fore				
Jib				
Spinnaker				

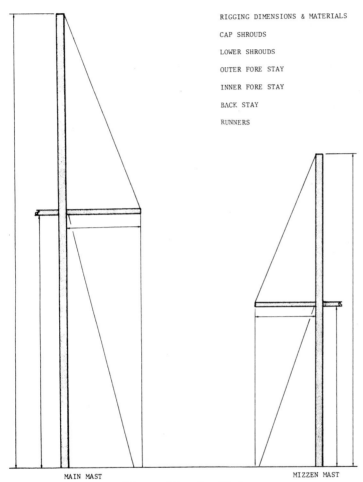

RIGGING DIMENSIONS & MATERIALS

CAP SHROUDS

LOWER SHROUDS

OUTER FORE STAY

INNER FORE STAY

BACK STAY

RUNNERS

MAIN MAST

MIZZEN MAST

45 Masts and Standing Rigging

Make of Main/Auxiliary Motor: _____

   Type: _____   Serial No.: _____

No. of Cylinders: _____   Cubic Capacity: _____

Shaft HP: _____   at _____ RPM

Fuel Grade: _____   Fuel Consumption (*Cruising Revs*):

   _____ gall/hour   _____ litres/hour

Fuel Tank Capacity: _____ *gallons* _____ *litres*

Range: _____ *miles at* _____ *knots*

Luboil Type: _____ Sump Capacity: ___ *pints/* ___ *litres*

Spark Plug Make/Type: _____

   Equivalents: _____

Fuel Filter Make/Type: _____

Oil Filter Make/Type: _____

Gearbox Type: _____

   Serial Number: _____   Reduction Ratio: _____

Oil Type: _____   Capacity: _____

Water Pump Type: _____   Flow Rate: _____

Generator Make/Type: _____

   Volts: _____ Amperes: _____ Watts: _____

Starter Motor Make/Type: _____

   V-Belt Types: _____

Propeller Diameter: _____ Pitch: _____

   Handed: _____ Material: _____

Prop Shaft Diameter: _____ Length O.A: _____

   Material: _____ Grease: _____

Outboard Motor Make/Type: _____

   Serial No.: _____   HP: _____

Fuel Grade: _____   Petroil Ratio: _____

   Consumption: _____

Spark Plug Make/Type: _____

   Equivalents: _____

MISCELLANEOUS DATA

Dinghy: *Length*_____ *Beam*_____ *Weight*_____

  *Builder*_____ *Year*_____

Liferaft: *Maker*_____ *Type*_____

  *Serial number*_____ *Next test due*_____

Trailer: *Maker*_____

  *Carrying capacity*_____ *Tyre size*_____

Anchors: (1) *Type*_____ *Weight*_____

     (2) *Type*_____ *Weight*_____

Anchor Chain: *Length*_____ *Size*_____

Mooring Lines: *Material*   *Length*   *Size*

        (1)_____

        (2)_____

        (3)_____

        (4)_____

        (5)_____

        (6)_____

Pyrotechnics: *Types*_____ *Expiry dates*_____

           _____   _____

           _____   _____

           _____   _____

           _____   _____

Insurance Renewal Due On:

EQUIPMENT SERIAL NUMBERS

	MAKE	TYPE	NUMBER
DF Radio:			
Depth Sounder:			
Patent Log:			
Sextant:			
Chronometer:			
Binoculars:			

PAINTS, VARNISH AND ANTIFOULING

Quantities for One Coat

HULL

Topsides: *Primer*_____ *Undercoat*_____

  *Enamel*_____

Underwater Surfaces: *Primer*_____

  *Undercoat*_____ *Antifouling*_____

Boot Topping: *Undercoat*_____ *Antifouling*_____

DECK AND CABIN TOP

*Deck paint*_____ *Varnish*_____

COCKPIT

*Varnish*_____

MAST AND SPARS

Mainmast: *Varnish*_____

Mizen Mast: *Varnish*_____

Main Boom: *Varnish*_____

Mizen Boom: *Varnish*_____

Spinnaker Boom: *Varnish*_____

Whisker Pole: *Varnish*_____

BILGES

*Bilge paint:*_____

USEFUL TELEPHONE NUMBERS

NAME	EXCHANGE/ CODE	NUMBER
Home:		
Yacht Club:		
Boat Yard:		
Marine Engineer:		
Sail Maker:		
Met. Office:		
Custom House:		
Coastguard:		
Harbourmasters:		
Insurance Co:		
Others:		

SUPPLEMENTARY NOTES

Appendix A

Buoyage Systems

46a Direction of Main Flood Tide.
(NOTE. On introduction of the new Buoyage System 'A', the convention will be *reversed* along the whole East Coast from the Thames Estuary to the Shetlands, and through the North Channel between Scotland and Ireland. The direction of buoyage in rivers and estuaries will continue to be from seaward inwards.)

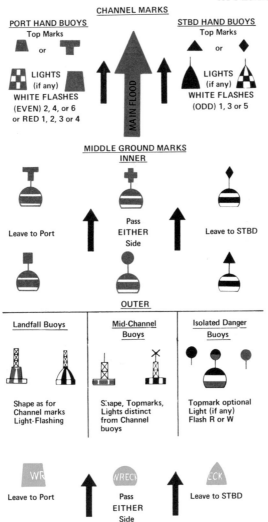

CHANNEL MARKS

PORT HAND BUOYS
Top Marks
or

LIGHTS
(if any)
WHITE FLASHES
(EVEN) 2, 4, or 6
or RED 1, 2, 3 or 4

MAIN FLOOD

STBD HAND BUOYS
Top Marks
or

LIGHTS
(if any)
WHITE FLASHES
(ODD) 1, 3 or 5

MIDDLE GROUND MARKS
INNER

Leave to Port

Pass
EITHER
Side

Leave to STBD

OUTER

Landfall Buoys

Shape as for
Channel marks
Light-Flashing

Mid-Channel Buoys

Shape, Topmarks,
Lights distinct
from Channel
buoys

Isolated Danger Buoys

Topmark optional
Light (if any)
Flash R or W

WR

Leave to Port

WRECK

Pass
EITHER
Side

ECK

Leave to STBD

WRECKS

46b Uniform System of Buoyage around
the British Isles

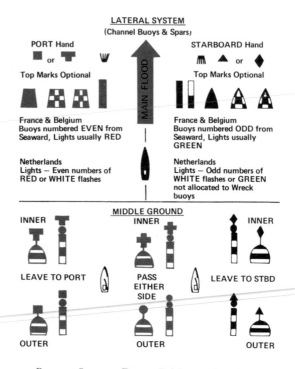

47a Buoyage Systems: France, Belgium and Netherlands

France and Belgium Light-Vessels off the North coast of France and Belgium are painted with RED and WHITE vertical stripes. They may be replaced by lighted buoys during summer months.

Wreck vessels, buoys and beacons are marked with a WHITE 'W' and the word 'EPAVE'

Netherlands Light-Vessels are painted RED with the name in WHITE.

Distinguishing buoys marking seaward approach to channels have no special colour.

Buoys marking channels are numbered in WHITE figures in natural sequence from seaward.

Spherical buoys are sometimes placed between channel buoys and conform to the appropriate colours. In inner channels, spar buoys are used when necessary.

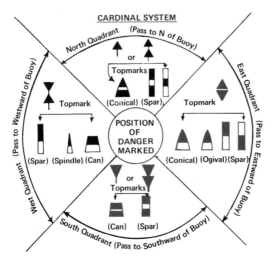

CARDINAL SYSTEM

North Quadrant (Pass to N of Buoy)

East Quadrant (Pass to Eastward of Buoy)

West Quadrant (Pass to Westward of Buoy)

South Quadrant (Pass to Southward of Buoy)

or Topmarks

(Conical) (Spar)

Topmark

POSITION OF DANGER MARKED

Topmark

(Spar) (Spindle) (Can)

(Conical) (Ogival) (Spar)

or Topmarks

(Can) (Spar)

Used to indicate dangers marked by compass quadrants - NORTH (NW-NE) — SOUTH (SE-SW) — EAST (NE-NW) — WEST (SW-NW). Thus, as diagram shows, a North Quadrant buoy lies North of the Danger. A vessel which passes to northward of the buoy puts it between herself and the danger. For WRECKS marked by CARDINAL system, only the EAST and WEST Quadrant characteristics are used.

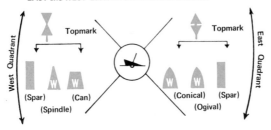

West Quadrant

East Quadrant

Topmark

Topmark

(Spar) (Can)
(Spindle)

(Conical) (Spar)
(Ogival)

47b Buoyage Systems: France, Belgium and Netherlands

291

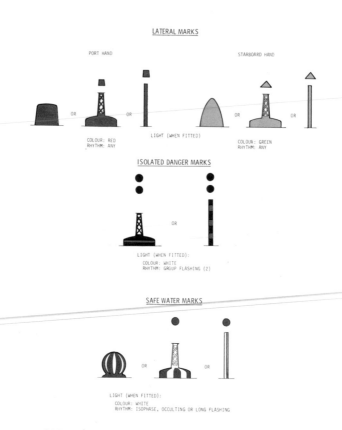

48 New Combined Cardinal and Lateral Buoyage System 'A'
(For Direction of Main Flood Tide, see note to Fig. 46.)

CARDINAL MARKS

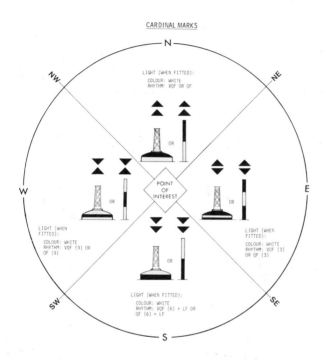

LIGHT (WHEN FITTED):
COLOUR: WHITE
RHYTHM: VQF OR QF

POINT OF INTEREST

LIGHT (WHEN FITTED):
COLOUR: WHITE
RHYTHM: VQF (9) OR QF (9)

LIGHT (WHEN FITTED):
COLOUR: WHITE
RHYTHM: VQF (3) OR QF (3)

LIGHT (WHEN FITTED):
COLOUR: WHITE
RHYTHM: VQF (6) + LF OR QF (6) + LF

SPECIAL MARKS

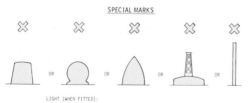

LIGHT (WHEN FITTED):
COLOUR: YELLOW
RHYTHM: ANY, OTHER THAN THOSE DESCRIBED AS NAVIGATIONAL MARKS

293

Appendix B

Signal Flags, Single-Letter Signals

(see p. 227)

ALPHABETICAL FLAGS

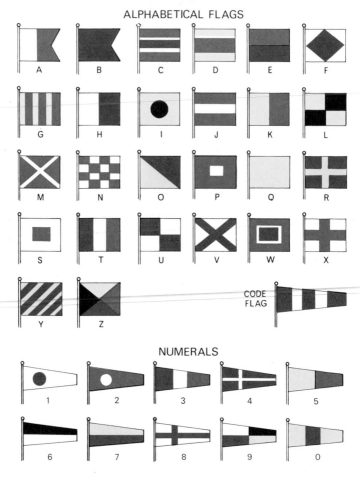

NUMERALS

SUBSTITUTES

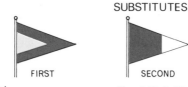

49 Signal Code Flags

A I have a diver down; keep well clear at slow speed.

*B I am taking in, or discharging, or carrying dangerous goods.

C Yes (affirmative or "The significance of the previous group should be read in the affirmative').

*D Keep clear of me; I am manoeuvring with difficulty.

*E I am altering my course to starboard.

F I am disabled; communicate with me.

G I require a pilot. When made by fishing vessels operating in close proximity on the fishing grounds it means: "I am hauling nets'.

*H I have a pilot on board.

*I I am altering my course to port.

J I am on fire and have dangerous cargo on board: keep well clear of me.

K I wish to communicate with you.

L You should stop your vessel instantly.

M My vessel is stopped and making no way through the water.

N No (negative or 'The significance of the previous group should be read in the negative'). This signal may be given only visually or by sound. For voice or radio transmission the signal should be 'NO'.

O Man overboard.

P *In harbour:* All persons should report on board as the vessel is about to proceed to sea.
 At sea: It may be used by fishing vessels to mean: 'My nets have come fast upon an obstruction'.

Q My vessel is 'healthy' and I request free pratique.

*S My engines are going astern.

*T Keep clear of me; I am engaged in pair trawling.

U You are running into danger.

V I require assistance.

W I require medical assistance.

X Stop carrying out your intentions and watch for my signals.

Y I am dragging my anchor.

Z I require a tug. When made by fishing vessels operating in close proximity on the fishing grounds it means: 'I am shooting nets'.

These signals may be made by any method of signalling, but those marked* may only be made by sound when used as manoeuvring or warning signals in strict accordance with the Collision Regulations. No meaning has been allocated to letter R.

Selected Book List

I

SEA SENSE

Richard Henderson: *Sea Sense*, International Marine Pub. Co (Patrick Stephens), 1973

2

DESIGN AND CONSTRUCTION

Jim Andrews: *Catamarans for Cruising*, Hollis & Carter, 1974

Juan Baader: *The Sailing Yacht*, Adlard Coles, 1965

D. Phillips-Birt: *Motor Yacht and Boat Design*, Adlard Coles, 1966

D. Phillips-Birt: *Sailing Yacht Design*, Adlard Coles, 1966

Eric Coleman: *Dinghies for All Waters*, Hollis & Carter, 1976

Fox Geen: *Fitting Out a Moulded Hull*, Hollis & Carter, 1974

Dave Jenkins: *The Dinghy-Owner's Handbook*, Hollis & Carter, 1975

Francis S. Kinney & D. Phillips-Birt, ed.: *Skene's Elements of Yacht Design*, A. & C. Black, 1963

Ian Nicolson: *Surveying Small Craft*, Adlard Coles, 1973

3

SHIP SAFETY

Denny Desoutter: *The Small-Boat Skipper's Safety Book*, Hollis & Carter, 1972

Guy Cole: *Safety in Small Craft*, H.M. Stationery Office, 1973

4
ROPES AND ROPEWORK

Clifford Ashley: *The Ashley Book of Knots*, Faber & Faber, 1944

Raoul Graumont: *Handbook of Knots*, Cornell Maritime Press (Souvenir Press), 1973

J. D. Sleightholme: *Yacht Ropes, the Marlow Standard Guide*, Marlow Ropes Ltd, 1964

C. L. Spencer: *Knots, Splices and Fancy Work*, Brown, Son & Ferguson, 1974

5
SAILS AND SAILCLOTH

Fox Geen: *Improved Keelboat Performance*, Hollis & Carter, 1975

J. Howard Williams: *Sails*, Adlard Coles, 1969

6
STANDING AND RUNNING RIGGING

Fox Geen: *Improved Keelboat Performance*, Hollis & Carter, 1975

8
MARINE ENGINES

H. & K. J. Wickham: *Motor Boating, A Practical Handbook*, Hollis & Carter, 1975

Dermot Wright: *Marine Engines and Boating Mechanics*, David & Charles, 1973

9
BOAT MAINTENANCE

Charles Jones: *Glass Fibre Yachts, Improvement and Repair*, Nautical Pub. Co, 1972

Ian Nicolson: *Surveying Small Craft*, Adlard Coles, 1973

J. D. Sleightholme: *Fitting Out, Maintenance and Repair of Small Craft*, Adlard Coles, 1972

Jeff Toghill: *Boat Owner's Maintenance Manual*, David & Charles, 1974

Michael Verney: *Boat Repairs and Conversions*, John Murray, 1972

H. & K. J. Wickham: *Motor Boating, A Practical Handbook*, Hollis & Carter, 1975

II

NAVIGATION

Mary Blewitt: *Celestial Navigation for Yachtsmen*, Stanford, 1973

Charles Cotter: *The Complete Coastal Navigator*, Hollis & Carter, 1964

Charles Cotter: *The Complete Nautical Astronomer*, Hollis & Carter, 1969

G. D. Dunlap & H. H. Shufeldt: *Dutton's Navigation and Piloting*, U.S. Naval Institute (Patrick Stephens), 1969

M. J. Rantzen: *Little Ship Astro-navigation*, Barrie & Jenkins, 1973

Reed's Nautical Almanac, Thomas Reed, annually

II

PILOT BOOKS

Admiralty Pilots, available for all parts of the world, consult your chart agent

P. Bristow: *Through the Belgian Canals*, Nautical Pub. Co, 1972

P. Bristow: *Through the Dutch Canals*, Nautical Pub. Co, 1974

P. Bristow: *Through the French Canals*, Nautical Pub. Co, 1970

K. Adlard Coles: *Channel Harbours and Anchorages*, Nautical Pub. Co, 1971

K. Adlard Coles: *Creeks and Harbours of the Solent*, Nautical Pub. Co, 1972

K. Adlard Coles & A. N. Black: *North Biscay Pilot*,
Adlard Coles, 1970

K. Adlard Coles: *North Brittany Pilot*, Adlard Coles, 1972

K. Adlard Coles: *Shell Pilot to South Coast Harbours*, Faber
& Faber, 1968

E. Delmar-Morgan: *North Sea Harbours and Pilotage*,
Adlard Coles, 1972

14
WEATHER

Elementary Meteorology, H.M. Stationery Office, 1969

Alan Watts: *Wind and Sailing Boats*, David & Charles,
1973

W. H. Watts: *Weather for Yachtsmen*, Adlard Coles, 1964

15

RADIO AIDS TO NAVIGATION

John French: *Electrical and Electronic Equipment for Yachts*,
Adlard Coles, 1974

Leo G. Sands: *Marine Electronics Handbook*, Foulsham, 1973

Reed's Nautical Almanac, Thomas Reed, annually

16

SEA SIGNALLING

B. P. Yachting Book No. 2: *Flags and Signals*, Pelham
Books, 1969

The International Code of Signals, H.M. Stationery Office,
1969

P. J. Russell: *Sea Signalling Simplified*, Adlard Coles, 1969

17

YACHTHANDLING AND BOATWORK

Denny Desoutter: *The Small-Boat Skipper's Safety Book*,
Hollis & Carter, 1972

Dave Jenkins: *The Dinghy-Owner's Handbook*, Hollis &
Carter, 1975

C. D. Lane & J. D. Sleightholme: *The New Boatman's Manual*, Adlard Coles, 1967

The Seaway Code, a Guide for Small Boat Users, H.M. Stationery Office, 1974

H. & K. J. Wickham: *Motor Boating, a Practical Handbook*, Hollis & Carter, 1975

Index